George Dixon, Nathaniel Portlock, Charles Banks Belt

A Voyage Round the World

but more particularly to the north-west coast of America - performed in 1785, 1786, 1787, and 1788, in the King George and Queen Charlotte, Captains Portlock and Dixon

George Dixon, Nathaniel Portlock, Charles Banks Belt

A Voyage Round the World

but more particularly to the north-west coast of America - performed in 1785, 1786, 1787, and 1788, in the King George and Queen Charlotte, Captains Portlock and Dixon

ISBN/EAN: 9783337198367

Printed in Europe, USA, Canada, Australia, Japan

Cover: Foto ©Andreas Hilbeck / pixelio.de

More available books at **www.hansebooks.com**

CAPTAIN PORTLOCK.

A

VOYAGE ROUND THE WORLD;

BUT MORE PARTICULARLY TO THE

NORTH-WEST COAST OF AMERICA:

PERFORMED IN 1785, 1786, 1787, AND 1788,

IN

THE KING GEORGE AND QUEEN CHARLOTTE,

CAPTAINS PORTLOCK AND DIXON.

EMBELLISHED WITH TWENTY COPPER-PLATES.

DEDICATED, BY PERMISSION, TO

HIS MAJESTY.

By CAPTAIN NATHANIEL PORTLOCK.

LONDON:

PRINTED FOR JOHN STOCKDALE, OPPOSITE BURLINGTON-HOUSE, PICCADILLY;
AND GEORGE GOULDING, JAMES STREET, COVENT GARDEN.

M,DCC,LXXXIX.

TO THE
KING.

SIR,

IT has been the invariable object of your Majesty's reign to enrich your people, by inciting their induſtry; to refine them, by encouraging the arts; to enlighten them, by the cultivation of ſcience; and to ſecure their enjoyments, by ſtrengthening the conſtitution.

But to a people, whoſe renown and whoſe ſafety are derived from their ſhipping and navigators,

DEDICATION.

navigators, the voyages of discovery, which your Majesty successively projected and atchieved, may be regarded as still more useful to your subjects, and beneficial to mankind. English seamen have been always celebrated for their bravery: your Majesty has, by those voyages, made them more skilful. They have ever been adventurous; but your Majesty has, by this wise policy, made them more safe. English sailors would at all times undertake and perform, on every sea, what mortals could execute: your Majesty has taught them by those salutary trials how to preserve their health in every climate. Yet, whatever glory and benefit have been thus derived to Great Britain, your Majesty's disinterestedness hath imparted, with a generous philanthropy, to every nation.

It was to those voyages (may I be permitted to add?) that I owe the perfect health, the perseverance, and the skill, however inconsiderable, which enabled me to conduct the
adventure

DEDICATION.

adventure that is recounted in the following sheets. But it was your Majesty's beneficence, which at all times has studiously noticed the humblest merit, that allowed me the honour of dedicating this narrative to your Majesty, as a tribute of the unalterable gratitude and profound submission, with which I shall continue through life,

Your MAJESTY's

most faithful Subject,

and most dutiful Servant,

LONDON,
April 19, 1789.

NATHANIEL PORTLOCK.

Directions to the BINDER for placing the CUTS.

Head of Captain PORTLOCK	To face the Title Page
General Chart	Page 1
Views of Bonavista, &c.	14
Yellow-winged Bunting	35
Rusty-crowned Plover, Male	36
Ditto, ditto, Female (the Bird looking over its Back)	37
Cinereous Lark	38
Graham's Harbour	102
View in Coal Harbour	108
Basket and God	176
Sketch of M'Leod's Harbour	206
Sketch of West Side of Montague Island	215
Sketch of Port Etches	226
Portlock's and Goulding's Harbour	258
View in Goulding's Harbour	270
View in Portlock's Harbour	280
Knives and Comb	294
White Tern	312
View in Sapan	317
Head of Tyaana	359

CONTENTS.

CHAP. I.

SHORT Account of the different Perfons who have engaged in the Fur Trade—The King George's Sound Company eftablifhed—Two Veffels purchafed—The Complements of their Crews, and Names of the Officers—Paffage from Gravefend to Portfmouth—In danger off the Cafkets—Arrival of the Ships at Guernfey,   Page 1

CHAP. II.

Various Refrefhments procured at Guernfey—Leave that Place, and proceed on the Voyage—Remarkable Rock at the Eaft End of Madeira—Send Difpatches from thence—Bonavifta—Mayo—Sal—Arrival at Saint Jago—Occurrences there—Refrefhments to be met with—Departure from thence—Precautions againft the Rain and fultry Weather near the Equator—Fortunate Prefervation of a Boy who fell over-board—Pafs a vaft Quantity of Shrimp Spawn—Arrival at Port Egmont—Falkland's Iflands,   -   -   10

CHAP. III.

Various Employments in Port Egmont—Ruins of a Town difcovered—Meet with two Ships employed in the Oil Trade—Method of extracting Oil from the Blubber of the Sea Elephant—Several Birds defcribed—Refrefhments obtained there—Leave Port Egmont and proceed to States Bay—Difference between the Sea Elephant and Sea Lion pointed out—Remains of a Wreck difcovered—Depart from Falkland's Iflands and proceed on the Voyage—Staten's Land—
Stormy

CONTENTS.

Stormy Weather in doubling Cape Horn—Pick up a Number of Turtle—Fruitlefs Search for Los Majos—Arrive in Sight of Owhyhee, - - - - Page 30

CHAP. IV.

Range along the Coaft of Owhyhee—Arrival in Karakakooa Bay—Unruly Behaviour of the Natives—Leave Karakakooa Bay—Refrefhments procured along the Coaft—Difappointed in coming to anchor at Morotoi—Arrival at Woahoo—Fruitlefs Search for a Watering-place—Supplied with Water by the Natives—Refrefhments obtained—Departure from Woahoo—Account of the prefent Government among the Sandwich Iflands—Pafs Atoui—Arrival at Oneehow—Tranfactions there, - - - 60

CHAP. V.

Continuation of Tranfactions at Oneehow—Method of falting Pork in tropical Climates—Departure from Oneehow—Method of brewing the fweet Root—Arrive in fight of the Coaft of America—Stand on for Cook's River—Meet with fome Ruffian Settlers—Arrival in Cook's River—Vifited by the Ruffian Chief—Anchor in Coal Harbour—Various Employments there—Abundance of Salmon—Vifit the Ruffian Settlement—Their Mode of Living defcribed—Proceed further up the River, - - 86

CHAP. VI.

Indians come to the Ships with Furs—Shew a Difpofition for thieving—Bring Salmon to barter—Short Defcription of the Country near Trading Bay—Climate—Produce—The Ships leave Trading Bay, and proceed down the River—Requefted by the Indians to join with them againft the Ruffians—Prefents given at parting—Leave Cook's River, and proceed for Prince William's Sound—Prevented from making it by bad Weather—Proceed along the Coaft—Difappointed in meeting with Crofs Sound, - - 112

CONTENTS.

CHAP. VII.

Fruitless Attempt to fall in with the Bay of Islands—Proceed along the Coast towards King George's Sound—Unsuccessful Attempt to make it—Passage from the Coast of America to Sandwich Islands—Saint Maria la Gorta—Arrival off Owhyhee—Refreshments obtained—Plan of future Proceedings—Departure from Owhyhee—Pick up a Canoe with some Indians in Distress—Anchor at Woahoo, Page 132

CHAP. VIII.

Visited by Taheeterre—Pernicious Effects of the Yava-root—Transactions at Woahoo—Wood purchased—An Eatooa erected—The Chiefs make offerings to their Deities—Meditate an Attack on the Ships—The King shewn the Effect of Fire-arms—Two Indians embark for Atoui—Take leave of Taheeterre and the Priest—Departure from Woahoo—Anchor in Wymoa Bay, Atoui—Excursion on Shore, - - - 154.

CHAP. IX.

Variety of Refreshments procured—Visited by the King—Presents given and received—Two Natives from Woahoo introduced to Ta-aao—Deplorable Situation of an old Warrior—Ceremony of the Tabooara—Excursion on Shore, accompanied by Abbenooe—A remarkably large Shark caught—Grateful Behaviour of Neeheowhooa—Arrival at Oneehow—Obliged to cut the Cables in a Gale of Wind—Leave three Invalids on Shore—Anchor again in Yam Bay—The Sick return on board—Leave Oneehow and arrive at Atoui—Remarkable Circumstance of a Woman with a Puppy at her Breast—Chiefs exercise with Spears—House built for Captain Portlock—Departure from Atoui—Arrival at Oneehow—Recover the King George's Anchors—Attempt made on the Life of an Atoui Chief—Final Departure from the Sandwich Islands, 174

CONTENTS.

CHAP. X.

Passage from the Sandwich Islands to the Coast of America—Good Effects of Beer made from the Sweet Root—Arrival at Montague Island—Anchor in Hanning's Bay—Boats sent on a trading Expedition—Meet with a Vessel from Bengal—Their distressing Situation—Refreshments sent to the Nootka—Plan of future Proceedings—Visited by a powerful Tribe of Indians—Their Propensity to Theft—Departure from Montague Island—The Ships separate—Arrival of the King George in Hinchinbrooke Cove, - - Page 201

CHAP. XI.

Indians visit the Ship with Sea-otter Skins—Boats sent on a trading Expedition—Plundered by the Indians—Return of the Boats—Arrival of the Nootka—Assist in getting her ready for Sea—Long-boat sent to Cook's River—Departure of the Nootka—Long-boat's Return—Sent a second Time—Visited by different Tribes of Indians—Various Employments carried on—Abundance of Salmon, Herrings, and Crabs—Arrival of the Long-boat—Departure from Port Etches, - - - - 226

CHAP. XII.

Run along the Coast of Montague Island—Short Account of Prince William's Sound—Description of the Inhabitants—Their Persons—Manners—Dress—Diseases—Ornaments—Food—Cookery—Situation for a Settlement—Produce—Weapons—Hunting Implements—Specimen of the Language—Proceed along the Coast—Anchor in Portlock's Harbour—Intercourse with the Natives—Long-boat sent on a trading Expedition—Visited by a distant Tribe of Indians, 244

CHAP. XIII.

A new Party of Traders from the East—Under the Necessity of exchanging Hostages—Part of the Ship's Company go on Shore—Meet

CONTENTS.

Meet with Indian Tea—Visit the Natives at their own Residence—Their Habitations and Manner of Living described—An Account of the Spaniards having been on the Coast, and left the Small-pox—The Long-boat returns from an Expedition to the Eastward—Examine the Sound—Another Visit from our North West Friends—Ceremonies to be observed before commencing Trade—Joseph Woodcock sent as an Hostage—Three Days in the Country—An Account of the Natives—Their Disposition, Ornaments, Dress, and Language—Observations on the Advantages likely to accrue from a Settlement on the Coast—Some Thoughts of an Expedition by Land—Leave Portlock's Harbour, - - Page 268

CHAP. XIV.

Passage from the Coast to Sandwich Islands—Transactions there—Letters received from Captain Dixon and Mr. Ross—Some Particulars received from Taa-boo-a-raa-ne respecting the Death of Captain Cook—Description of the White Tern—Cruelty of the Chiefs to their Inferiors—Observations on a Trade to Botany Bay from these Islands—Final Departure from them—Passage to China—Arrival there, - - - - 297

CHAP. XV.

An Account of a Court of Enquiry held at the Request of Captain Greer of the Belvidere, on his People who mutinied in his Absence—The Court's Determination thereon—Punishment inflicted on the Mutineers—Account of meeting with Tyaana at China—His Behaviour there—Attention paid him—Returns to his own Country with a valuable Cargo—A short Description of his Person, - - - - 327

CHAP.

CONTENTS.

CHAP. XVI.

Leave Macao—Proceed through the Straits of Banca and Sunda—Anchor at North Island—The Veſſels part Company—Arrival at Saint Helena—Departure from thence—Five of the People nearly poiſoned by eating Fiſh—Arrival in England—A Liſt of Plants, Birds, and Foſſils ſeen in Cook's River, - - Page 364

A VOY-

A VOYAGE

TO THE

North West Coast of *America*.

CHAP. I.

Account of the different Persons who first carried on the Fur Trade.—The King George's Sound Company established.—Two Vessels purchased.—The Complements of their Crews, and Names of the Officers.—Passage from Gravesend to Portsmouth.—Employments there.—Departure from Portsmouth.—In Danger near the Caskets.—Arrival at Guernsey.

THOUGH that illustrious navigator, Captain Cook, did not, with all his skill and all his perseverance, obtain the great object of his voyage to the western coast of America, the discovery of a practicable passage from the North Pacific to the North Atlantic Ocean, he furnished philosophy with many additional facts, and he opened to commerce several extensive prospects. The voyages

CHAP. I. voyages of the present reign, as they were prosecuted with views the most disinterested, were exposed to the world without reserve. And every nation and every individual had thus an opportunity of forming new designs, either for the cultivation of science, or for the advantage of traffic.

If Great Britain owe something to France for her discoveries in former times, the French are much indebted, in the present, to the British mariners for laying open the whole globe to human eyes and to human industry. The French king, with a noble emulation, seems to have sent out several officers with suitable accommodations, to follow the tracts of the successive voyages which had been so happily atchieved under his Majesty's auspices; though an English seaman may be allowed to say, that the French navigators sailed in their wake at a great distance astern. No sooner were the voyages of Cook, of Clerk, of Gore, and of King accomplished, and their narratives published, than a new expedition was, in 1785, dispatched from France, under the conduct of Messrs. Peyrouse and De Langle, in order to glean on this ample field what the misfortune of Cook had left unattained.

As early indeed as 1781, a well-known individual, Mr. Bolts, attempted an adventure to the North Pacific Ocean from the bottom of the Adriatic, under the emperor's flag; but this feeble effort of an imprudent man failed prematurely, owing to causes which have not yet been sufficiently explained. The project of Bolts appears to have been early adopted by the British subjects who are settled in Asia, and who stand high in an active age for knowledge and for enterprise. They were naturally struck with the suggestion of captain Cook, what a gainful trade might be carried on from America to China for furs. And a brig of sixty tons, with twenty men, under the command of James Hanna, was, in pursuit of this flattering object, dispatched from the river of Canton in April 1785; and after coasting Northward, and traversing the Southern extremity of Japan, this brig arrived in the subsequent August at Nootka Sound, the American mart for peltry. Whatever may have been the success of Hanna in 1785, he performed, in a larger vessel, a similar voyage in 1786. In this year, the merchants of Bombay sent two vessels under the direction of James Strange, while the traders of Bengal dispatched two ships, which were commanded by the lieutenants Mears and Tipping, to the American coast for furs, in the hope of Indian profits. These several adventures, the gains of which were no doubt greatly amplified, incited to similar pursuits the torpid spirit of the Portugueze at Macao, whose fathers had been the discoverers, the conquerors, and monopolists of the East.

These enterprises have proved extremely important to the world, though their profits, considering the capital and the risques, were not enviously great. These enterprises, however, by enlarging the limits of discovery, made navigation more safe in the North Pacific Ocean. They familiarised the South Sea islanders to European persons, and manners, and traffic. They taught the American savages, that strength must always be subordinate to discipline: and, having discovered the Ahooa Indians

CHAP. I.

Indians on the borders of Nootka Sound, who had so far advanced from their savage state as to refuse to sell to Mr. Strange, for any price, the peltry which they had already engaged to Mr. Hanna, these enterprises have ascertained this exhilarating truth to mankind, that civilization and morals must for ever accompany each other.

In the effluxion of ages, periods often arise, when mankind, by a consentaneous spirit, pursue with ardour analogous enterprises. At the same epoch Columbus and Gama were employed, the one in discovering the lands in the West, the other in exploring the regions of the East. In the present times the British, the French, and the Spaniards, have, at the same moment, busied themselves in searching every coast and every creek, with the glorious purpose of benefiting the human race, by adding to their happiness. While those adventures were thus performed from the Eastern extremities of Asia to the Western shores of America, private persons undertook a more arduous voyage of a like kind from England. It was in May 1785, that Richard Cadman Etches and other traders entered into a commercial partnership, under the title of *The King George's Sound Company*, for carrying on a fur trade from the Western Coast of America to China. For this purpose they obtained a licence from the South Sea Company, who, without carrying on any traffic themselves, stand in the mercantile way of more adventurous merchants. They procured also a similar licence from the East India Company, who at the same time engaged to give them a freight of Teas from Canton. This enterprise of *The King George's Sound Company* alone evinces what English copartner-

ships

ships and English capitals could undertake and execute, were they less opposed by prejudice and restrained by monopolies.

In order to execute this design, *The King George's Sound Company* purchased a ship of 320 tons, and a snow of 200 tons; having thus a size and burden which captain Cook, after adequate trials, recommended as the fittest for distant employments; and which, owing to the merchants experience, England happily enjoys in the greatest numbers. These vessels were immediately put into dock, in order that they might be completely fitted for so long a voyage. With all the skill and diligence of the shipwrights of the Thames, it was not, however, till the 8th of July, that these vessels were moored at Deptford, for the convenience of fitting their rigging, engaging seamen, and taking on board such stores and other necessaries as were judged needful for a voyage of such length and variety. The best provisions were purchased, as being the cheapest in the end; and great attention was used in providing those articles which were thought most likely to preserve the health of the crews, by adding to their comforts.

In the mean time the owners appointed me commander of the larger vessel, and of the expedition; and George Dixon of the smaller: both of us having accompanied captain Cook in his last voyage into the Pacific Ocean, were deemed most proper for an adventure which required no common knowledge and experience. Other officers of competent talents were at the same time appointed, in order that they might know each other and facilitate the outfit.

outfit *. The novelty of this enterprise attracted the notice of several persons, who were eminent either for talents or station, and who promoted this voyage by their countenance, or strengthened the company by their approbation When Sir Joseph Banks and Lord Mulgrave, Mr. Rose and Sir John Dick, came on board, the Secretary of the Treasury named the largest vessel *The King George*, and the President of the Royal Society called the smallest *The Queen Charlotte*. Exclusive of the profits of traffic, or the advantages of discovery, this voyage was destined to other national objects. Several gentlemen's sons, who had shewn an inclination to engage in a seafaring life, were put under my care, for the purpose of being early initiated in the knowledge of a profession which requires length of experience, rather than supereminence of genius †. I at

* King George.

Officers and Men.	Officers Names.
Captain,	Nathaniel Portlock,
Mates,	William M'Leod, John Christleman, Samuel Hayward.
Surgeon,	James Hoggan.
Assistant Traders,	Robert Hill, William Wilbye.
Boatswain,	Archibald Brown.
Carpenter,	Robert Horne.
Seamen and Boys,	50
Total,	59

Queen Charlotte.

Officers and Men.	Officers Names.
Captain,	George Dixon.
Mates,	John Ewen Carew, James Turner, George White.
Surgeon,	William Lauder.
Assistant Trader,	William Beresford.
Steward,	Henry Forrester.
Boatswain,	John Gatenby.
Carpenter,	John Sadler.
Seamen,	24
Total,	33

† Walter Adams was sent out by Sir John Dick.
John Penetire, by Mr. Salt, deputy governor of the South Sea Company.
John Gore, by Captain Gore of Greenwich Hospital.
David Gilmore, by Mr. Ch. Gilmore.
Charles Gilmore, by Mr. S. Gilmore.
William Biron, by Mr. Edward Biron.
John Webb,
William Kirby, } by Mr. Hanning.
Thomas Thompson, by Mr. Wilbye.

the same time engaged William Philpot Evans and Joseph Woodcock, two of the pupils of Mr. Wales, the master of the mathematical school in Christ's Hospital, who were at once able to assist in teaching the boys the rudiments of navigation, and might be usefully employed in taking views of remarkable lands, and in constructing charts of commodious harbours.

Having got most of our stores on board, we proceeded down the river, and arrived off Gravesend on the 29th of August. This evening I read articles of agreement respecting the voyage to both the ships companies, which some of them at first refused to sign; but, after a proper explanation, they all cheerfully consented, except two of my own crew, whom I immediately discharged; as I had resolved to engage no seaman who was not perfectly satisfied with the articles, and altogether contented with his station. The next morning the crews were paid their river-wages, with a month's advance; and, having stood towards the Downs with a fresh South Westerly breeze, the ships came to an anchor the same evening in Margate Roads.

Early in the morning of the 31st we got under sail and proceeded towards the Downs, having still a fresh breeze at South West; and at eight the same morning we anchored off Deal in 8½ fathom water; the South Foreland Point bearing South West, distant five miles, and Deal Castle North West, two miles distant. We lay at anchor during the 1st September, employed in procuring fresh beef and various refreshments.

8   A VOYAGE TO THE

CHAP.
  I.
1785.
September.
Friday 2.
Saturday 3.

NEXT morning at one o'clock we weighed anchor, and stood towards the channel; but meeting with gales at once fresh and contrary, we were obliged to anchor under Dungeness in the evening of the 3d, with the light-house bearing South West by West, about four miles distant. A remarkable circumstance happened whilst we lay here: Charles Gilmore (one of the boys under my care), being at the maintopmast-head, attempted to come down by the topmast backstay; but losing his hold when he was almost at the top, he fell directly into the main chains; yet he providentially received no hurt, and was not the least frighted with his fall.

Sunday 4.

Wednes. 7.

AT three o'clock in the morning of the 4th we weighed anchor and stood towards Spithead, where we arrived at one o'clock on the seventh.

DURING our stay here, the crews were constantly served with fresh beef and plenty of vegetables; the employments which principally engaged us were, setting up the rigging, and replacing the water that had been expended. Several spare anchors, and a variety of such other stores were purchased, which we judged would be necessary during so long a voyage, and with which we had not been supplied in the Thames.

Thurs. 15.

Friday 16.

EVERY necessary business being completed, on the 15th all hands were employed in getting the vessels ready for sea; and at seven o'clock in the morning of the 16th we got under sail with light variable winds. By noon we were close in with Dunnose, which caused us to ply occasionally.

At

At four in the afternoon, having a fresh gale, and very hazy weather, we bore up for St. Helen's, and soon afterwards anchored in St. Helen's road, Bembridge Point bearing South West by West, three miles distant.

At six in the morning of the 17th we weighed, and made sail with moderate variable winds, the weather hazy with rain; at noon St. Catherine's Point bore North West, five miles distant. From this to the 19th, we had little variety; the weather in general was thick and hazy, with frequent showers of rain. About seven o'clock in the evening of the 19th, the Caskets bore East North East three leagues distant; it being then nearly calm, a rapid tide set us strongly towards them; and at one time we were not two miles distant from those very dangerous rocks; however, before nine o'clock, the tide turned, and at ten we could just discern the lights, bearing South West by South, distant about three leagues.

At ten in the morning of the 20th we saw the island of Guernsey bearing South, at the distance of three or four leagues. Our latitude at noon was 49° 39′ North, the North East point of Guernsey bearing South South East, five miles distant.

At six o'clock we came to anchor in Guernsey Road with the best bower, in 13 fathom water, the castle bearing West, by South half a mile, and St. Martin's Point South South West, one mile distant. We moored with the kedge to the East South East.

CHAP. II.

Various Refreshments procured at Guernsey.—Leave that Place, and proceed on the Voyage.—Remarkable Rock at the East End of Madeira.—Lay-to in Funchal Bay, whilst Dispatches are sent on board one of his Majesty's Ships.—Bonavista.—Mayo.—Sal.—Arrival at St. Jago.—Occurrences there.—Refreshments to be met with.—Departure from thence.—Precautions against the Rain and sultry Weather near the Equator.—Fortunate Preservation of a Boy who fell over-board.—Pass a vast Quantity of Shrimp Spawn.—Arrival at Port Egmont.—Falkland's Islands.

AS it was the intention of our owners to have the same quantity of spirits daily served out to the ships companies as is customary on board his Majesty's vessels, our principal business at Guernsey was to procure a proper supply of liquor for that purpose; accordingly we received on board a considerable quantity of spirits, together with Port wine and cyder; various stores were at the same time taken from my vessel, and put on board the Queen Charlotte. These different employments engaged the whole of our time till the afternoon of the 24th, when all hands were busied in getting ready for sea.

AT five o'clock in the morning of the 25th a breeze sprung up at South East, and soon afterwards the pilot came on board; at eight we unmoored and got ready to heave a-head, when

when the wind suddenly chopped round to South South West. At noon we had very strong gales and squally weather. About one o'clock the wind veering to West South West it was my intention to have weighed and gone to sea, but the weather in an instant changing its appearance, and beginning to blow very hard, prevented me. The gale still increasing, I gave orders for the topgallant-masts to be struck and got down upon deck. I likewise caused preparation to be made for striking the topmasts, and spliced one of the new cables to the best bower; intending, should the gale continue till the evening, to lower the topmasts, to have veered to a cable and half on the best bower, and half a cable on the small one. If the ship had not held fast under these precautions, I should have run through the Little Russels, as I had a pilot on board; and by having the lower yards aloft, might have brought her under the courses, and on occasion, the topsails close reefed; but fortunately towards evening the wind got round to the Northward, though it continued blowing in sudden gusts through the night.

CHAP. II.

1785.
September.
Sunday 25.

AT nine o'clock in the morning of the 26th, having a moderate breeze at North North West, we weighed anchor and got under sail; at noon St. Martin's Point bore North East by North, distant one mile and a half; our observation gave 49° 20′ North latitude. At four in the afternoon the pilot left us. Salt provisions were first served out to the crews on the 27th, at a pound a man a day, together with half a pound of potatoes. At noon we saw Seven Isles, which bore South, eight or nine leagues, and the Isle of Bass South West by South, seven leagues distant: our latitude was 49° 6′ North, and the longitude, by lunar observation, 3° 50′ 45″ West.

Monday 26.

12   A VOYAGE TO THE

CHAP.   IN the evening of the 28th a heavy gale came on at
 II.   South East by South, attended with drizzling rain, which
1785.   brought us under close-reefed topsails. The gale still in-
September. creasing, we handed the fore and mizen top-sails: at half
Wednes. 28. past eleven we hauled round, in consequence of seeing a
        light bearing about South West, which had much the ap-
        pearance of a light-house, and which, if a real one, must
        have been Ushant light. We judged ourselves to be about
        two leagues from it. The gale continued during the night
        with unceasing violence, attended with heavy rain. As we
Thursday 29. saw no land on the morning of the 29th, it is probable
        the light which was seen the preceding evening was the
        stern light of some vessel which stood on a contrary tack.

Friday 30.   AT six o'clock in the morning of the 30th I acquainted
        captain Dixon with my intention of steering West South
        West as long as the wind continued favourable. This day
        portable soup was served to the ship's company, with half
        a pint of peas each man three times per week. We saw a
        number of land birds, one of which was caught; I suppose
        them to have been driven off the French coast by the heavy
        South East gales which we recently had met with. Our
        latitude at noon was 47° 58′ North, and the longitude
        9° 0′ West. In the afternoon we sounded with a line of
        130 fathom, but got no bottom. During the afternoon
        and night we had light variable airs with frequent calms.

October.   AT ten o'clock in the forenoon of the 1st of October
Saturday 1. we passed a Danish galliot. On this occasion our Com-
        pany's ensign was hoisted, in hopes she might take notice
        of us, and mention it on her arrival in Europe.

                                                              IN

IN the afternoon of the 2d, a heavy gale of wind came on at North West, which occasioned us to close-reef the topsails; towards evening, the weather growing more moderate, we made and shortened sail occasionally, in order to give the Queen Charlotte an opportunity of coming up with us. Indeed we have often been obliged to take this step since our departure from England, as we found the King George to have greatly the advantage of her in sailing, either when going large or by the wind.

CHAP. II.
1785.
October.
Sunday 2.

TOWARDS evening on the 3d, the weather having a very unpromising appearance, I kept under an easy sail, and hauled up to West South West, for fear of being too near Cape Finisterre; as I judged, if a strong breeze came on in the night, I should pass its latitude; but we had a light North Westerly breeze, the clouds looking black and lowering.

Monday 3.

DURING the whole of the 4th and part of the 5th we perceived a considerable ripling on the water which I have reason to think was occasioned by a current, and our observation giving, for the last 24 hours, 24 miles *less* westing than the longitude by account, and the observed latitude giving 23 miles *more* than by account, I judged this current set to the South East at a considerable rate. Our latitude at noon was 41° 48′ North, and the longitude 11° 40′ West. On the 7th, having very fine weather, the crew's bedding was got up to air, and every part below was thoroughly cleaned.

Tuesday 4.
Wednes. 5.

Friday 7.

FROM this to the 12th nothing particular occurred; but at eight o'clock that morning we saw the island Porto Santo

Wednes. 12.

CHAP. II.

1785.
October.
Wednes. 12.

Santo bearing West by North about 20 leagues distant. On this we hauled up, to have a nearer view of it, with a moderate breeze at North North East. At noon the North point of the island bore North 68° West, distant 14 leagues. I now changed our course to West by South, and steered for the East end of Madeira, which, having been one of the first of the Western discoveries, has facilitated future voyages. Our observation at noon gave 33° 7' North latitude, and the longitude was 15° 29' West. During the afternoon we kept standing for Madeira, the West end of which, at six o'clock, bore due West about 12 leagues distant.

As I wished to look into Funchal Bay, and was not willing to lose the opportunity of doing it, we shortened sail and brought-to during the night with the ship's head to the Northward. At five in the morning of the 13th we bore away and made sail.

Thursday 13.

THE East point of the island of Madeira, when it bears about West by North, has a most remarkable appearance; the land seems to be divided by many extraordinary chasms, and there is a large rock at the extreme East point, in the shape of a sphere, which is perforated so as to form an uncommon arch. There is also a rock greatly resembling a spire, which seems entirely detached from the island, and which, one might suppose, could never resist the heavy surfs that constantly beat against it.

By noon we were close in with the island, and kept standing for Funchal Bay, with a fine breeze at North East. Soon after five o'clock, being abreast of the bay, we found riding there his Majesty's ship Grampus, of fifty guns, commo-

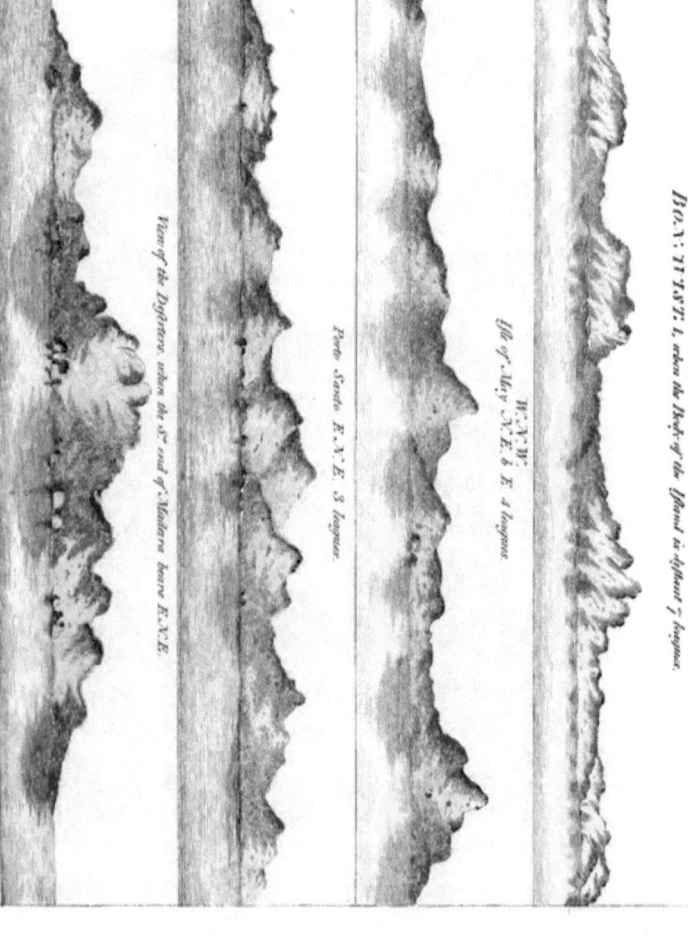

commodore Edward Thomson; and under his command his Majesty's ship Nautilus of 16 guns, which were bound on the African station. We hove-to, and I sent Mr. M'Leod, my chief mate, on board the commodore with dispatches, in order to desire that he would be so obliging as to send them on shore to the British consul, with a request that he would forward them to England by the first conveyance. At the same time I discharged one of my crew, and sent him on board the commodore at his own request. Mr. M'Leod returning about eight o'clock, we made sail and stood to the South West with a fine Easterly breeze and clear weather.

NOTHING occurred worthy of note till the 22d; when the water appearing remarkably coloured, we sounded at noon with 130 fathom line; but got no bottom. Our latitude was 17° 19′ North, and the longitude 22° 55′ West.

AT five in the afternoon we saw the Isle of Sal, bearing West North West half West, 11 leagues distant: at six o'clock we shortened sail and stretched to the Northward under the topsails; being apprehensive of falling in with some rocks which are laid down in the charts about 10 or 12 leagues to the Eastward of this island.

AT six in the morning of the 23d we made sail and bore up South by West with a fine trade breeze: in the forenoon we were in sight of Bonavista, the extremes of which bore from North 49° West to North 86° West, distant about seven leagues. Our meridional observation gave 16° 7′ North latitude, and the mean result of several lunar observations, taken in the morning, gave the longitude at noon 22°

22° 27′ 45″ West; in this situation, the Isle of Sal appears altogether as one high mountain, and Bonavista as a number of detached hillocks.

Monday 24.

At two in the morning of the 24th the Isle of Mayo appeared in sight, bearing West, about three leagues distant. On this we hauled up to South South East, in order to give the island a good birth. At five we again made sail and stood for St. Jago, which we saw soon after seven o'clock, bearing West by North.

The Isle of Mayo is considerably elevated, and the land seems capable of yielding most of the productions which are natural to tropical climates; but it does not appear that the inhabitants take any great pains to cultivate it: formerly this place was much frequented for salt, which was purchased by British ships and carried to America; but since salt has been so plentifully gathered on the Bahamas, that trade has greatly declined.

With a fresh trade breeze we stood well in for St. Jago, and at noon anchored in Port Praya Bay in eight fathom water over a sandy bottom; the fort bearing North West by North, the East point of the bay East by South, and the South point South West by West. I ordered the ship to be moored with the stream anchor to the South West a cable each way: our distance from the bottom of the bay, when moored, was about one mile and a quarter.

Soon after we were moored, there arrived in the bay the Hammet, captain Clark, and a brig commanded by a captain Hawkins, which were both from London on the Southern whale

whale fishery. Captain Clark had been out fourteen months, and had 100 tons of oil on board; the brig was outward bound.

CHAP. II.
1785.
October.
Monday 24.

THE filling up our water, and providing ourselves with such fresh provisions as the island afforded, being principal objects here, I went on shore in the afternoon, accompanied by captain Dixon, to learn the best method of facilitating our various purposes.

AFTER waiting on the commander of the fort, who is styled the " *Captain Moor*," and paying a port charge of four dollars for each vessel, I went to inspect the wells, of which there are two, and both afford excellent water: one of them indeed is rather inconvenient for watering, being situated at a considerable distance from the shore; but the other is not more than 200 yards from the beach, with a good rolling-way for casks. I am inclined to think it is better water than the other, as I observed it the most frequented by the inhabitants.

I WAS informed that a market would be held at Praya on the morrow, where I might have an opportunity of furnishing myself with live stock and various kinds of refreshments, which were brought by the inhabitants from several parts of the island.

AT day-light in the morning of the 25th the long-boat was hoisted out, and I dispatched Mr. Hayward, my third mate, with a party, to fill water, following them immediately myself in the whale-boat. When we got near the beach,

Tuesday 25.

D

CHAP. II.

1785.
October.
Tuesday 25.

beach, the surf running pretty high, I ordered Mr. Hayward to bring the boat to an anchor, as I did not think it prudent for them to land with her.

HAVING set the people busily to work in filling watercasks and rafting them off to the boat, I again waited on the *Captain Moor*, accompanied by captain Dixon. Whether he was dissatisfied with us the preceding afternoon, or what other reason he might have I cannot say, but he now behaved in a very haughty manner, seemed disposed to prevent us from procuring any refreshments, and even refused us a little water to drink, though the day was extremely sultry; but on my intimating a design of waiting on the governor (who I was given to understand resided at some distance from Praya), to inform him of this improper treatment of the subjects of a friendly power, he relaxed a little, and suffered us to trade with the inhabitants without molestation. The people in general appeared well-disposed and ready to serve us. The remainder of the day was taken up in purchasing hogs, goats, sheep, and oranges, which were brought to market in tolerable plenty.

Wednesf. 26.

EARLY this morning I dispatched two of my mates with the long-boat and a watering party, following myself soon afterwards; they immediately got to work, and by nine o'clock a boat-load of water was sent on board; I likewise sent some sheep, goats, hogs, and oranges for the ship's company. The boat returned at eleven o'clock, and by one in the afternoon a second load was sent on board, which completed our water.

UNDER-

UNDERSTANDING there were bullocks on the island, and being desirous to purchase some for the crews, I waited on a gentleman who acts here as agent for a mercantile house in Lisbon, and who I found was the only dealer for beef: on inquiring the price of bullocks, I was told ten dollars each; but as they were very small, I thought the price too high, and I only engaged one, and it was with difficulty I prevailed on this merchant to take money for it; he behaved politely and treated us hospitably. This behaviour from a stranger called for a similar return, and we sent him tea, brandy, wine, and a few other presents.

CHAP. II.
1785.
October.
Wednes. 2^d.

THE watering of both the ships being completed, I determined to stay here two days longer, in order to give the crews an opportunity of recreating themselves on shore; being convinced this recreation would be of infinite service to them, especially at a place where there is no great quantity of spirituous liquors to be procured; accordingly, on the 27th and 28th, both the ships companies had liberty given them to go on shore, the half one day and the half the other; while those on board were employed in getting the vessels ready for sea.

Thursday 27.
Friday 28.

AN officer from each ship was always sent on shore with our sailors, and had particular orders given them to prevent, if possible, any disputes with the natives; these directions were strictly attended to, and not a single quarrel happened; our people conducting themselves on shore with the greatest regularity.

IN the afternoon of the 28th arrived in the bay the Diana, captain Barrett, from London, bound to the coast

CHAP.
II.
1785.
October.
Friday 28.

of Brazil, and a brig from Martinico commanded by captain Clark. The Diana, in letting go her anchor, got foul of the Hammet's cable, on which I sent my long-boat to her assistance, and she was extricated without much difficulty.

Saturday 29.

EVERY business at this place being now completed, and the crews in excellent health, I determined to leave it the first opportunity. At daylight in the morning of the 29th we unmoored, and at ten o'clock weighed and made sail, standing out of the bay with a moderate easterly breeze. Previous to this I took my leave of captain Clark of the Hammet, to whom I acknowledge myself greatly indebted for his assistance on many occasions during our stay at Port Praya. At noon the extremes of the island bore from North 53° West, to North 33° East, distant from the harbour about three miles.

SAINT JAGO is generally mountainous, and appears to be a very fine island: but our short stay here, and my professional duties, prevented me from making excursions into the interior parts. The vallies appear to be fertile; there is a great quantity of land which is fit for producing sugar-cane, and I have no doubt but that with proper care they might cultivate some of the finest in the world; they raise cotton, and some of the natives appear to be industrious, but are exceedingly oppressed by the Portuguese soldiers, who exact an exorbitant toll from the unhappy countrymen who bring their commodities to market, their sheep, hogs, goats, turkeys, fowls, oranges, lemons, limes, bananas, and plantains; all which are tolerably plentiful, and might be purchased at very reasonable prices,

prices, were it not for those oppressions, which seem to be without remedy from an inattentive government. On the whole, the variety of refreshments which Saint Jago supplies, renders it a very eligible station for those vessels to touch at, which are employed in the Southern whale fishery, or for those which are bound, as we were, round Cape Horn.

HAVING for some days past observed a rippling on the water, in the morning of the 4th November the whale-boat was lowered down, in order to try the current; and we found it setting South East by East, at the rate of five fathoms an hour. Our latitude then was 7° 44′ North, and the longitude 21° 55′ West.

ON the 11th one of our seamen caught a sparrow-hawk, which had settled on the mizen-topsail-yard. I could scarcely find any difference between this bird and that of the same species to be met with in England. The observation at noon gave 4° 39′ North latitude, and 21° 30′ West longitude.

SINCE our departure from Saint Jago we had seldom been favoured with a steady North East trade; the wind frequently was variable, at times blew very fresh and in heavy squalls; the weather was close and sultry, attended with violent showers of rain.

SUCH heavy rains and close sultry weather very often bring on sickness among seafaring men, and too much care cannot be taken to guard against their fatal effects; accordingly every precaution was taken that could be thought of for preserving the crews in good health; their
clothes

CHAP. II.
1785.
November.
Friday 11.

clothes and bedding were brought upon deck to air, whenever the weather permitted; great care was taken to keep the ships between decks clean and well aired; and krowt, sweet-wort, borcole, and portable soup, were alternately served to the ship's company. These methods, with the blessing of Providence, succeeded to the utmost of my wishes; so that there was not one person sick on board during this passage, although we laboured under the disagreeable circumstance of our decks and upper works leaking so much, that many of the sailors could scarcely lie dry in their beds, and the rain prevented the caulkers from being set to work so constantly as our situation required: this inconvenience arose from the vessel being new, and consequently having never been in a warm climate.

Tuesday 15.

On the 15th David Gilmore, a boy about ten years old, fell overboard from the weather main shrouds, and not being able to swim, dropped a-stern. Every effort was used to save him; but all had proved ineffectual, had not Providence enabled him to keep above water till the boat picked him up, when he was near two hundred yards from the vessel, and had been eight or ten minutes in the ocean; and when he was almost dead with fright and fatigue.

Wednes. 16.

Early the next morning we caught a shark, which had the greatest part of a large porpoise in his maw; this circumstance gave us fresh cause of thankfulness for the preservation of Gilmore, and additional reflections on the various accidents to which a seafaring life is subject.

THE

NORTH WEST COAST OF AMERICA.

THE same day we crossed the equator in the 25th degree of West longitude with a moderate trade wind at South East, and pleasant weather.

CHAP. II.
1785.
November.
Wednes. 16.

IN the afternoon of the 24th captain Dixon came on board the King George, and I signified to him my intention of touching at Port Egmont in Falkland's Islands, in order to refit and water our ships; as we then should be enabled to prosecute the voyage without attempting to make any harbour near Cape Horn, a circumstance which would most probably be attended with difficulty and delay. This point being determined on, captain Dixon returned on board his own vessel about five o'clock; and we stretched to the Southward with a favourable breeze.

Thursday 24.

TOWARDS evening on the 27th, two sand-pipers of the striated species were seen about the ship; after staying near an hour, they flew away in the direction of East North East. John Hamilton Moore, in his chart of the Atlantic Ocean, lays down an island called Ascencas, about 19° 45′ South latitude, and 35° 25′ West longitude; and judging myself at this time nearly in the same latitude, and not being certain of its situation as to longitude, I brought-to and lay by during the night; at daylight next morning we bore away and stood South West till ten o'clock, and afterwards West South West until noon, when our observation giving 20° 1′ South latitude, which is more than five leagues to the Southward of Ascencas, and it being only a needless waste of time to search for that island, I altered our course to South West by South, in order to make Port Egmont as speedily as possible. Several large flocks of boobies and sheerwaters were hovering about

Sunday 27.

Monday 28.

about to the Northward of us, and it is possible that there may be land not far from this situation.

IN the morning of the 29th we passed a large quantity of rock-weed, which I supposed had been driven from the island of Trinidada and the small islands adjacent to it; a land bird, about the size of a wild duck, and very much like one, was seen flying about; we at that time were in 21° 14' South latitude, and 35° 5' West longitude.

THE same precautions that I have already taken notice of were still strictly observed in regard to the preservation of health amongst our ships companies, and were attended with the happiest effects, as we had not at this time one sick person on board.

THE trade wind left us on the 3d December, about 24° South latitude, and was succeeded by a fresh gale at South West; on this we stretched to the Eastward, but the wind gradually shifting to the Southward, we were again enabled to steer South West by South.

IN the evening of the 6th, being in 26° 24' South latitude, and 39° 26' West longitude, we steered South West during the night, as there is a rock laid down in Moore's chart nearly in that situation. Fortunately, however, we saw nothing of it; and next morning we again steered our proper course with a fresh Easterly breeze.

ON the 12th we passed through a prodigious quantity of spawn, some of which was taken up, and on examination it was found to be the spawn of shrimps; each separate particle

NORTH WEST COAST OF AMERICA.

particle was about the fize of a fmall bean, of a fubftance like blubber or jelly, quite tranfparent, and contained a fmall fhrimp alive but not matured.

I HAVE reafon to fuppofe this fpawn comes out of the river Plata, as we were nearly oppofite its mouth; our latitude being 34° 35′ South, and the longitude 45° 37′ Weft; the great numbers of fpermaceti whales which are generally met with here, are doubtlefs induced by thefe tranfparent fubftances to frequent a fituation where they conftantly find fuch abundant food.

ON the 15th, being in 37° 44′ South latitude, and 48° 20′ Weft longitude, we paffed a great number of fpermaceti whales; a large piece of bark, which appeared to have been recently feparated from the tree, was feen floating in the water; and albatroffes, fheerwaters, and a number of birds which were entirely white, and greatly refembled a pigeon, were flying about in every direction. During the forenoon of the 20th the water was very much coloured; but as there is no *known* land near the fituation we then were in, and having a brifk favourable gale, I did not chufe to interrupt our progrefs by founding; we faw a number of albatroffes, fheerwaters, and filver-coloured birds, a fhark, and feveral whales. Our obfervation at noon gave 42° 26′ South latitude, and the longitude was 53° 39′ Weft.

IN the evening of the 21ft we had a frefh gale of wind at Weft South Weft, and the fea breaking in a very extraordinary manner, we founded, but got no bottom, with a line of fixty fathom. The next morning large patches of rock-

CHAP.
II.

1785.
December.
Thursday 22.

rock-weed were floating on the water, and great variety of birds, such as albatrosses, sheerwaters, and stormy petrels, were flying about the vessels. The latitude then was 45° 26′ South, and the longitude 54° 3′ West.

1786.
January.
Monday 2.

From this to the 2d January we in general had very tempestuous weather, attended with violent squalls; variety of birds in great numbers were daily seen, such as Port Egmont hens, albatrosses, petrels, penguins, &c. large quantities of rock-weed constantly floating in the water; and it being much coloured, we were frequently induced to sound, but we never got any bottom with 120 fathom line: at length, early in the morning of the 2d, we got soundings in 72 fathom water, over a bottom of fine grey sand, and immediately afterwards saw Falkland's Islands, the land then in sight bearing from South to South East, about seven leagues distant. During the whole day we had light variable winds, and very hazy weather, which obliged us to ply occasionally, and prevented our getting in with the land.

Tuesday 3.

About eleven o'clock in the forenoon of the 3d, being about six leagues distant from the land, we saw something from the mast-head which had greatly the appearance of a ship under sail bearing South East of us, but on a nearer approach it was found to be a rock whitened over with the dung of birds; it is situated about three leagues from the land. Our latitude at that time was 51° 1′ South, and the longitude 58° 48′ West; in this situation we had soundings in 72 fathom water over a bottom of fine sand, and as we stood in shore they lessened gradually.

It

IT happened rather unluckily, that we had not a separate chart of Falkland's Islands on board of either vessel. This circumstance, together with the variable winds and foggy weather we constantly had, occasioned us to ply with caution, though I was very desirous to make a harbour as soon as possible; what water we could get at being nearly expended, without breaking up the hold, which I did not like to undertake in such stormy weather as we had recently had. At six o'clock in the afternoon, seeing the appearance of an harbour to the South South West, I sent my whale-boat on board the Queen Charlotte for captain Dixon, and communicated to him my intention of standing in for it next morning, as we (having then nearly a calm) had no chance of coming to anchor whilst daylight continued. We now had soundings in twenty-six fathom water, over a bottom of soft sand inclining to mud; the white rock just mentioned bore North 41° East, distant four or five leagues; the Easternmost point of land in sight North 61° East, and the Westernmost point South 65° West, about seven miles distant. We tacked during the night as occasion required, and soon after two o'clock in the morning of the 4th, stood for our expected harbour; but on our getting well in with the land, we found ourselves disappointed, the inlet not affording any shelter for vessels to lie at anchor. On this we stood to the Westward, as I judged we were too much to the Eastward for Port Egmont, which I wished to make. In the morning we had light airs, and so thick a fog, that no land could be seen, but at ten o'clock some high land made its appearance over the fog-bank, and presently afterwards we saw low land bearing from South by East to South by West, about four miles distant: we had soundings in thirty-two fathom water,

water, over a bottom of mud covered with fine yellow sand.

THE low land was situated about three miles from shore, and seemed to form two islands; but on a nearer approach I found that they were joined by a reef, and that a rocky shoal ran out from each extreme nearly a mile.

WE plied along shore with variable winds and foggy weather until daylight in the morning of the 5th, when, having a favourable breeze from the Northward, we stood well in for the land; soon afterwards a fine opening presented itself to the South West, which promised an excellent harbour. On this I ordered the whale-boat to be lowered down, and sent Mr. M'Leod, my chief mate, with orders to sound the entrance, and to direct captain Dixon to keep a-head of the King George.

BY five o'clock we approached the opening very fast; on which I made a signal for the whale-boat to push on and look out for an anchoring place. Soon after six o'clock, the boat being about four miles a-head, made the signal for shoal water, which occasioned us to haul the wind and stand off: after sounding directly across the entrance, the boat proceeded on and presently disappeared within the East point of the opening; notwithstanding which, I stood in under a very easy sail, being doubtful whether we should meet with a harbour; Mr. M'Leod not having as yet made the appointed signal for finding one. At the same time we were within some small islands, with an increasing wind, which blew directly on shore, and there was every appearance of an approach-

ing

ing gale: however, foon after nine o'clock I had the plea- CHAP. II.
fure of feeing the union flag flying on the top of a high
hill over the Eaft point of the opening, which was the   1786.
fignal for a fafe harbour; I immediately made a fignal for January.
the boat to return, not thinking it prudent to run in until Thursday 5.
I had the mate's report; but that no time might be loft,
I requefted captain Dixon to fend his whale-boat a-head
to found, and, fhould they meet with fhoal water, to
continue on it as a mark for the veffels to fail by.

ABOUT ten o'clock Mr. M'Leod returned, and reported
that he had found a good harbour, and a place tolerably
convenient for watering. When the fignal was made for
fhoal water, he was in feven fathom water, over a bed of
rocks covered with weeds, which came up to the furface,
and which were fituated near the middle of the channel.

WE ftood in for the harbour under an eafy fail, and at
eleven o'clock came to anchor with the beft bower on the
Eaft fhore in twelve fathom water, over a fandy bottom,
but under the furface I judge it to be a ftiff mud.

THE fhip was moored with the ftream-anchor to the
Southward: when moored we were land-locked, except
at the entrance we came in by, the Eaft point of which
bore North Weft by Weft half Weft, and the Weft point
Weft by North, diftant from the land to the Northward
about three quarters of a mile.

CHAP. III.

Various Employments in Port Egmont.—Ruins of a Town discovered.—Meet with two Ships employed in the Oil Trade.—Method of extracting Oil from the Blubber of the Sea Elephant.—Several Birds described.—Refreshments obtained there.—Leave Port Egmont, and proceed to States Bay.—Difference between the Sea Lion and Sea Elephant pointed out.—Remains of a Wreck discovered.—Leave Falkland's Islands and proceed on the Voyage.—Pass Staten's Land.—Stormy Weather in doubling Cape Horn.—Pick up a Number of Turtle.—Fruitless Search for Los Magos.—Arrive in Sight of Owhyhee.

CHAP. III.
1786.
January.
Thursday 5.

IMMEDIATELY after we were moored, I ordered the whale-boat to be lowered down, and went on shore, accompanied by captain Dixon, to inspect the watering-place pointed out by my mate, and which was situated on the North shore: it afforded excellent water, which runs through an immense bed of large stones; but the path to the watering place being also very stony, and liable to hurt our casks very much, I was induced to look out for a more eligible spot. We walked along shore to the Eastward, and fell in with several runs of good water, but the access to every one of them was equally stony. As these stones occupy a number of vallies whose declivity is confiderable, and which are separated by high mountains, I think it

very

very probable that they have been collected together by impetuous torrents of rain, though this seems not to have happened very lately, as they are universally covered with a kind of white moss.

CHAP. III.

1785. January. Thursday 5.

In the course of our walk we met with a number of sea lions on the beach, several of which were killed for the sake of their fat or blubber to make oil for our lamps, and various other purposes: by the time they were got into the boat the day was far spent, which occasioned us to repair on board.

During the afternoon we had fresh gales from the Northward with frequent squalls, but at night the wind shifted to South West, and the weather grew moderate.

Early in the morning of the 6th I went in the whale-boat, in order to look for a convenient watering-place on the West side the harbour, not being well satisfied with any I had hitherto seen, and likewise to sound the bay to the Southward. Captain Dixon also went in his boat upon the same service, taking the Northern shore.

Friday 6.

We carried soundings from twelve to ten fathom water, over a sandy bottom, until we got within a quarter of a mile of the shore; the water then shoaled to five and six fathom, with a bottom of rocks. Round the point of land to the Southward we had still a rocky bottom with six and seven fathom water.

After proceeding to the Westward for about two miles, we met with a sandy bar that runs quite across, and forms a bay within the other: small vessels might go over this

bar

CHAP. III.
1786.
January.
Friday 6.

bar at high water and lie perfectly secure; but it not answering our purpose, we landed and walked into the country, which was all in a wild state, without the least appearance of cultivation, and not a stick of wood to be seen as far as the eye could reach; but a good substitute, as fuel, may easily be procured, which is the root of a long coarse grass, that grows in many places quite to the water's edge, and when dry would make excellent turf. In our walk we picked up an iron hoop, and saw some dung which appeared like that of an hog; but our principal design in making this excursion was not answered, as we could not find any water so convenient as that to the Northward of our present situation; on which I returned on board at one o'clock, and determined to make the ship as secure as possible, in order that we might proceed on our watering business without the least delay.

Saturday 7.

At two o'clock the wind blowing very strong at South West, we got the topgallant-masts down upon deck, the top-masts were struck close down to the rigging, and the lower yards kept aloft. In the night the weather grew more moderate, and at four o'clock in the morning of the 7th, the long-boat was hoisted out and sent on shore with a watering party; the cables were got upon deck, in order to get at the empty butts under them. At eleven o'clock the boat returned with a load of water which filled thirteen butts in the main hold; she was immediately dispatched for another turn of water. During the afternoon we had fresh gales and very squally weather, so that it was with great difficulty the long-boat got a second turn of water on board; this completed the main-hold, and the cables were again coiled down.

NORTH WEST COAST OF AMERICA.

CHAP.
III.
1786.
January.
Sunday 8.

On the 8th I gave as many men as could be conveniently spared from the ship leave to recreate themselves on shore, and a boat to remain with them all day, in order to bring them on board in the evening. The 25th December being at sea, and the weather very unsettled, we declined celebrating Christmas until a more favourable opportunity; and this being a very convenient time, I gave all hands a double allowance of brandy, and some fresh pork which I killed for the occasion: these indulgences, together with a good walk on shore, made the Christmas pass very pleasantly; and in the evening I had the satisfaction of seeing my ship's company in good spirits; not a single man incapable of doing his duty from drunkenness or any other cause.

Our people, when on shore, made excursions into various parts of the country, and some of them discovered the ruins of a town, with some garden ground adjoining, in which were a few flowers; several sorts of vegetables in small quantities, such as horseradish, shalots, a few small potatoes, and some celery, which was in a degenerate state: they likewise saw a hog, but he was so wild they could not catch him.

Monday 9.

This forenoon we completed our water, and the longboat was sent for a load of stone ballast; the people who remained on board yesterday, had liberty given them to go on shore; they landed on the West side of the harbour, near the ruins of the town I have already taken notice of; and at some distance in the country saw a bullock, a cow, and several hogs, which probably were left behind when the place was evacuated.

F   From

CHAP.
III.
1786.
January.
Saturday 14.

FROM this to the 14th we were engaged in various necessary employments. About seven tons of stone ballast were taken on board, and our boats likewise assisted the Queen Charlotte in the same business, as she required a much larger quantity of ballast than the King George. A number of seals and sea lions were killed for the sake of their skins and blubber; and the carpenters were fully employed in caulking the quick-work and other parts that were found defective, in order that we might proceed to sea as soon as possible. I gave the people liberty to go on shore at every opportunity, being convinced that land-air and exercise conduce very much to preserve the health of seamen in long voyages.

DURING this interval we in general had fresh gales at South West, with squally weather and frequent rain.

Sunday 15.

AT nine o'clock this evening a sloop arrived in the harbour, and anchored off the town. Early next morning, captain Coffin came on board the King George, and informed me that his sloop is named the Speedwell, and is tender to a ship called the United States, commanded by captain Hussey, and now lying in a good harbour at Swan Island, in company with the Canton, captain Whippy: both these vessels were employed in the oil trade, and had nearly completed their cargoes; the United States having 300 tons of oil on board, and the Canton about half that quantity.

THE chief part of their oil is procured from animals they call sea elephants. These creatures are certainly amphibious,

YELLOW WINGED BUNTING.

NORTH WEST COAST OF AMERICA.

phibious, as they generally frequent fandy bays, or the points of bays that are compofed of fmooth flat ftones. A good fea elephant yields near half a ton of oil, which is produced without boiling, the blubber is fo exceedingly free: if put into cafks, the blubber will foon run to oil, and afterwards it may be ftrained off into other cafks; but this procefs being rather tedious where there are very large quantities of blubber, captain Coffin informed me they had difcovered a better and more expeditious method.

CHAP. III.
1786.
January.
Sunday 15.

They build a tank on fhore, of a fize fufficiently large to contain any quantity of oil they expect to procure. Over this tank a grating work is fixed by way of ftrainer; the blubber is then thrown on the grating, and weights being put on it, the oil is foon preffed out. Adjoining to the large tank is a fmaller one, into which the oil is ftrained a fecond time; by this means it is rendered perfectly fine, and may be put into cafks at pleafure.

From the defcription given by the late captain Cook of an animal he faw at New Georgia, I have no doubt but it was a fea elephant; and there is every reafon to fuppofe they may be found at that ifland in great plenty: the fame may be faid of Kerguelen's Land, where we touched during captain Cook's laft voyage, and found a number of thefe animals, which we then fuppofed to be fea lions; but this was certainly a miftaken notion, for they were very tame, and killed with the greateft eafe, whilft the fea lions met with at this place are quite furious, and ought not to be attacked without great caution.

F 2   THE

CHAP. III.

1786.
January.
Sunday 15.

The feathered tribe which inhabit thefe iflands are very numerous and in great variety, but moft of them are already well known: however, I procured fpecimens of the *yellow-winged bunting*, the *rufty-crowned plover*, and the *cinereous lark*. Since my arrival in England I have got correct drawings, from which the annexed engravings are taken, and a defcription of them may perhaps not be improperly introduced in this place.

The *yellow-winged bunting* is nearly the fize of a *yellow-hammer*; length five inches and a half; the bill is brown; the plumage on the upper part of the body, a reddifh brown; the fides of the head, quite round the eye, the cheft and fore-part of the neck, white; at the lower part of the laft a bar of reddifh brown; the breaft yellowifh; the reft of the under-part dufky white; the leffer wing-coverts yellow; the reft of the wing, like the back and edges of the feathers, yellowifh; the tail reddifh brown, all but the two outer feathers on each fide, which are yellow; legs yellow.

The *female* is much like the *male*, but the leffer wing-coverts incline to yellowifh afh-colour; the fides of the head, the cheft, and throat, dufky white.

Rufty-crowned plover.—Size of the *ringed plover*; length feven inches and a half; bill three quarters of an inch long, and black; the forehead, cheft, all the fore-part of the neck, the upper part of the breaft, and the belly, white; acrofs the top of the head is a bar of black paffing downwards on each fide of the neck in an irregular manner to the wings, and from thence forwards acrofs the lower part

THE RUSTY CROWN'D PLOVER, MALE.

From Falkland's Islands.

Rusty Crowned Plover, Male.

Published May 1. 1789. by J. Stockdale & G. Goulding.

of the breast, forming thereon a broad bar; behind the black bar on the top of the head is a circle of a rusty iron-colour surrounding the back part of the head as a wreath; the crown of the head within this, as well as all the upper parts of the body and wings, are cinereous brown, except the greater quills and tail, which are black: the legs are also black.

The *female* is greatly similar to the *male* in colour, but wants the rusty-coloured wreath at the back part of the head.

Cinereous lark.—This species is smaller than the sky-lark; length six inches; the bill and legs are black; the plumage and upper parts of the body are ash-colour, and the under part the same, but much paler, inclining to white near the vent; the quills and tail are black, the outer edges of the feathers of both margined with white. This species is a variety of the lark found at New Zealand.

Every necessary business being now completed, it was my determination to get to sea immediately, although we had fresh gales at South West, attended with rain; but having occasion to send one of my mates on board the Speedwell, he returned with a message from captain Coffin, informing me that captain Hussey had on board the United States, six or seven thousand fur seal skins, and that he had reason to suppose they would be disposed of at a moderate price. An opportunity of procuring such a quantity of skins was by no means to be lost, especially as there was a great probability of their selling well in China; I therefore sent for captain Dixon immediately, and consulted

him

him on the business: he was entirely of my opinion, and we agreed to purchase them, if the price was not too high; and, that this affair might delay us as little as possible, we determined to request captain Coffin to pilot the vessels to Swan Island, where, as I have already observed, the United States lay at anchor.

At four o'clock in the morning of the 16th, the Speedwell sailed for a bay on the East side of Keppel's Island; at five o'clock we unmoored and got under sail, in order to run farther into the bay. About ten, we anchored in twelve fathom water, over a muddy bottom, the town bearing West North West, distant one mile and a half, the stony valley where we watered, North, three miles and a half, and the South East end of Keppel's Island, East North East, six miles distant. We moored with the best bower to the Westward and the stream to the Eastward.

At noon I went in my whale-boat, accompanied by captain Dixon, after the Speedwell, to have some conversation with captain Coffin respecting the skins; we got on board about two o'clock, but the information he gave us about them was little more than I had already received by his message; however, he very readily undertook to pilot us to Swan Island, through the inner passage, as soon as he had got a quantity of elephant blubber on board, which then lay at one of the outer keys.

The day being far spent, and our distance from the ships considerable, we remained on board the Speedwell all night; and at five o'clock in the morning of the 17th set

CINEREOUS LARK OF FALKLANDS ISLANDS.

set off for our vessels, with an intention of surveying the bay to the Eastward; at the same time the Speedwell sailed for the key where their blubber was left.

At one o'clock I got on board my own ship, and the Speedwell arriving soon afterwards, I sent for captain Coffin, and we agreed to sail in the morning if the wind and weather permitted; he then returned on board his own vessel. Some of my people that were on shore for recreation, returned in the evening with a large sow and several small pigs, which they had caught at some distance in the country; and also great plenty of geese, ducks, and various kinds of birds, caught chiefly near the sea side. During the night we had strong gales from the South South West, with squalls and rain.

Next morning I sent my boat on board the Speedwell for captain Coffin; he came immediately on board the King George, but was of opinion that it would not be prudent for us to sail with the present unsettled weather; I therefore determined to keep my present situation till a more favourable opportunity. The wind blew very strong all day at South South West, attended with frequent squalls, but towards evening the weather grew moderate.

At four o'clock in the morning of the 19th we unmoored, and at seven got under sail with a moderate breeze at South, shaping our course for Swan Island: the Speedwell took the inner passage, and we stood round Saunders's Island.

CHAP.
III.
1786.
January.
Thursday 19.

By eight o'clock we were just in the entrance of Port Egmont, and the wind inclining to South West, we plied to windward, and at noon were working through the passage between Saunders's Island and Low Islands. During the afternoon we had variable winds, with fogs and clear weather by turns. At eight o'clock the West end of Saunders's Island bore East by South three leagues, a ridge of rocks which extends from it, East North East five miles, the West end of Low Islands four leagues, and the East end of Carcass Island South by West four leagues distant. Soon after ten o'clock we anchored off Carcass Island Bay, in 15 fathom water, over a bottom of coarse sand and broken shells.

Friday 20.

The morning of the 20th was ushered in with a thick fog and quite calm, but about seven o'clock, a breeze sprung up from the Westward, and the weather cleared up; on which captain Coffin came on board the King George, in order to pilot us into West Point Harbour; the passage from our present situation to that place being amongst a number of small islands: he likewise put a pilot on board the Queen Charlotte. On this we immediately weighed, and at nine o'clock passed between Beachy Island and the Easternmost of the middle rocks. There is a most excellent harbour on the South side of Carcass Island, well sheltered, which may easily be known by a small island that lies in the middle of it, within which a vessel may anchor with the greatest safety. At noon we anchored with the best bower in West Point Harbour, in seven fathom water, over a sandy bottom, and moored with the kedge. When moored, the North point of the harbour

bour bore West North West one mile distant, and the West point of West Point Island, West half North, distance three leagues. This harbour is certainly one of the finest in the world, being sheltered from every wind, and easy of access.

CHAP. III.
1785.
January.
Friday 20.

THE wind being unfavourable, and the weather very hazy during the afternoon, we kept our situation; but the morning of the 21st proving fine, we weighed and got under sail at seven o'clock. Soon afterwards, being directly opposite the South West point of West Island, the gusts of wind came on so very heavy from the high land, that we were obliged to clew all up and keep the ship large; however, after we had rounded the point, and got clear of the high land, we had a moderate steady breeze from West North West. The weather being very hazy, we steered South West by South, to make the Middle Islands; and at half past ten o'clock the South end of Middle Islands bore South East by East half East, one league distant, and Swan Island, South half East, four leagues distant. At noon we had an observation, which gave 51° 44′ South latitude. In this situation, Loop's Head (which is the East point of the entrance into Swan Island Bay) bore South East half East, distant about two leagues, and the Westernmost of the Middle Islands East South East, three miles distant. At one o'clock we passed Loop's Head, and stood into States Bay, so named by captain Benjamin Huffy, who first discovered it when on a whaling voyage to these islands some years ago.

Saturday 21.

WITHIN this bay are several fine harbours, the principal of which I shall distinguish by the name of *Huffy's Harbour*,

G

CHAP. III.
1786.
January.
Saturday 21

bour, in honour of the difcoverer. Here we found riding at anchor the United States, the Canton, and the Speedwell and Maria floops, tenders to the United States.

AT three o'clock we anchored with the beft bower in States Bay, in eighteen fathom water, over a muddy bottom, and moored with the kedge. When moored, the outer end of a reef without us bore North half Eaft, one mile diftant; the entrance of the Bay Eaft by North, one mile and a half; and a fmall ifland South by Weft half Weft one mile and a half diftant.

As foon as the fhip was fecured I went in my whaleboat, accompanied by captain Dixon, on board the United States, to have fome converfation with captain Huffy, refpecting the purchafe of his fur feals, but we found he was not difpofed to part with them; and I am inclined to think he meant them for an Eaftern market, as he mentioned to me his intention of going to China immediately on his return home.

THE bufinefs which had detained us here for fome days paft being now finally put an end to, nothing prevented us from getting to fea immediately; however, as our next paffage was likely to prove a long one, I was induced to give the failors a day's liberty on fhore previous to our leaving thefe iflands; accordingly, on the 22d, moft of the people from both veffels had a walk on fhore, and the weather proved very favourable.

Sunday 22.

I WENT along with captain Huffy over to the North fide of States Bay, and there found a fea elephant, which

at

at once convinced me that those animals we saw at Kerguelen's Land were really sea elephants, and that we were totally mistaken in calling them sea lions. I have already taken notice how very different these animals are in their nature, and I now had a most convincing proof of it; for the elephant was killed with all the ease imaginable, but at the North point of the bay a number of sea lions were drawn up in a kind of rank on the beach, and disputed our passage with the greatest ferocity; far from attacking them, we acted only on the defensive, and it was not without difficulty we got round the point.

CHAP. III.
1786.
January.
Sunday 22.

IN the course of our walk we found several pieces of white wax, and saw a top, some spars, and various other pieces of a wreck. I mention this circumstance more particularly, as it may possibly throw some light on the following accident.

SOME years ago two Spanish vessels came round Cape Horn, bound to Buenos Ayres, laden principally with white wax; one of them arrived safe, the other has never yet been heard of, but there is too much reason to fear that she was lost on Falkland's Islands.

THE day being pretty far advanced, I repaired on board my ship with a determination to put to sea at daylight in the morning, if the weather permitted.

HAVING a fine Southerly breeze, at four o'clock in the morning of the 23d we unmoored, and at five weighed and came to sail. We run clear of Ball Island, which is situated on the West side of the entrance into Swan Island Bay,

Monday 23.

Bay, and then shaped our course for New Island, which from Ball Island bears West half North, four leagues distant. On the East side of New Island are three good bays; its greatest extent is from North to South. Good water is scarce at this island, except in a bay on the South side, and there it is easily found, as it is a boiling spring, situated nearly at low-water mark. I was informed by captain Hussy, that most of the springs at New Island are rendered brackish by a very heavy sea, which constantly sets in with a Westerly wind, the spray of which flies over the beach and mixes with the fresh-water springs.

At noon the Northernmost point of Round Island bore East South East half East, ten miles distant; the South West point of New Island, South East half South, eight miles; and the South West point of all Falkland's Islands South South East half East, six leagues distant. We had an observation, which gave 51° 36′ South latitude. The wind hauling to the Westward at four o'clock, occasioned us to tack, the weather moderate and hazy. At eight o'clock Cape Peribal (the Westernmost point of Falkland's Islands) bore East South East, six leagues, and the North point of New Island East North East half East, eight leagues distant.

Having a moderate breeze to the Northward in the morning of the 24th, I steered South West, being well clear of all the Islands, Cape Peribal at this time bearing East North East, about ten leagues distant. The weather was hazy, and in the afternoon a very thick fog came on, but we were fortunate enough not to lose company. We saw numbers of whales, and variety of birds, such as penguins,

silver–

silver-coloured birds, and small divers. About seven o'clock the only hen turkey I had flew overboard, but the weather being very foggy, and a heavy swell from the Northward, I did not think it safe to venture my boat from the ship, though I was sorry for the accident; as I had reserved her and a cock, together with some other poultry, to leave as breeders at any place where I thought there was a probability of their breeding and being taken care of.

ON the 25th, being then in 52° 33′ South latitude, and 63° 12′ West longitude, the variation was 23° 6′ East. In the evening we sounded with sixty fathom of line, but got no bottom.

AT six o'clock in the afternoon of the 26th we saw Staten's Land very high, bearing South, distant about five or six leagues; soon afterwards it came on to blow very strong and in squalls, attended with rain, and the weather so thick that we lost sight of the land; this brought us under close-reefed topsails and reefed courses; the topgallant-masts were also struck. The weather clearing up at half past seven o'clock, the land again appeared in sight, on which we made sail and run in for it: this however was of short continuance, for presently afterwards there was every appearance of a bad night; so that I judged it prudent to shorten sail, and haul our wind to the Northward. We sounded at eight o'clock in forty-five fathom water, over a muddy bottom: the lead was kept going, but did not strike the ground with sixty fathom of line. At midnight we tacked, and at two o'clock in the morning of the

CHAP. III.
1786.
January.
Friday 27.

27th again saw Staten's Land; the extremes bearing from South South West to South East by South, distant about six leagues. The weather being moderate, we made sail, and shaped a course for the East end of it. At eight o'clock the East end of Staten's Land bore South South West five miles, and the small island opposite New-year's Harbour, West South West, about seven leagues distant. Soon afterwards we passed through a strong rippling, which I found was occasioned by a current setting to the Northward.

IMMEDIATELY after we doubled the East point of Staten's Land, I steered South by West by compass, in order to get a good offing; not chusing to keep near the shore, on account of the strong current which sets through the Straits of La Maire. At noon Cape Saint Juan, which is the East cape of Staten's Land, bore North West by West half West, about six leagues distant. Our latitude was 54° 57′ South, and the longitude 63° 33′ West. Staten's Land is high, but the mountains near the summit being very uneven, it gives them greatly the appearance of saddle lands.

NEW-YEAR's Harbour is already well known; besides which, there is an appearance of a harbour on the North side near the East end; there also seem to be two openings, one near the West end, the other about the middle of the island, and which is situated within two small round islands that are detached from Staten's Land. There was a patch of snow on the summit of the highest mountain, but not any wood to be seen.

SEALS

NORTH WEST COAST OF AMERICA.   47

SEALS were seen in prodigious numbers, and there is no doubt but the sea elephant frequents this place; so that certainly it would be a lucrative employ for one or two ships to be sent annually for oil. During the afternoon we had a moderate breeze at West by North, and cloudy weather. At six o'clock Cape Saint Juan bore North 40° West, about eight leagues distant. Presently after this, the wind shifted gradually to the Southward, and blew a very strong gale, which brought on a heavy cross sea, and caused the ship to labour exceedingly; the wind was however by no means steady, but veered from South to West, still blowing a fresh gale, with frequent heavy squalls, which occasioned us to tack as occasion required.

CHAP. III.
1786.
January.
Friday 27.

WE still had stormy tempestuous weather, the wind continuing to the Westward; on which I determined to stand well to the Southward, by which means, after running down our Southing, we were certain of gaining, either from a Southerly or Westerly wind.

Sunday 29.

OUR latitude at noon on the 30th was 56° 53′ South, and the longitude 63° 35′ West. A number of very large albetrosses, and many small pieces of rockweed, were seen about the ship. As I was apprehensive that a current set us to the Eastward, I steered South West when the wind permitted.

Monday 30.

THE weather, which for some days had been very stormy, now grew moderate, and we had light breezes from the Southward, attended with a thick fog and drizzling rain. This morning I struck a very remarkable fish; the hind part and tail were exactly like those of a shark,

February.

Wednes. 1.

and

and its nose had the resemblance of a porpoise. I should gladly have got this fish on board, that I might have been able to describe it more minutely; but in struggling he extricated himself from the harpoon, after being struck near half a minute.

THE morning of the 3d being clear and the weather fine, I took this opportunity of getting the seamen's chests up, and had the ship well cleaned and scraped fore and aft, and thoroughly aired with fires. Towards noon it grew cloudy, and a strong gale came on at North West, attended with squalls, which increased to a violent degree towards night; this caused us to hand the topsails and foresail, and bring-to under a reefed mainsail, fore and mizen staysails. The morning of the 4th was more moderate, but the wind still blew a fresh gale from the Westward. An observed distance of the sun and moon gave 68° 1' West longitude, the latitude was 60° 19' South.

ON the 5th I ordered the people one pound and a half of fresh pork a man, in addition to their allowance of salt provisions, together with an extra half allowance of brandy: this, and every indulgence in my power, I gave them with the greatest pleasure, as their behaviour has given me great satisfaction ever since they have been under my command.

IN 60° 9' South latitude, and 70° 13' West longitude, the mean result of six azimuths gave 26° 19' Easterly variation. Being now well to the Southward, I steered West by South whenever the wind permitted.

WE

WE continued our voyage without making much progress, as the wind was generally in the Western board, blowing fresh and in squalls; the weather very stormy and unsettled. Our latitude at noon on the 18th was 55° 31' South, and the mean result of several lunar observations gave 82° 22' West longitude.

CHAP. III.
1786.
February.
Saturday 18.

DURING this interval every change of wind was preceded by a sudden squall, which generally was of short continuance, and succeeded by a calm: not being able to carry topgallant-sails in such critical weather, I kept the yards down, and the topgallant-masts struck close down to the topsail-yards, swaying them up, or lowering them down, as we had occasion to take reefs in the topsails: indeed I find this method of great advantage to the ship, not only as it serves to ease the topmast-heads, but makes her hold a much better wind.

ON the 22d, the weather being very fine, I ordered the sailors hammocks to be brought upon deck and their bed-clothes to be well aired; being well assured that inattention to things of this nature often occasions fatality amongst seamen. Our observation at noon gave 54° 4' South latitude, and the longitude by lunar observation was 81° 19' West; in this situation we found the variation to be 22° 56' Easterly. We still had squally unsettled weather with Northerly and Westerly winds.

Wednes. 22.

IN the afternoon of the 25th a very strong gale came on at North West; notwithstanding which we were under the necessity of carrying more sail than the ship could well

Saturday 25.

H

CHAP. III.
1786.
February.
Saturday 25.

well bear, in order to prevent our being driven to the Eastward.

It is the general opinion of navigators that South West winds prevail in this part of the Pacific Ocean constantly, but we have experimentally found this opinion to be erroneous; the wind for a considerable time past has blown from the Northward and Westward; generally in strong gales attended with squalls.

Tuesday 28.

In the morning of the 28th some seals were seen about the ship; a parcel of rockweed and the branch of a tree were floating in the sea. Our latitude was 52° 20' South, and the longitude 83° 59' West; we here found 19° 49' Easterly variation. The wind still continued Westerly; frequently blowing a fresh gale, with hazy weather; how-

March.
Sunday 5.

ever, the 5th of March proving very fine, I ordered the ship to be well cleaned between decks, and properly aired with good fires. At that time we were in 45° 58' South latitude, and 80° 45' West longitude *. During the late tempestuous weather the water had found its way into the sail-room, and our spare sails and canvas were much wet:

Tuesday 7.

the weather on the 7th being pretty favourable, they were got upon deck and well aired; the same opportunity was taken to repair our rigging, some of which was much damaged.

For some days past the wind had inclined to the Southward, and I began to conceive hopes that we should be

favoured

* The longitude being invariably West, no distinction will be made hereafter, in order to avoid repetition.

NORTH WEST COAST OF AMERICA.

favoured with a steady breeze at South West or South South West; especially as we had a prodigious swell from that quarter, and the clouds moved briskly towards the North East, but now it again hauled to the Westward. Indeed appearances of this nature are not to be depended on in these seas, as we have been regularly disappointed in them for three weeks past. Towards noon the water changed colour and had the appearance of soundings; if so, it must be a considerable distance from shore, our latitude being 44° 20′ South, and the longitude 79° 49′.

ON the 10th we had 10° 41′ Easterly variation, and on the 12th it was 15° 7′ East. As the variation had gradually been decreasing for some time past, I cannot account for so material a difference, except that on the 10th we were rather more to the Eastward, and consequently nearer the land, which possibly might have some effect on the compass. The wind still continued to the Westward, and brought on so thick a fog that we seldom saw each other; yet we were fortunate enough not to part company. On the 15th, the weather clearing up, we got a meridian altitude, which gave 42° 14′ South latitude; the longitude by lunar observation was 85° 4′, and the variation 12° 3′ East.

THE fog was succeeded by squally unsettled weather, with frequent heavy rains, and sometimes light snow storms, which, however, were of short duration, and the weather gradually became temperate and pleasant, but the wind still continued to the Northward and Westward.

ON the 21st the latitude was 36° 17′ South, and the mean result of several sets of human observations gave 85°

CHAP. III.

1786.
March.
Tuesday 21.

88° 7' longitude. In the afternoon I sent a boat on board the Queen Charlotte for captain Dixon; he came on board the King George, and we determined to stand on directly for Los Majos, an island discovered by the Spaniards, and situated about 20° North latitude, and 135° longitude. This island being very little out of our track, induced me to steer for it, as there was a probability of meeting with a good harbour and water; so that we should be able to refit our vessels and refresh the crews, without running down to the Sandwich Islands, which were considerably out of our course. At the same time we appointed Owhyhee as our place of rendezvous in case of separation before we arrived at Los Majos; there to wait for each other ten days; and if not joined during that time, to sail for King George's Sound.

Saturday 25.

ON the 25th, being in 32° 28' South latitude, and 91° 51' longitude, we had a moderate steady breeze at East South East, with very fine weather, and I began to entertain hopes that we had fallen in with a trade-wind. This forenoon the ship was well scraped fore and aft, aired with fires, and afterwards washed with vinegar; cyder was also served to the people at the rate of a pint a man, besides their usual allowance of spirits.

WITH a light Easterly breeze we steered North West by West; and at six o'clock in the afternoon a sail was seen from the mast-head, or a rock which had greatly the appearance of one, bearing North West by West half West. Not being certain whether what we had seen really was a vessel, I changed our course to West by North, and stood under an easy sail; so that we could easily haul our wind in case of danger during the night; but soon after nine o'clock our doubts were changed into certainty; for we plainly perceived the object in doubt to be either a brig or a snow, standing to the Southward. The Queen Charlotte, on seeing this vessel, shewed a light, and on our answering it, the strange sail hoisted a light, and tacked to the Northward. By this time she was rather abaft our larboard beam; and as I did not think it prudent to make ourselves, or our business, known to strangers, I kept on my course, and by half past ten o'clock we lost sight of her. There is reason to suppose that this strange sail was a Spanish vessel, and from her plying to the Southward, she certainly was bound either to Baldivia or Conception on the coast of Chili; though I was rather surprised at meeting with a vessel of this description in such a situation; we being at this time 300 leagues from the coast.

We continued our course to the North West, without meeting with any thing worthy of notice. On the 2d of April we were well within the tropics, our latitude being 21° 44′ South. At the same time, the longitude by lunar observation was 102° 9′, and the variation 4° 58′ East.

From this till the 10th we had little variety: that afternoon we passed a turtle, and being very anxious to procure a fresh meal for my ship's crew, I brought the ship to, and ordered the whale-boat to be lowered down, and sent Mr. M'Leod, my first mate, after it. He brought it on board, but it had been dead some time, and was almost in a state of putrefaction; so that we threw it overboard, and were much disappointed in our expected dainty. However, to make us some amends for this disappointment, we picked up

CHAP. III.
1786.
April.
Saturday 15.

up a very lively one on the 15th, which weighed sixty-five pounds, and was caught just in time for us to celebrate Easter, the next day being Easter Sunday.

The cyder, which had been regularly served to the ship's company for some time past, being expended, I ordered some sweet wort to be made, and served out at the rate of half a pint per man each day. Our latitude at noon was 7° 4′ South, and 111° 59′ longitude.

We saw a large flock of white birds about the size of a tern, and which I am inclined to think are of the same species with those we met with in great abundance at Christmas Island during captain Cook's last voyage. Several turtle passed us, and great numbers of dark-coloured birds were flying about. From these appearances I conjectured we were passing near some land; but, though the day was clear, we could see nothing of the kind from the mast head.

Thursday 20.

On the 20th we crossed the equator, in 115° 10′ longitude; the variation here was 3° 28′ East.

Saturday 22.

In the latitude of 3° 33′ North, longitude 116° 35′, we found a current setting to the Eastward, at the rate of one mile and a half per hour, in which I changed our course from North North West to North West half West. A cross swell from every direction inclined me to think that we were rather too near the great bay of Panama. However, I was under the necessity of keeping well to the Eastward, that we might be enabled to fetch the islands Los Majos, which, should they afford good water, and some

other

NORTH WEST COAST OF AMERICA.

other refreshments, may be hereafter of the greatest importance to any ships coming round Cape Horn to the Western coast of America, as they lie directly in the track for that coast, and consequently are more conveniently situated than the Sandwich islands.

I HAD conceived hopes, that when the South East trade wind left us, it would have been succeeded by that at North East; but we did not get a steady North East trade till the 1st of May in 8° 53′ North latitude, and 120° 29′ longitude.

DURING this interval, we had light variable winds and calms by turns, with close sultry weather and frequent heavy rains. Notwithstanding every precaution, the scurvy made its appearance amongst us; and the boatswain in particular was so bad for some days, that I almost despaired of his recovery; but it fortunately happened, that some small sallad, such as mustard and cresses, which I had sown in several casks of mould procured at Falkland's Islands, was now in great perfection. I planted some horse-radish in a cask before we left England, which was in an improving state, and some potatoes, planted since we left Falkland's Islands, began to sprout very finely. These things were given to the boatswain, and they had every good effect that could be wished; they checked the disorder, and he began to recover his health daily. This unwholesome weather had likewise affected the health of several seamen on board the Queen Charlotte; and captain Dixon in particular being very bad, I went on board the Queen Charlotte, and found his disorder to be the scurvy. At my return, I sent him a cask of fine mould, with sallad growing

ing in it, together with some krout, garden seeds, and a few bottles of artificial mineral water, which was prepared by Dr. Melville, in imitation of Seltzer water, and supposed to be a most excellent antiscorbutic. We frequently caught turtle, which were constantly served out amongst the ship's company, and I sent some on board the Queen Charlotte. This, with the addition of krout, portable soup, and sweet-wort, contributed greatly to preserve the health of the ships crews.

Sunday 7.

IN the forenoon of the 7th, we were near the situation of the island Partida, according to captain Cook's general chart, but no appearances of land were seen. Indeed, this island was not seen by captain Cook, but copied into that chart from the authority of the Spaniards.

TOWARDS noon the wind inclining more to the Northward, we steered North North West, in order that we might get into the latitude of Los Majos, without being to the Westward of it, which I was afraid might be the case, if the wind hauled to the Northward as we increased our latitude.

Friday 12.

ON the 12th, being in the latitude of 20° 1' South, and 134° 11' longitude, I expected to have fallen in with the Los Majos islands, as we were now exactly in the centre of them, according to the chart just mentioned, but not the least appearance of land was to be seen. The sickly situation of our people rendered it however absolutely necessary for us to make land as soon as possible; on which account we lay-to in the night-time, and spread during the day; so that (as we were favoured with fine

clear

clear weather, and a steady breeze) it was impossible for us to miss them if they really existed.

We stood to the Westward between 19° 46′ and 20° North latitude, till the 15th, by which time we were considerably to the Westward of Los Majos, but no such islands were to be found. On which I determined to stand directly for the Sandwich Islands, as there was a certainty of our procuring whatever refreshments we wanted.

The scurvy now attacked a number of the ship's crew. The first symptoms were a stiffness about the knees and hams, afterwards the shin-bones became sore; and in a few days those parts which before were stiff began to swell and turn black, and the mouth grew sore. My boatswain had all these appearances to a great degree, attended with a fever and a violent pain in his head, notwithstanding which he recovered in a surprising manner.

As I never knew an instance of a person recovering from an advanced stage of the scurvy whilst at sea, I shall take the liberty of mentioning the regimen he was under during his illness, especially as it may be of great service to persons in the same situation. Besides the assistance he received from Mr. Hogan my surgeon, who was very skilful in his profession, he had for breakfast a pint of sweet wort, with some soft bread, which I ordered to be made for him. About ten o'clock he gathered some small sallad from the little garden I have just mentioned; this he ate with vinegar; for dinner he had portable soup with barley, celery seed, mustard, cress, and rape seed boiled in it; besides which, he ate plentifully of krout. These things

CHAP. III.

1786.
May.
Monday 15.

things had so good an effect, that in a fortnight he was able to do his duty as usual: Captain Dixon likewise grew better, though slowly; and he attributed this favourable turn in his disorder chiefly to the mineral water prepared by Dr. Melville; a few bottles of which I sent him, as already has been related.

Tuesday 23.

WITH a fine trade breeze we steered West by South, in order to make Owhyhee, the principal of the Sandwich Islands. Our latitude on the 23d was 19° 10′ North, and 153° 21′ longitude. In this situation we found a current setting to the Southward.

Wednes. 24.

I EXPECTED to have made the land before night came on; but towards evening the weather turned very hazy, on which we shortened sail, and brought-to during the night. At daylight in the morning of the 24th, we bore away and made sail, and at seven o'clock Owhyhee made its appearance, the East point bearing North West by West, about six leagues distant. Soon afterwards, having an uninterrupted view of the island, I kept away along shore down the South side, and at noon the East point bore North half West, three leagues distant. The East and South East parts of this island appear fertile and very pleasant; but that part which lies South and South West is quite barren, and seems to be covered with a kind of lava.

By two o'clock, being within three miles of the land, and running along shore with a moderate breeze, a number of the natives came off in their canoes, and brought with them some small hogs and a few plantains, which I bought

I bought for beads and small pieces of iron. A number of their fishing lines were purchased, many of which were from three to four hundred fathoms long, and perfectly well made. Some were made with two and others with three strands, and much stronger than our lines of twice the size.

CHAP.
III.
1786.
May.
Wednes. 24.

CHAP. IV.

Range along the Coast of Owhyhee.—Arrival in Karakakooa Bay.—Unruly Behaviour of the Natives.—Leave Karakakooa Bay.—Refreshments procured along the Coast.—Disappointed in coming to anchor at Morotoi.—Arrive at Woahoo.—Fruitless Search for a Watering-place.—Supplied with Water by the Natives.—Refreshments obtained.—Departure from Woahoo.—Account of the present Government amongst the Sandwich Islands.—Pass Atoui.—Arrival at Oneehow.—Transactions there.

THE Indians traded with cheerfulness, and did not shew any disposition to act dishonestly: after disposing of every thing they had got to sell, and viewing the ship all round, they returned to the shore perfectly well pleased. As Karakakooa Bay was the only harbour we knew of at Owhyhee, I determined to make it as soon as possible; and at eleven o'clock in the forenoon of the 25th we passed the South point; but soon afterwards the wind grew variable, and frequently blew in squalls.

During the afternoon we stood to the Northward along the West side of the island; and being well in with the land, a number of canoes came off, bringing hogs and other refreshments, which we chiefly purchased with small pieces of iron. I had conceived hopes that we should have

have come to anchor in Karakakooa Bay this evening; but there was very little wind, and that little was unfavourable: indeed the trade-wind is not to be expected after hauling round the South point of the ifland, as the high land to the Eaftward entirely breaks it off, and light breezes prevail from the Northward and Weftward.

CHAP.
IV.
1786.
May.
Thurfday 25.

Soon after the day was clofed in we obferved a great number of fires all along fhore, and I was inclined to think they were lighted in order to alarm the country: indeed it is cuftomary for the natives at this ifland to light fires when they make offerings to their gods for fuccefs in war; and this might poffibly be the cafe at prefent; but I had obferved a fhynefs in the natives the nearer we approached Karakakooa; they frequently enquired after captain King, and feemed by their behaviour to think that we were come to revenge the death of captain Cook.

Soon after daylight on the 26th, Karakakooa bore North Eaft by Eaft, about fix leagues diftant; and a light breeze fpringing up at North Weft, we ftood in for the bay. In the forenoon an inferior chief came on board, from whom I learned that Tereeoboo, who was king of Owhyhee when we laft were at that ifland, was dead; and that the prefent king's name was Maiha Maiha. He importuned me very ftrongly to go on fhore; but on my declining it, and making him a prefent, he informed me that Maiha Maiha would pay me a vifit on the morrow; but I paid little regard to this piece of intelligence, as it was not likely that Maiha Maiha would venture on board after the active part he took in that unfortunate affray which terminated in the much-lamented death of captain Cook.

Friday 26.

MANY

CHAP.
IV.
1786.
May.
Friday 26.

MANY canoes now came along-side, and the people were very importunate to come on board; they behaved in a very daring infolent manner; and it was with difficulty they were prevailed on to quit the ship; however, I bore all this with patience, being unwilling to ufe violence if it could poffibly be avoided; though at the fame time I was much afraid from thefe appearances, that we fhould not be able to do our bufinefs at Karakakooa with eafe and fafety, particularly to fill our water and get the fick people on fhore.

As we approached the harbour, great numbers of canoes joined us, and many of them hanging by the fhip, retarded our progrefs fo much, that it was near four o'clock in the afternoon before we came to an anchor. I moored with the beft bower to the Weftward in nine fathom water, over a bottom of white fand, and the fpare anchor to the Eaftward, in feven fathom, over the fame bottom. The Weft point of the bay bore Weft, and the South point South half Weft, diftant from the beach at the bottom of the bay about a quarter of a mile.

Soon after our anchor was gone, we were furrounded by an amazing number of the natives, both in canoes and in the water; they grew very troublefome, conftantly crawling up the cable and the fhip's fides; fo that moft of the feamen were employed in keeping the veffel clear, and it was not without fome difficulty that we got moored.

DURING this time no chief who had any command on the people made his appearance, which was rather unfortunate; for if I could have got a perfon of confequence

on

NORTH WEST COAST OF AMERICA.

on board, he would have kept the reft in order, and our bufinefs would have been carried on with eafe and dif- patch.

CHAP. IV.
1786.
May.
Friday 26.

In the courfe of the afternoon we procured a number of fine hogs, and a good quantity of falt, together with plantains, potatoes, and taro, which laft was the fineft I ever faw, and not in the leaft inferior to yams: bread-fruit was fcarce, and the little we got was not in a perfect ftate; fo that I conclude this is not the proper feafon for it.

At night fires were lighted all round the bay, and the people on fhore were in conftant motion; feveral canoes continued near the fhip, and about midnight one of the natives brought off a lighted torch, feemingly with an in- tention of fetting fire to the veffel: on our driving him away, he paddled to the Queen Charlotte, but there they were equally on their guard; on which he again went on fhore.

By daylight the next morning we were vifited by a vaft multitude of the natives; but ftill no chief was to be feen who had power fufficient to keep them in order, and they grew fo daring and infolent, that I was under the neceffity of placing centinels with cutlaffes to prevent their board- ing us.

Saturday 27.

This unexpected reception convinced me that we could do nothing with fafety on fhore without the protection of a ftrong guard; and our taking a ftep of that kind might probably be attended with fatal confequences; fo that I deter-

CHAP.
IV.
1786.
May.
Saturday 27.

determined to leave Karakakooa as soon as possible. I acquainted captain Dixon with my intention of sailing, and the reasons I had for it: his opinion respecting the disposition of the inhabitants exactly agreed with my own.

NOTWITHSTANDING the vast concourse of Indians that were assembled about the ships, we saw great numbers collected in bodies on shore; some on the beach, and others on the top of a hill which commands the watering-place; and there appeared to be many chiefs among them.

AT nine o'clock I gave orders to unmoor, but the crowd of people around the ship was so great, that our boats could scarcely pass to the buoys: in this situation it was absolutely necessary for us to drive them away, and I was desirous of using some method that would frighten, without hurting them; accordingly, after drawing out the shot, we fired six four-pounders and six swivels; at the same time our colours were hoisted, and the ship tabooed, by hoisting a white flag at the main-topgallant-mast-head: this had the desired effect; for, immediately on our beginning to fire, the Indians made for the shore with the utmost precipitation; in the hurry and confusion occasioned by this alarm, many canoes were overset; the owners, however, did not stay to right them, but swam immediately on shore.

WE now had an opportunity of unmooring without molestation, and soon after eleven o'clock, having light baffling winds, began to warp out of the bay to the Westward; at five o'clock, judging myself in a good situation to wait for the land-breeze, which usually blows off towards

wards evening, we let go an anchor, and presently were visited by a number of canoes, who brought us some good hogs, a quantity of salt, and vegetables of various kinds.

CHAP. IV.
1786.
May.
Saturday 27.

AT seven o'clock a breeze springing up from the land, we weighed and stood to the South West until our distance from Karakakooa was about three leagues: I then brought-to, with an intention of standing off and on for twenty-four hours, in order to traffic with the natives; being convinced that it is the best and safest method of procuring any refreshments the island of Owhyhee affords.

EARLY next morning we were surrounded by canoes, and a brisk trade commenced, in the course of which we purchased a number of fine hogs, and vegetables of various kinds. Many of our people were employed in killing and salting down hogs for sea-store; our present situation being much better calculated for carrying on that business than in harbour; for now we had a fine free air, whereas in Karakakooa Bay the weather is so extremely close and sultry, that there is a great probability of the meat being spoiled even after it is salted.

Sunday 28.

AT noon we were standing along shore to the Northward, with a light westerly breeze and fine weather. Karakakooa Bay then bore East half South, distant three leagues, and the high land of Mowee North North West.

MANY canoes still kept about the ships, and some of the natives brought off water in calabashes, which we purchased for nails. Indeed water now began to be an article of the first consequence to us; our 52d butt being

K   a-broach,

a-broach, and there was as yet no certainty of our watering amongst these islands: the refreshments, however, that we already had procured, were of great service to the sick people, all of whom daily got better.

During the night we stood off and on, with variable winds and hazy weather. In the morning of the 29th the Southernmost part of Owhyhee in sight bore South South East half East, twelve leagues distant; the Northernmost part North by East, ten leagues; and the body of Mowee North North West half West, nine leagues distant. The natives of Owhyhee still followed the vessels with hogs and vegetables, and we stood to the North North West under an easy sail, that the canoes might be enabled to keep up with us.

At six o'clock in the afternoon a fresh breeze sprung up at North East, which brought on a cross swell, and obliged all the canoes to leave us and make for the shore.

During the night we had fresh gales and cloudy weather, which occasioned us to shorten sail and tack occasionally. Towards morning the weather moderated. At eight o'clock Mowee bore from North half East to East North East, distant four leagues, and the West end of Ranai North North West, two leagues distant.

The unsettled state of the weather, and the uncertainty of our being able to water the ships at these islands, induced me to put the ship's company to an allowance of water, at the rate of two quarts a-man a-day. Towards noon a few canoes came off from Ranai, but brought nothing of any

any confequence to barter. At three o'clock, being about one mile and a half from fhore, we founded with a line of 100 fathom, but got no bottom. The Wefternmoft point of Morotoi now bore North Weft by Weft, eight or nine leagues diftant; and foon afterwards a frefh breeze coming on at North Eaft, I ftood directly over for that ifland: by fix o'clock the Weft end, which is low and rocky, bore North Weft, diftant three leagues; and I had fome hopes of getting round the point, and anchoring in a bay fituated on the Weft fide of Morotoi, but the breeze rather failing, we had not daylight fufficient to accomplifh our purpofe; on this, we hauled up the courfes and brought-to, the Queen Charlotte being confiderably aftern.

CHAP. IV.
1786.
May.
Tuefday 30.

At half paft feven o'clock, the Queen Charlotte being well up, we filled and ftood to the South Eaft under the topfails; at the fame time the Weft point of Morotoi bore North Weft two leagues, and the Eafternmoft point North Eaft, fix leagues diftant.

At three o'clock next morning we wore and ftood in for the land; but when daylight came on, I was greatly furprifed to find that we had been driven in the night eight or nine leagues to the South Weft; fo that inftead of fetching in with the Weft point of Morotoi, as I expected, the wind being well to the Eaftward, I found we fcarcely fhould be able to weather the Eaft point of Woahoo, round which we knew there was anchorage.

Wednef. 31;

These difappointments mortified me a good deal, as I was very defirous to look for water in the bay on the Weft fide

CHAP. IV.

1786.
May.
Wednef. 31.

side of Morotoi, where, from the appearance of the land, it was likely we should find some. Had that plan failed, we then should have been able to get round the East point of Woahoo with a large wind; but finding now that it would be a work of some days to get in with the West end of Morotoi, I gave it up, and stood for the East point of Woahoo, which then bore North West, under all the sail we could carry, with a moderate breeze at East North East. For some time appearances were greatly in our favour. Indeed I believe we should easily have fetched round the point; but about ten o'clock, the Queen Charlotte being a considerable way on our lee quarter, I was afraid she would not be able to weather the island, as I could plainly perceive we had a strong current setting to the South West. On this we tacked and stood towards her, and soon afterwards wore and stretched to the Northward. Just at this time the wind hauled round to the Eastward, and we again stood on, in hopes of fetching our intended situation. However, about half past eleven o'clock, the Queen Charlotte drove in shore, and captain Dixon finding he could not weather the point, tacked, which occasioned us to tack immediately afterwards. At noon, the outermost rock off the North East point of Woahoo bore North North West about four leagues, and the Southernmost part of the island in sight South West half West, five miles distant.

The island of Woahoo between the South East and North East points appears high and craggy, forming into several high rocks, within which there appears to be tolerable shelter; but as the wind blew fresh, and right on shore,

shore, I did not think it prudent to run in with a lee shore to look for anchorage.

We plied in this uncertain state till noon on the 1st of June, when finding it would be impracticable for us to get round the North East point of the island without wasting more time than could be spared, we bore away for the South East point; and at one o'clock being well up with it, a fine bay made its appearance, which promised to afford good anchorage. We hauled round the point, and stood in for the bay. Soon afterwards, the whale-boat was lowered down, and sent in shore to sound. At half past two o'clock we came to an anchor in the bay, which I distinguished by the name of King George's Bay, in twelve fathom water, over a bottom of speckled sand and broken shells, and moored with the best bower to the Eastward, and a kedge to the Westward. The East point of the bay, which I distinguished by the name of Point Dick, in honour of Sir John Dick, the first patron of this voyage, bore East by North one mile and a half; the West point, which was named Point Rose, after George Rose Esq. secretary of the treasury, the second worthy patron of our undertaking, bore West South West half West, about two leagues, and the bottom of the bay North, two miles distant.

Soon after our arrival, several canoes came off and brought a few cocoa-nuts and plantains, some sugar-cane and sweet root; in return for which we gave them small pieces of iron and a few trinkets. Towards evening, a fresh breeze coming on at East North East, our visiters left us, and returned on shore.

NEXT

CHAP.
IV.
1786.
June.
Friday 2.

NEXT morning at daylight we had several canoes about the ship, which brought us a few small hogs and some vegetables. Great numbers of both sexes were in the water, impelled by curiosity to pay us a visit, notwithstanding our distance from shore.

As watering the ships was now become an object of the first consideration, I went on shore early in the morning, accompanied by captain Dixon, in order to find out a convenient spot for that purpose. We landed on some rocks just round Point Dick, quite dry, and met with no opposition from the inhabitants; on the contrary, they received us with great kindness, and answered every question we asked them very readily. On our inquiring for fresh water, they conducted us to some, which was lodged in a kind of bason, formed by the rocks, about fifty yards from the place where we landed; but the quantity was so small, that it would not afford even a temporary supply. On this we continued our inquiries along shore, and were informed that there was no fresh water to be met with but at a considerable distance to the Westward.

AFTER making the Indians some trifling presents, we returned to the boats, and rowed to the Northward, close to a reef, which appeared to run quite across the bay, about a quarter of a mile distant from the beach. Having proceeded nearly a mile in this direction, a small opening in the reef presented itself, for which we steered. The channel was narrow, but in the middle we had two fathoms water; and after getting through, there was from three to four fathoms over a bottom of fine sand, and good room between the reef and the beach for a number of vessels

to

NORTH WEST COAST OF AMERICA.

to ride at anchor. We landed on a fine sandy beach amidst a vast number of the inhabitants, who all behaved with great order, and never attempted to approach nearer to us than we desired. They informed us that there was no water near our landing-place, but that we should find plenty farther down along shore, and one of the natives accompanied us as a guide: however, our progress was soon impeded by a little salt water river that has a communication with King George's Bay. This putting a stop to our progress by land, we again had recourse to our boats, and attempted to get to the Westward within the reef; but the water was so shallow that it was impracticable; so that we returned through the passage we came in at, and afterwards rowed to the Westward, keeping close along the outside of the reef, until we got near the watering-place pointed out to us by the Indians. In this situation, seeing a small opening in the reef, we made for it; and the moment we entered, a breaker overtook us, which almost filled and nearly overset our boats. However, through the good management of the steersmen, who were mine and captain Dixon's third mates, we escaped without any misfortune; though we had the mortification, after getting over the reef, to find the water so shoal, that our boats could not get within 200 yards of the shore.

UNDER these circumstances, I found that we could not water at this place without an infinite deal of trouble, besides the danger of losing our casks, getting the boats dashed to pieces against the rocks, and the inconvenience of carrying our casks so far amongst a multitude of Indians, which would make it necessary to have an armed force on shore, the ships lying at too great a distance for them

CHAP.
IV.
1786.
June.
Friday 2.

them to cover or secure a watering party; I therefore gave up the idea of watering at this spot, and determined to send two boats the first opportunity to examine the Western part of the bay for a good landing place and convenient watering.

I RETURNED on board at noon, and found a pretty brisk trade carrying on for small hogs, sugar-cane, and vegetables; having given orders to Mr. Hill, on my leaving the ship, to purchase every refreshment which the natives brought alongside.

No time was now to be lost in coming to some conclusive determination respecting our future transactions; I saw but little probability of watering the ships with our own boats: but captain Dixon, as well as myself, was of opinion, that the Indians might be induced to bring off water to the ships, sufficient at least for a temporary supply. At all events, I knew there was enough in each vessel to serve near three months with proper care, but it was all in the ground tier; I therefore determined to have all our water got to hand, and the ground tier filled with salt water. In the mean time, our spare hands could be well employed in repairing the rigging, and making the vessels in every respect fit for the further prosecution of our voyage, so soon as the crews were well refreshed; and our present situation being the most eligible one we knew of at these islands, we resolved not to quit it before all our business was completed.

Saturday 3.

EARLY in the morning of the 3d I dispatched Mr. Hayward and Mr. White in a boat from each ship to examine the

the West part of the bay for a landing-place and fresh water. They likewise had orders to land, and make an excursion to that part of the island round Point Rose, as there appeared from the ship to be a fine deep bay in that situation. The natives now began to bring us water pretty briskly, and some of their calabashes contained near ten gallons; for one of these we gave a tenpenny nail, which was much cheaper than we could possibly procure the water ourselves, allowing for the damage our boats would sustain, and the presents we should be obliged to make on shore to the chiefs.

CHAP.
IV
1786.
June.
Saturday 3.

The weather being very fine, our ailing people were sent on shore under the care of my surgeon; and as the inhabitants had hitherto behaved in a quiet inoffensive manner, there was no great danger of their being molested.

No chiefs of consequence paid us a visit as yet: the inferior chiefs indeed came on board without any scruple, and some of them slept with us every night. Amongst the rest I had a daily visit from an old priest, who always brought by way of present, a small pig, and a branch of the cocoa-nut tree. From him I learnt, that their present king's name was Taheeterre, and that he was also king of Morotoi and Mowee. The old man informed me, that his residence was in a bay round the West point, and importuned me very much to carry the ships there, as that place, he said, afforded plenty of fine hogs and vegetables. Indeed, I had some reason to think, that the inhabitants on that part of the island were more numerous than in King George's Bay, as I observed most of the double canoes came round the West point; but as the people now brought us plenty of water, I determined to keep my present situation, it being in many respects a very eligible one; for we hitherto had been favoured with a most refreshing sea breeze, which blows over the low land at the head of the bay; and the bay all round has a very beautiful appearance, the low land and vallies being in a high state of cultivation, and crowded with plantations of taro, sweet potatoes, sugar-cane, &c. interspersed with a great number of cocoa-nut trees, which renders the prospect truly delightful.

In the afternoon the boats returned, and Mr. Hayward reported that he had landed in the West part of the bay, where he found a pond of standing water; but it was very inconveniently situated, and could not be got at without difficulty. He afterwards walked up to a rising ground, from which he could perceive the land round the West point of King George's Bay to fall in and form a fine deep bay running well to the Northward; and the Westmost land stretching out to the Southward: this however by no means induced me to change our situation.

Towards evening the surgeon returned on board with the convalescents, and informed me, that the inhabitants had behaved in a very quiet inoffensive manner, though they were rather incommoded by the multitudes which curiosity brought about them.

By this time all our water from the ground tier was got to hand, and the cables coiled down. The inhabitants now brought us water in such plenty, that by noon on the 4th all our empty casks were filled, having procured twenty-nine butts, eight hogsheads, and three brandy-pieces, which contained

contained 130 gallons each. As good water in any quantity may be procured at this island with the greatest facility for small nails and buttons, it undoubtedly must be the safest and most expeditious method any person can adopt who may chance to touch here, to barter for their water in the manner we did. Potatoes and taro are likewise met with here in great plenty, but I never observed any bread-fruit, and scarcely any yams; so that there is reason to suppose they are not cultivated by the inhabitants of Woahoo.

Having completed our water, and procured such refreshments as Woahoo afforded, I determined to proceed to Oneehow without loss of time, in order to get a supply of yams, which I knew that island produced in great plenty and perfection. Accordingly, at seven o'clock in the morning of the 5th, we weighed and stood to the Westward under an easy sail, with a moderate breeze at North East. As we approached Point Rose, a vast number of double canoes joined us, which came out of that bay to the Westward, seen by Mr. Hayward, and which obtained the name of Queen Charlotte's Bay. An excellent bay it appears to be, stretching well both to the Northward and Southward. The Southern extreme forms itself into a flattish point, which I distinguished by the name of Point Banks, in honour of Sir Joseph Banks. Point Banks bears West by North from Point Rose, distant about twelve miles. From each of these points there runs a ridge of rocks for about three quarters of a mile; but they always shew themselves by breakers, and coloured water.

CHAP.
IV.

1786.
June.
Monday 5.

WHEN we were a-breast of Point Rose, my old visiter the priest came on board in a large double canoe; bringing with him a very good feathered cap, as a present for me from Taheeterre; in return for which, I sent him two large towees and some other trifles of little value; I also gave the old priest a light-horseman's cap, and another to a young chief who had almost constantly been on board since my arrival at the island; being desirous to shew any future navigators who might happen to touch here, that this place had recently been visited by British ships. My guests were highly delighted with their presents, and after many professions of friendship, they took their leave and went on shore. At noon Point Dick, which is the South East point of Woahoo, bore East by North seven leagues, and Point Banks, the South West Point, North West half West, four leagues distant. After passing Point Banks, we hauled to the North West, and with a moderate Easterly breeze, stretched along the Western part of the island, accompanied by several canoes, who brought some flying fish to sell, the largest I ever saw; many of them measuring from ten to twelve inches in length, and thick in proportion. These fish are caught in nets, which the people here manage with great dexterity.

THE West side of Woahoo is very high and uneven, and near the shore there appear to be several small detached islands, within which there is a probability of meeting with good anchorage. From the North West, to the South West points, the land trends North West and South East, and, likewise seems to promise well for anchoring ground; but the day being very hazy, we were prevented from

NORTH WEST COAST OF AMERICA.

from examining it distinctly. Before I quit Woahoo let me observe, that I think it the finest island in the group, and most capable of being turned to advantage, were it settled by Europeans, than any of the rest; there being scarcely a spot which does not appear fertile. Here we found a great number of warriors and warlike instruments; many of the warriors were tattooed in a manner totally different from any I ever took notice of amongst the Sandwich Islands; their faces were tattooed so as to appear quite black, besides great part of the **body being** tattooed in a variety of forms.

The greatest part of the daggers left by us at these islands during our last voyage, at present seem to centre here; for we scarcely ever saw a large canoe that the people in her had not one a-piece; and at Owhyhee I do not remember seeing more than two or three.

As they are very dangerous and destructive weapons, I did not suffer any to be made in either ship, though strongly importuned to it by many of the natives: indeed I always thought it the last voyage a very imprudent action to furnish the Indians with weapons which, at one time or other, might be turned against ourselves; and my suspicions were but too well founded; for with one of the daggers given by us to the natives of Owhyhee my much lamented commander captain Cook was killed; and but for them, that ornament to the British nation might have lived to have enjoyed the fruits of his labour in ease and affluence, after a series of years spent in the service of his country, and for the benefit of mankind in general: he, however, unfortunately set the example, by ordering

some

CHAP. IV.
1786.
June.
Monday 5.

some daggers to be made after the model of the Indian Pahooas; and this practice was afterwards followed by every person who could raise iron enough to make one; so that during our stay at these islands, the armourer was employed to little other purpose than in working these destructive weapons; and so liberally were they disposed of, that the morning we were running into Karakakooa bay, after the Resolution had sprung her foremast, I saw Maiha Maiha get eight or nine daggers from captain Clarke, in exchange for a feathered cloak; though since our arrival at Woahoo, I have purchased some cloaks considerably better than that of captain Clarke's, for a small piece of iron worked into the form of a carpenter's plane-bit: these the Sandwich islanders make use of as adzes, and call them *towees*; and to them they answer every purpose wherever an edge-tool is required.

SINCE the year 1778, at which time the Sandwich Islands were discovered, there appears to have been an almost total change in their government: from every thing I now have been able to learn, Taheeterre, the present king of Woahoo, is the only surviving monarch we left amongst the islands at that period; he then was king of Morotoi only; and Pereeoranne, who then governed Woahoo, was at war with him, and had sent a number of fighting canoes to attack his dominions. It seems that Pereeoranne's forces were worsted on this occasion; for presently afterwards, Taheeterre took possession of Woahoo; and, flushed with this success, he attacked and conquered the island of Mowee; which, as already has been observed, is now annexed to his dominions. Tereeoboo, who at that time was king of Owhyhee

hee and Mowee, fell in battle whilst defending his dominions. I have no reason to doubt the truth of these relations; for Maiha Maiha, the present king of Owhyhee, at the time we last were there, was only an inferior chief, and is now, as I understand, in some measure subject to Taheeterre; besides which, the Woahoo chiefs having in their possession most of the daggers we left at Owhyhee, is a most convincing proof that they have been victorious; for I am very certain the natives at these islands will never part with their weapons but at the expence of their lives. From the best account our short stay would permit me to obtain, the principal of the Sandwich Isles were at this time governed by the following persons: Woahoo, Morotoi, and Mowee, were subject to Taheeterre; Maiha Maiha governed Owhyhee and Ranai; and a chief whose name I understand is Ta'aao, was king of Atooi and Oneehow.

CHAP. IV.
1786.
June.
Monday 5.

WITH a light breeze at North East we stretched to the North West during the afternoon, and were followed by canoes, bringing small hogs and vegetables, although our distance from the land was considerable.

AT eight o'clock in the morning of the 6th the North part of Woahoo bore East North East, nine leagues; and the South West part South East by East, ten leagues distant; the island of Atooi appeared in sight, bearing North West by West, distant twelve leagues. We now had light variable winds, with calms by turns; the weather very close and sultry. Our observation at noon gave 21° 36′ North latitude: in this situation we found a pretty strong current setting West North West.

Tuesday 6.

AT

80   A VOYAGE TO THE

CHAP.   At eight o'clock the extremes of Atooi bore from
 IV.   North Weſt, to Weſt half North, the neareſt land about five
1786.   leagues diſtant. The night was ſpent in ſtanding off and
June.   on; as I wiſhed to run well in with the South ſide of
Tueſday 6. Atooi on the morrow, in order to give the natives an op-
        portunity of bringing us vegetables, the ſtock we pro-
        cured at Woahoo beginning to run ſhort.

Wedneſ. 7.   At five o'clock in the morning of the 7th we bore away
        and made ſail with a fine breeze from the Eaſtward, which
        brought us by eight o'clock within two leagues of the
        land.

        The land on the Eaſt and South Eaſt part of Atooi,
        riſes gradually from the ſea-ſide till it terminates in high
        land, which ſeems ſituated near the centre of the iſland;
        theſe hills are clothed to the ſummits with lofty trees,
        whoſe verdure has a beautiful appearance; the land next
        the ſhore affords a few buſhes, but ſeems quite uncult-
        vated, and deſtitute of inhabitants.

        On the Eaſtern ſhore there are a few ſmall ſandy bays,
        but they afford no ſhelter for ſhips to ride in; being
        quite expoſed to Eaſterly winds, which blow directly on
        ſhore, and generally prevail here.

        After paſſing the South Eaſt point, we found the land
        cultivated in general, and houſes were ſcattered here and
        there all along ſhore to the Weſtward: by noon we had
        ſeveral canoes about the ſhip, from whom we procured a
        few vegetables; but the ſurf ran ſo high on the beach,
                              8   that

that the natives could not bring off any considerable quantity.

As I knew Atoui afforded plenty of fine hogs, and a variety of other refreshments, we stood on for Wymoa Bay, where captain Cook anchored the last voyage; as I was desirous of procuring some good hogs for salting, and also some to carry with me to sea. By three o'clock we were nearly a-breast of the bay, when the wind inclined to the Southward, and blew so fresh, that the anchoring-ground was very unsafe to ride in; being entirely exposed to Southerly winds, which send in a heavy cross-sea: I therefore did not think it prudent to trust the ships in such a situation; so wore, and stood for Oneehow, under all the sail we could carry. At four o'clock the extremes of Oneehow bore from North North West half West, to South West by West, about four leagues distant from the nearest land.

The South point of this island forms a remarkable high bluff, rising on all sides to a considerable height, and breaking off abruptly. About five leagues to the Eastward, it has the appearance of a detached island, being joined to the main by a low slip of land, which is not seen more than three leagues distant. At seven o'clock the South point bore West by North about two miles, and the Easternmost part of the island, North North East, four leagues distant. Finding we had not sufficient daylight to bring us into the bay on the West side of Oneehow, we shortened sail, and hauled on a wind to the Southward; intending to spend the night in standing off and on. At eleven o'clock we wore, and made the signal to the Queen Charlotte,

M

CHAP.
IV.
1786.
June.
Wednef. 7.

Charlotte, but she not observing it, continued standing to the Southward; soon afterwards having nearly lost sight of each other, we wore, and stood after her. Having joined company, we again wore at one o'clock, and stood to the Northward. This mistake nearly occasioned us to miss Oneehow; for, by standing too long to the Southward, we got into a current which set us so strongly to the South West, that at daylight next morning, though the wind hung well to the Eastward, we could scarely fetch a league to the Eastward of the West point.

Thursday 8.

At six o'clock the South and East points of Oneehow in one, bore North East half North; our distance then from the nearest land was about two miles. I now perceived that we could weather well to the Eastward of the road; therefore stretched along shore, about the distance of one mile, and had regular soundings from twenty to sixteen fathoms water, over a bottom of fine sand. The wind still continuing well to the Eastward, I was tempted to run down and look into the West bay. At nine o'clock we hauled round the West point, and opened a bay, which I found to be a very good one; the soundings from fifteen to seventeen fathoms water, over a fine sandy bottom, and distant at least two miles from shore. After running a-breast the South West part of the bay, we anchored with the best bower in eighteen fathoms water, over a sandy bottom, and moored with a kedge to the Westward in twenty-four fathoms water: the extremes of the bay bearing from North by South to South East; from which last point we were not more than half a mile distant. From the North point of the bay a ledge of rocks extend themselves in a direction nearly East and West, for more than half a mile; some of of which appear above water, and the extent of the rest may easily be known by the surf that continually breaks over them.

CHAP. IV.
1786.
June.
Thursday 8.

ABOUT the middle of the bay is a fine sandy beach, within a quarter of a mile of which a ship may moor in seven and eight fathoms water, over a bottom of fine sand; and boats may land with great ease and safety.

No sooner were we moored, than several canoes visited us, bringing yams, sweet potatoes, and a few small pigs; for which we gave in exchange nails and beads. Amongst the people in these canoes were several whose faces I remembered to have seen when at this island before; particularly an old priest, in whose house a party of us took up our abode, when detained all night on shore by a heavy surf, and who treated us in a very friendly manner.

OUR principal business here was to procure a good stock of yams; and these I had the pleasure to see brought to us in tolerable plenty. I was also desirous to obtain a further supply of good hogs for salting; but this at present was very doubtful: for as yet we had seen very few, and the largest did not weigh more than twenty pounds. I expected to find no difficulty in getting water, at least sufficient for our daily use; as Mr. Bligh, who was master of the Resolution during our last voyage, and discovered the bay we now lay in, went on shore in order to examine this part of the island, and met with two wells of fresh water in the neighbourhood of our present situation.

EARLY next morning we were surrounded by canoes, who brought a plentiful supply of yams, and some sugar-cane.

Friday 9.

cane. A chief, named Abbenooe, whom I knew when at this island before, also paid me a visit, and recognized his old acquaintance the moment he came on board. Having appointed six persons to trade with the natives for yams, and given orders to have them dried and stowed away, I went on shore in search of the wells mentioned by Mr. Bligh, accompanied by Abbenooe as a guide.

When we landed, a number of the natives who were assembled on the beach retired to a considerable distance, and we walked to the wells without the least molestation. I found one of them brackish and stinking; the other afforded good water, but in no great quantity. The good water was situated about half a mile to the Eastward of the beach, and the direct path to it was over a salt marsh: to avoid which a considerable circuit must be taken, which renders the situation very inconvenient. Indeed, a ship in distress for water might procure it here, though much time must be spent in doing it. I would recommend it to all ships watering amongst Indians, to have a sufficient number of casks hooped with wood instead of iron, for the purpose of filling on shore. These might afterwards be started into other casks in the boats. By this means much mischief might be avoided; for the Indians, having no temptation to steal them, probably would behave in a peaceable manner, and might safely be trusted to assist in rolling the casks.

After examining these wells, I made an excursion into the country, accompanied by Abbenooe, and a few of the natives. The island appears well cultivated; its principal produce is yams. There are besides, sweet potatoes, sugarcane, and the sweet root which is called *tee* by the natives.

A few

A few trees are scattered here and there, but in little order or variety. Some that grew near the well just mentioned were about fifteen feet high, and proportionably thick; with spreading branches, and a smooth bark; the leaves were round, and they bore a kind of nut somewhat resembling our walnut. Another kind were nine feet high, and had blossoms of a beautiful pink colour. I also noticed another variety, with nuts growing on them like our horse chesnut. These nuts, I understand, the inhabitants use as a substitute for candles, and they give a most excellent light.

HAVING viewed every thing remarkable on this side the island, I repaired on board, accompanied by my good friend Abbenooe, and found a brisk trade carrying on for vegetables. A few hogs had also been purchased, sufficient for daily consumption.

CHAP. V.

Continuation of Transactions at Oneehow.—Method of salting Pork in tropical Climates.—Departure from Oneehow.—Method of brewing the sweet Root.—Arrive in sight of the Coast of America.—Stand on for Cook's River.—Meet with some Russian Settlers.—Arrival in Cook's River.—Visited by the Russian Chief.—Anchor in Coal Harbour.—Various Employments there.—Abundance of Salmon.—Visit the Russian Settlement.—Their Mode of Living described.—Proceed farther up the River.

CHAP. V.
1786.
June.
Friday 9.

I HAVE already observed, that Oneehow belonged to Ta'aao, king of Atoui. I now learnt that he was there at present, and that Abenooe governed Oneehow in his absence. I made the old man a present of some red baize, and two large towes, which he sent away immediately to Ta'aao at Atoui, and gave me to understand that I might expect plenty of hogs and vegetables from that place in consequence of this present. I placed no great reliance on this

Saturday 10. piece of information; but in the afternoon of the 10th I was agreeably surprised to see Abbenooe's messenger return, accompanied by several large double canoes, which brought a number of fine hogs to be disposed of, together with taro and sugar-cane.

THE messenger gave me to understand, that Ta'aao himself meant to have paid me a visit; but that he could not
leave

NORTH WEST COAST OF AMERICA.

leave Atoui under fix or seven days, being detained there during that time, in order to perform some religious ceremonies for one of his wives, who was lately dead; and this intelligence was also confirmed by Abbenooe. However, I had no great reason to regret the absence of his Majesty, for Abbenooe kept the natives in very good order, encouraged them to bring us whatever the island afforded; and after the people from Atoui had disposed of their commodities, he sent them back for a fresh supply.

CHAP. V.
1786.
June.
Saturday 10.

BEING desirous to make Ta'aao some further acknowledgment for his supplying us with the various refreshments Atoui afforded, though at such a considerable distance, I sent him as a present a light-horseman's cap; this however Abbenooe scarcely thought sufficient, and strongly importuned me to send along with it an armed chair, which I had in the cabin, as it would be, he said, peculiarly useful to one of the king's wives who had lately lain in. I willingly complied with my friend's request, and he dispatched the chair and cap to Atoui, under the care of special messengers. Our business now went regularly and briskly forward; the trading party were well employed in bartering for yams and other refreshments, and others were busied in killing and salting hogs for sea store. Observing the natives to break the yams in bringing them off, which prevents them from keeping for any length of time, I sent my second mate on shore on the 11th in the yaul to purchase some; by which means we procured a large quantity of very fine ones. Since our arrival here, such of the seamen whose recovery from sickness was scarcely confirmed were daily sent on shore, and found vast benefit from exercise and land air. Indeed, the inhabitants at

Sunday 11.

this

CHAP. V.
1786.
June.
Sunday 11.

this island are not numerous, and they were kept in such excellent order by Abbenooe, that our people walked about wherever inclination led them, without the least molestation.

Besides hogs and vegetables, we purchased some salt fish of various kinds, such as snappers, rock-cod, and bonetta, all well cured and very fine. The natives likewise brought us water in calabashes, sufficient for daily use, and to replace what had been expended since we left Woahoo. Curiosities too found their way to market, and I purchased two very curious fly flaps, the upper part composed of beautiful variegated feathers; the handles were human bone, inlaid with tortoiseshell in the neatest manner, which gave them the appearance of fineered work.

Monday 12.

By the 12th we had purchased near thirty hogs, weighing on an average sixty pounds each; the principal part of which were brought from Atoui: these were salted for sea store, as we daily got a supply of a smaller sort for present consumption.

The method of curing pork in tropical climates was first brought to perfection by captain Cook; yet his plan seems not to be generally known; on which account I shall here take notice of the mode I adopted, as I found it answer my most sanguine expectations.

Three different parties were employed in this business; and the best times for killing we found to be about three o'clock in the afternoon, and again in the cool of the evening. An awning was fixed over those employed in killing and

and salting, to prevent the sun from damaging the meat. After one party had cleaned the hogs well, they were handed to another set, who took the bones entirely out, cut away all the bruised parts and blood-vessels, and cut the meat into four or six pound pieces; at the same time making incisions in various parts of the skin, so as to admit the salt freely. These pieces were then given to the salters, who rubbed them thoroughly with good white salt, and afterwards stowed them on some hatches, that were fixed as a kind of temporary stage, about two feet from deck.

A sufficient quantity of meat being placed on this stage, it was covered with canvass and boards, on which heavy weights were placed. In this state it remained till morning, by which time all the blood was pressed out, and the meat was hard and firm. Every piece was then carefully examined, and if any parts appeared the least tainted, they were cut away, and fresh salt rubbed on. The pork was then packed in casks filled up with strong pickle, and pressed with weights as before. After remaining in casks twenty-four hours, it was repacked, filled up with fresh pickle, and put away for future use. Some pork that we salted at Owhyhee was examined after it had been packed a week, and found perfectly sweet, and the finest I ever saw. The bones were broke, rubbed well with salt, and afterwards put into strong pickle; and the flesh being cut from the heads, it was dry-salted, and kept exceedingly well.

I also salted several whole sides after the bones were taken out, without pickle, and they made very fine bacon.

SINCE our arrival at the Sandwich Iſlands, we had ſalted on board the King George ſeven tierces and two hogſheads of pork, beſides two tierces of bones, and had not twenty pounds of meat ſpoiled amongſt the whole quantity. In addition to the above, I ſhall juſt obſerve, that after the hogs are killed, they cannot be too expeditiouſly cleaned and ſalted; for on that the ſafety of the meat principally depends, though I believe in moſt countries where much pork is cured, they uſually leave it to cool before the ſalt is laid on. This method, however, is certainly a bad one; for I have known a houſe in Virginia, by following it, to loſe near 600 hogs at one time; whereas, had they begun ſalting while the meat was warm, and the blood running, I have every reaſon to think that the greateſt part, if not all of it, would have been preſerved.

By this time we had procured near ten tons of fine yams, and captain Dixon had got about eight tons on board the Queen Charlotte. The health of both ſhips crews was well re-eſtabliſhed, and every neceſſary buſineſs being completed, no time was loſt in getting the ſhips ready for ſea, as the ſeaſon for commencing our operations on the American coaſt was already begun.

AT five o'clock in the morning of the 13th we unmoored, and at eight o'clock we weighed and got under ſail, ſtanding out of the bay (which obtained the name of Yam Bay, from the great quantity of yams we procured in it), with a freſh breeze at North Eaſt.

As our viſit to the Sandwich Iſlands was a very tranſient one, I had little opportunity of obtaining any information reſpecting the manners and cuſtoms of the natives;

natives; so that the reader may collect what little intelligence I can give him on that head from the foregoing detail of our transactions.

Hogs, sweet potatoes, taro, sugar-cane, and yams, may, as has already been shewn, be procured in any quantity; and water is so easily obtained at Woahoo, that in little more than one day we got upwards of thirty tons on board. But amongst the refreshments these islands abound with, the sweet root, or tee, which we met with in great abundance at Woahoo, must by no means pass unnoticed, as it makes very good beer, which, after two or three trials, I brought to perfection. The great utility of this root was not known to us during the last voyage; so that the method I made use of in brewing it may not improperly be mentioned in this place.

The root was peeled very clean, cut into small pieces, and put into a clean kettle, and six of the large roots were found a sufficient quantity for twelve gallons of water. This was put on the fire at three o'olock in the afternoon, and after boiling an hour and a half, was put away to cool. By the time the liquor was lukewarm, a gill of prepared yeast was added, and afterwards it was put into a cask. It generally begun to work about midnight, and by nine o'clock the next morning it was excellent drinking. I found it necessary to make use of yeast only once; the grounds fermented the liquor afterwards; and I am inclined to think, that when yeast cannot be procured, a little leaven would answer as a substitute.

This beer was constantly drank by such of our sailors as were affected with the scurvy, and they found great benefit from it; so that in addition to its being very useful as common drink, I may safely call it a most excellent antiscorbutic. Having succeeded so well in brewing the sweet root, I tried sugar-cane by the same method, and made a good wholesome drink from it, though much inferior to the other.

We stood to the North North West, along the West side of Oneehow, which forms several fine sandy bays, that seem to afford good shelter and anchorage. At ten o'clock my worthy old friend Abbenooe took his leave of me, and all the canoes left us; on which occasion we hoisted our colours, and fired ten guns, by way of taking leave of this little friendly island. At noon Yam Bay bore South East eight or ten miles, and the West point of Oneehow, South by East, six leagues distant.

Thursday 15. In the forenoon of the 15th we saw great numbers of the tropic and man-of-war birds, together with terns and boobies; so that I conjectured we then were sailing at no considerable distance from some uninhabited island. Our latitude at noon was 24° 14′ North, and 160° 24′ longitude.

Tuesday 20. For some days the weather was close and sultry, attended with frequent heavy rains; but on the 20th the weather became clear and pleasant, with a fine Easterly breeze. This gave us an opportunity of examining our yams, and it was very fortunate that we did so;

for

NORTH WEST COAST OF AMERICA.   93

for they began to decay, occasioned by heat; and in a few days would certainly have been spoiled.

CHAP.
V.
1786.
June.

IN the forenoon of the 22d we saw a great number of petrels, about the size of a pigeon, and of a sooty colour; and passed two large pieces of a substance which appeared to be a part of the cuttle-fish: they were very much torn, probably by whales, who feed on the cuttle-fish. Our latitude at that time was 32° 4′ North, and 160° 8′ longitude.

Thursday 22.

THE wind now gradually shifted to the Southward, and afterwards hauled to West and North West, with rain and a heavy cross swell, which indicated that the trade-wind had left us.

Friday 23.

ON the 27th, being in 38° 14′ North latitude, and 155° 56′ longitude, we found 15° 30′ Easterly variation. In the year 1778, when nearly in the same latitude, and about three degrees to the Eastward of the above longitude, the variation was found to be 16° 30′ Easterly; a difference of one degree, which is very considerable. In the forenoon of the 28th I went on board the Queen Charlotte, in order to appoint a rendezvous for the ships in case of separation, as the weather now was constantly thick and hazy. We fixed on a situation in Cook's River, near Cape Bede; which cape forms the South side of a deep inlet, and Anchor Point the North side. This situation was a very eligible one, not only as there was a great probability of finding a good harbour, but whichsoever vessel arrived there first, would be able to make signals to the other

Tuesday 27.

Wednes. 28.

other on her entering the river. Having settled this point, I returned on board my own ship.

IN the afternoon the water altered its colour, and had the appearance of foundings; on which we founded with a line of 120 fathoms, but got no bottom.

NEXT morning a number of seals were seen playing round the ship, but our distance from the coast of America was so considerable, that I cannot think those animals came from thence, or from any known islands near the coast. On the contrary, there is great reason to suppose that we were near some land which has not as yet been discovered; for during our last voyage, in 1778, when in 41° 50′ North latitude, and 142° 30′ West longitude, we passed a piece of wood which appeared to have been but a short time in the water, and drifted from the Westward; and in the same year, when in 40° 15′ North latitude, and 157° 55′ West longitude, we saw a shagg, which bird is never known to fly far from land; and as our present situation was nearly in the midway between those just mentioned, I had great reason to expect we should fall in with some.

THE weather for several days was constantly thick and hazy, attended with drizzling rain; so that had we passed within five miles of any land, it would have been impossible for us to have seen it; and the advanced season of the year not permitting me to waste any time in searching for undiscovered islands, I kept on my course to the North.

TOWARDS noon on the 3d July the weather cleared up, and our observation gave 44° 4′ North latitude, and 151° 12′ longitude.

SINCE the 29th we had daily seen seals, whales, and porpoises, together with a great number of petrels, and various other birds; we frequently sounded with a line of 150 fathoms, but found no bottom, neither was there any appearance of land. I struck one of the seals that were playing about the ship, and got it on board; at first sight I imagined it to be a sea-otter; its fur was very close and fine.

FOR some time past the wind had kept to the Northward and Westward, which greatly retarded our progress; but on the 7th, in 46° 11′ North latitude, and 147° 8′ longitude, it shifted to the Southward, which enabled us to shape a course North West by North, for the entrance of Cook's River. We kept standing for that place without meeting with any particular occurrence. The weather in general was cloudy, with alternate fogs and heavy rain. Vast numbers of different kinds of birds, such as divers, gulls, petrels, and albetrosses, were constantly about the ship, and we frequently passed pieces of wood and patches of sea-weed, called by the sailors sea-leek.

THE weather on the 14th being tolerably fine, I took the opportunity of cleaning the ship well, fore and aft; and afterwards every part was aired with good fires; a most necessary precaution, after the foggy, wet weather we so recently had experienced.

IN

CHAP. V.

1786.
July.
Saturday 15.

IN the morning of the 15th the water altered its colour, and at ten o'clock, judging we were in soundings, and willing to strike the edge of them, as a future direction in coming on the coast, we tried soundings, but had no ground with 190 fathoms of line. Our latitude then was 57° 2′ North, and 148° 32′ longitude. In this situation we found 22° 21′ Easterly variation.

Sunday 16.

THE weather being thick and foggy, we frequently tried for soundings, but got no bottom; at length, about eight o'clock in the morning of the 16th, we struck the ground in seventy fathoms water, over a bottom of fine grey sand with black specks; and at seven o'clock in the evening the fog dispersing, we saw the coast of America extending from North by East to West by North, distant from the nearest land, and which appeared to be a projecting point, about twelve leagues. In this situation we had fifty-seven fathom water, over a bottom of shells and mud.

AT eight o'clock the land in sight, from North to South South West, appeared to be entirely detached from the land in sight to the Westward; this induced me to suppose, that the land bearing South South West was Cape Saint Hermogenes, and another point, which bore West by North was Cape Elizabeth. A very great number of Gallicia whales were seen near the shore, and indeed in every direction as far as the eye could reach.

Monday 17.

DURING the night we sounded with a line of fifty-five fathoms, but got no bottom. The next day at noon the

land

NORTH WEST COAST OF AMERICA.

land in sight, bore from West by North to North, twelve or thirteen leagues distant. The latitude then was 58° 23′ North, and 149° 43′ longitude. We continued during the afternoon to stand in for the shore, but the wind grew light and variable; so that we gained ground very slowly.

AT noon on the 18th our latitude by observation was 58° 29′ North. Cape Elizabeth then bore North West by West, distant fifteen leagues; the barren Isles West North West, about the same distance; and Cape Saint Hermogenes South West, distant twelve leagues. With a moderate breeze at West North West, we stood towards Cape Saint Hermogenes; but by six o'clock the wind entirely failed us, and it grew calm. Cape Saint Hermogenes then bore South West, six leagues distant. In that situation we had soundings in forty fathoms water, over a bottom of gravel and dark sand. At nine o'clock a light breeze springing up at South East, I changed our course from West North West to North West by West; being apprehensive, should it again fall calm, that the tide might draw us in between the Isle Saint Hermogenes and the land to the Westward; a situation I wished to avoid, particularly in the night and with light winds. During the night our soundings varied greatly; when the Isle Saint Hermogenes bore South South West, six leagues distant, we had forty-five fathoms water; after the island was brought to bear more to the Southward, we had from sixty-five to seventy fathoms water, over a bottom of dark grey muddy sand.

AT two o'clock in the morning of the 19th I again steered West North West, with a moderate breeze from

South

South East by East: soon afterwards the South point of the Isle Saint Hermogenes bore South by West, six leagues distant. The morning proved so very foggy, that we lost sight of land; however, towards eleven o'clock, the fog dispersing, we saw the Barren Islands, bearing North North West, about three leagues distant; on this I steered North West by North, in order to run to the Westward of them; intending, if possible, to make the inlet, already mentioned, near Cape Bede; as we had thick, rainy weather, with signs of an approaching gale. Whilst standing on in this direction, the lead was kept going; but we got no bottom with thirty fathoms of line. At one o'clock the Westernmost part of the Barren Isles bore East North East, three miles distant; on this I stood over for Cape Bede, steering North by East, under double-reefed topsails, with a strong breeze from the East South East, and thick foggy weather. At four o'clock we saw the land near Cape Bede, bearing North North East, about three leagues distant. In running from the Barren Isles we passed several strong ripplings of a tide; and on standing well in with Point Bede, the wind shifted to North East and East North East, blowing in sudden puffs from the land, with rain and dark gloomy weather.

I HAULED in as near the shore as the wind would permit; and when we had brought Cape Bede to bear South 34° East, four miles distant, an appearance of a harbour presented itself, with a small island situated directly in the entrance, and bearing from South 87° East, to South 81° East, distant three miles. We stood for this opening, but made little progress, the wind growing light, and the little we had being directly against us. Just at this time we were greatly surprised to hear the report of a great gun from the shore; it was now very thick over the land, which prevented us from seeing the smoke of the gun; however, we fired a gun and hoisted our colours, and presently afterwards fired another, expecting it would be answered. Immediately after our firing the second gun another was fired from the shore, in the direction of East, three quarters South. It was now very evident, that some nation or other had got to this place before us, which mortified me not a little. Soon after this we perceived a boat rowing out towards the ships; on which, we tacked and stood in shore, in order to meet her: by seven o'clock the boat came on board, and I found the people to be Russians.

As we had no person who understood the Russian language, the information we got from this party was but little. If I understood them right, they came last from Kodiac, an island near the Schumagins, on a trading expedition; that they left their vessel at Kodiac, and proceeded to Cook's River in boats. The harbour which I intended to make, they gave me to understand, was a very good one; and they offered to take a person from the ship in their boat to examine it. I accepted their offer, and sent Mr. M'Leod along with them to examine the harbour and found the entrance, there being some rocks near it. The Russians left us at half past eight o'clock, and immediately afterwards we came to anchor in thirty-five fathoms water, over a bottom of coarse sand and shells; Point Bede bearing South 31° East, distant two leagues, and a small rocky island detached from it, in the same direction. At the time we anchored it was high water; and on the ebb making, I found it to set from the North

CHAP. V.
1786.
July.
Thursday 20.

by compass, and run at the rate of two knots per hour, and fall fourteen feet perpendicular. The flood set directly from the South, and run nearly at the same rate as the ebb. At four o'clock in the morning of the 20th the Russian boat returned with Mr. M'Leod, who informed me that the harbour was a very good one, and that there was a safe passage into it on either side the small island at the entrance.

AFTER examining the harbour, Mr. M'Leod landed on a beach just without the South entrance of it, where the Russians had taken up their abode. It should seem that they only continue here during the summer season, as they had nothing more than tents covered with canvas or skins to live in. He observed but few sea-otter skins amongst them, and they were mostly green, and appeared as if recently taken from the animal. The Russian party consisted of twenty-five men; they had also a number of Indians along with them, who had skin canoes, and seemed to be on the most friendly terms with the Russians, which inclined me to think they were not natives of this place, but brought here from Kodiac or Oonalaska, for the purpose of hunting; especially as Mr. M'Leod could not perceive any Indian habitations near the Russian settlement.

THE Russian chief brought me as a present a quantity of fine salmon, sufficient to serve both ships for one day; in return for which I gave him some yams, and directed him how to dress them; and likewise some beef, pork, and a few bottles of brandy. He made his acknowledgments in the best manner he was able, and returned on shore, perfectly pleased with his reception.

THESE

These people, quite contrary to the Russian custom, were particularly careful not to get intoxicated; but I have reason to think, that this caution proceeded rather from a fear of being surprised by the neighbouring Americans in a state of intoxication, than from any dislike they have to liquor; for Mr. M'Leod informed me that they were constantly on their guard, with their arms always ready, and that no man slept without a rifle-barrelled piece under his arm, and his cutlass and a long knife by his side.

We now began to be in want of wood, and the crews stood in need of some exercise on shore, therefore I determined to get into the adjacent harbour, and more particularly as there was not the least appearance of any inhabitants near it; so that our business could be carried on without danger or molestation. An additional reason for making this harbour was, that during the time our various business was going forward, I might probably learn from the Russians how long they had been at this place, and what time they intended to stay; also the place where their sloops lay, as they had none in Cook's River; I likewise particularly wished to know whether they procured their furs, by bartering with the natives, or killing the animals themselves.

At three o'clock in the afternoon a light breeze springing up from the North North West, we weighed anchor, and stood in for the North entrance of the opening. After we were got some distance into the harbour, the wind failed us, and we were obliged to drop an anchor under foot, as there was a strong current setting directly out,
although

CHAP.
V.

1786.
July.
Thursday 20.

although it was flood-tide. This I could no way account for, but by supposing that we were in the entrance of a streight, leading out directly to sea.

A LIGHT breeze coming on soon afterwards, enabled us to work well into the harbour; and at half past seven o'clock we anchored in eleven fathoms water, over a bottom of black muddy sand, and moored with the best bower to the sea, and the stream cable bent to a spare anchor towards the shore. When moored, the inner point of the bay bore East South East, distant about three cables length, and the point forming the North entrance into the harbour, West North West, half a mile distant; Volcano Mount, in Cook's River, West North West, half North, and Mount St. Augustine, South West by South.

Friday 21.

EARLY in the morning of the 21st, I went on shore in search of a convenient place for wooding and watering the ships. I landed on a fine smooth beach at the head of the bay, and about a mile distant from the ship; near which I found a run of good fresh water. An opening, which from the ship had the appearance of a creek, was found to be a narrow entrance leading to a salt water lake. Here was wood of different kinds in great abundance, such as pine, black birch, witch hazle, and poplar. Many of the pines were large enough for lower masts for a ship of 400 tons burden; and in every place were plants and shrubs of various sorts growing with great strength and vigour. However, this not being a very convenient situation for getting wood to the boats, I proceeded up the harbour to look for a place better adapted for our purpose.

I FOUND

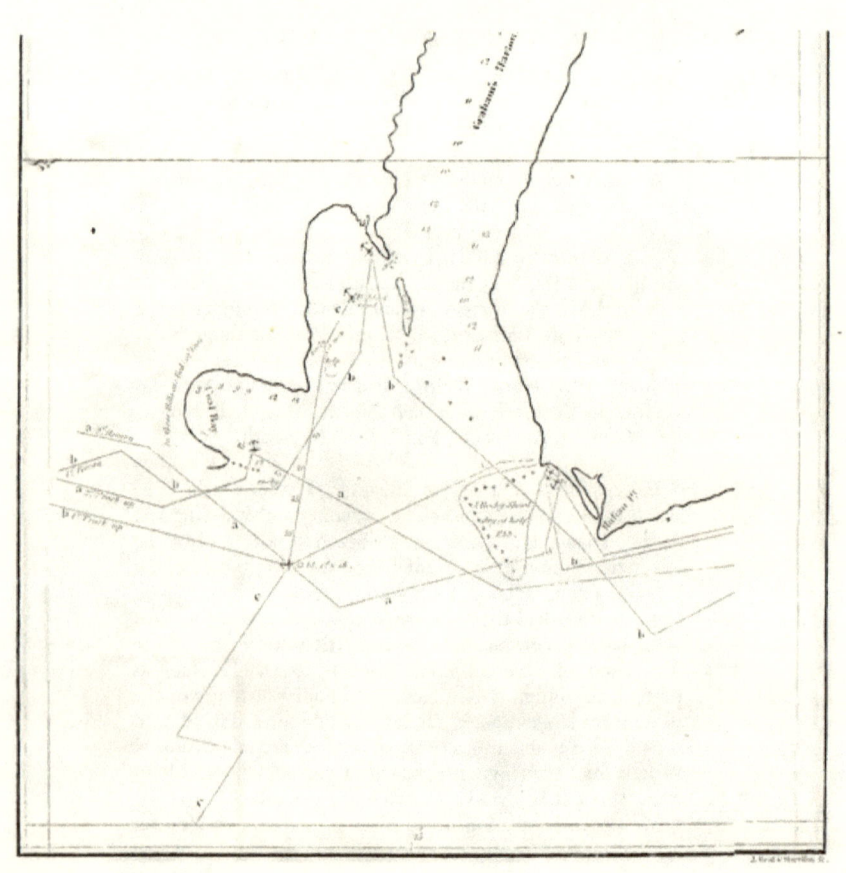

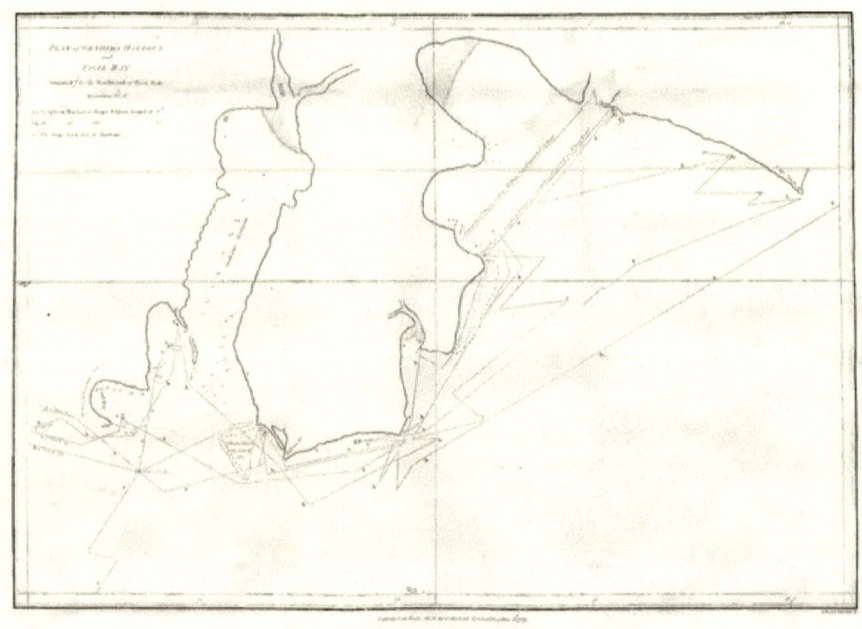

I found it a most excellent one indeed, with great plenty of wood every where, and several fine runs of water. For a confiderable diftance it runs up nearly Eaft South Eaft, and then bends rather to the Southward, with fourteen fathoms water, over a bottom of muddy fand. The Eaft fide affording plenty of black birch, and other kinds of wood, which grew clofe to a beach where the boats could have eafy accefs, I fixed on it for a wooding place, and returning immediately on board, I fent the carpenters to get fome fpars, and another party to cut firewood.

None of the natives as yet had made their appearance; but as the Ruffians were conftantly on their guard for fear of being furprifed by the Americans, I judged it prudent that we fhould be fo likewife; and accordingly fent a cheft with arms along with the parties on fhore. By noon we got feveral boat loads of wood on board.

In the afternoon the feine was hauled at the head of the bay where we lay, but with little fuccefs, only a few colefifh being caught. Whilft we were engaged in this bufinefs, the Ruffian chief paid me a vifit, and informed me, that the place where we hauled the feine was not ftocked with fifh, but that near his refidence plenty might be caught. I accordingly took the feine thither, and in feveral hauls caught about thirty falmon, and a few flat fifh. This indifferent fuccefs was owing, as my friend the Ruffian told me, to the time of tide, it being then low water, when, for hauling the feine, it fhould be nearly high water. However, he affured me, if I would leave the feine all night, and a man along with it, I fhould have

have plenty of fish the next morning. I embraced this offer with great pleasure, and left one of my sailors, who had some little knowledge of the Russian language.

THE Russian settlement, if I may be allowed to call that one where the residence is only temporary, was situated on a pleasant piece of flat land, about three miles in length, and 200 yards over, bounded by a good sandy beach on one side, and a small lake of fresh water, which empties itself into the sea, on the other. In this lake they catch plenty of fine salmon. The beach terminates at each end in high points of land, which form a snug bay, where small craft might lie with great safety.

THE Russians were twenty-five in number, exclusive of the Indians, which I now found were brought from Kodiac and Oonalaska. They had two skin boats, each calculated to row twelve oars, and the thwarts were double banked. I understood that the chief and the Indians took up their abode in a small tent covered with canvas, and the remainder slept under the two boats just mentioned.

THEY have no bread; their diet seems to consist principally of fish, and a mess is made of the root of a plant, called by Steller the Serena, which would taste very well, were it not rendered unpalatable, by being mixed with animal oil: they had also some very good tea.

AMONGST the party were three Indian women; one of whom I was informed came from Oonalaska, the others from Kodiac.

I COULD

I could perceive that they procured no furs by bartering with the Americans, and that they got no sea otter skins, nor indeed furs of any kind, but what the Kodiac Indians caught in hunting.

During my stay amongst the Russians, they were all very busily employed. Some were dressing green sea otter skins, others repairing their boats, and cleaning arms. Most of the Indians were out on a hunting party; the few left behind were busied in fitting darts to their spears, and making snuff from tobacco, of which they seem very fond, and their women in cooking and repairing canoes.

It was very evident that this little party were under great apprehensions from the Americans. Indeed, the chief gave me to understand, that they had attempted to surprise them several times, which made it absolutely necessary for them to be constantly on their guard. He told me, that they were a set of savage, cruel people, but spoke much in favour of the Oonalaska and Kodiac Indians.

Having procured all the intelligence I could from the Russian chief, I returned towards evening on board my own vessel.

During the night the weather was very unsettled, and the wind variable; blowing at times in heavy squalls from the land, with calms by turns.

At seven o'clock next morning I sent the whale-boat to the Russian settlement, to learn what success they had had with the seine. The boat returned at nine o'clock, deeply

deeply loaded with fine salmon; part of which I sent on board the Queen Charlotte; and now having a plentiful supply of good fish, the people were no longer upon salt provisions, but in lieu of it had fish and yams served to them. Part of the ship's crew were sent to cut firewood, and others had liberty given them to recreate themselves on shore.

Towards noon the Russian chief returned my visit. The service he had rendered us in pointing out a situation where we at any time could catch plenty of fish, demanded some addition to my former present, and I gave him several articles, which in my opinion would be serviceable; such as salt, vinegar, port wine, and brandy; and observing when I was at his residence that they had boiled some of the yams I had given them, which seemed to please them very much, I added to my present about four hundred weight more.

Though my new acquaintance and myself understood each other but very imperfectly, yet he seemed very much pleased with this mutual exchange of friendly offices, and after staying on board a short time, he took his leave, and returned on shore.

Soon afterwards I went in the whale-boat, accompanied by captain Dixon, to take a survey of the harbour. On our first setting out, we expected to find a strait leading out to sea, but we presently found ourselves mistaken. The harbour, from the small island at the entrance, and which obtained the name of Passage Island, runs up about nine miles, nearly in an East South East direction, and afterwards

wards terminates in a fresh water river that branches out in several directions. There are several projecting points on each side the harbour that form very snug and good bays, with excellent beaches, where a ship might, if necessary, be hauled on shore with the greatest safety; the depth of water close to the beach seven and eight fathoms. In our way we called on the wooding party, whom we found busily employed. My carpenter informed me, that he had seen a tree with two holes through it, which appeared to have been made by swivel shot; if so, they probably were fired from a Russian sloop when hereabouts at the American Indians, who I am certain have recently inhabited this neighbourhood, and fled at the approach of the Russians; for we saw a number of huts scattered here and there, some of them very large, and several appeared to have been but lately deserted. After determining the extent of the harbour, we landed, and walked up to the fresh water river; being at that time low water, the river was very narrow; it abounded with salmon, and on the banks we could perceive the tracks of bears and the moose deer. The flood-tide making soon afterwards, we embarked, and rowed into one of the branches, intending to proceed as far up it as possible; but on getting into the mouth of the largest branch, our attention was taken up by a large brown bear coming down to the river. I was in hopes that we should have come within musquet-shot of him, but he got sight of us, and made off into the woods with much greater speed than I imagined a bear could run, and was presently out of sight.

In the course of an hour we saw more than twenty bears, but they were all so shy, that we could not shoot one.

CHAP.
V.
1786.
July.

Tuesday 25.

one. Night now coming on, we left the shore, and got on board about ten o'clock.

By the 25th we had completed our wood and water, and the ships were ready for sea; so that I waited with impatience for an opportunity of proceeding up the river, as there was a probability of meeting with inhabitants, and consequently we stood a chance of procuring furs. At present, however, the wind was light and variable, frequently inclining to calm, and the weather thick and foggy. In the afternoon I went along with captain Dixon to look into a bay situated to the Eastward of the North point of the harbour. We found it a pretty good one, carrying soundings in fourteen, twelve, and eight fathom water, over a bottom of fine black sand. We landed on the West side of the bay, and in walking round it discovered two veins of kennel coal, situated near some hills just above the beach, about the middle of the bay; and with very little trouble several pieces were got out of the bank, nearly as large as a man's head. From this bay we rowed across for the entrance leading into the harbour to the Southward of Passage Isle, and found plenty of water; but the passage much narrower than the Northern one. The best time to run into this harbour is as near low water as possible. Whatever danger there is may then be seen either from the beds of kelp, or the rocks shewing themselves above water. In the evening we returned on board, and I tried some of the coal we had discovered, and found it to burn clear and well.

Wednes. 26.

At six o'clock in the morning of the 26th, the weather, which for some time had been very thick, cleared a little,

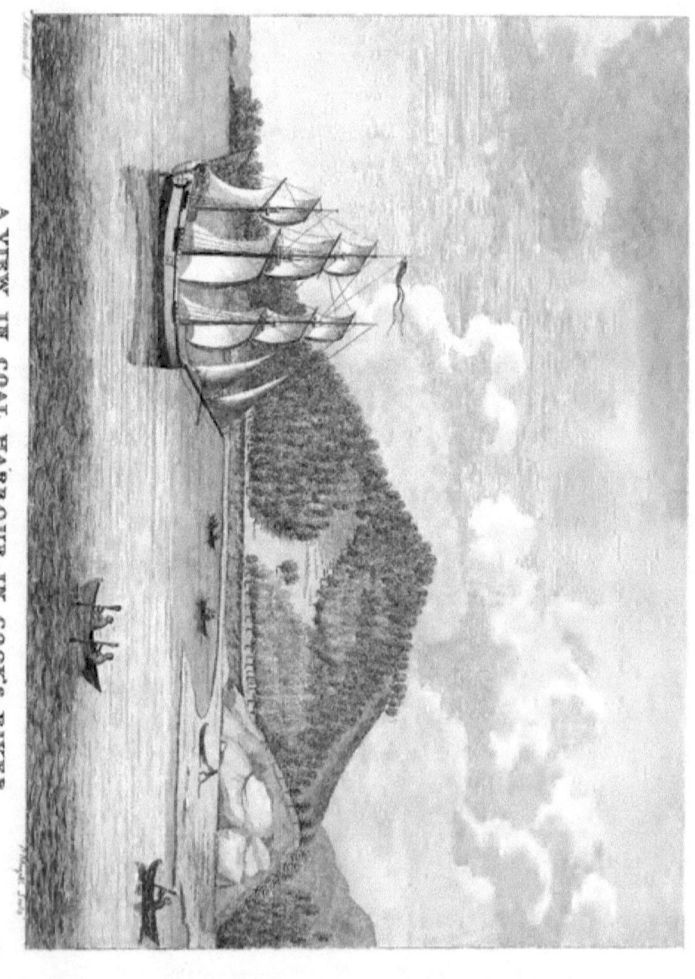

A VIEW IN COAL HARBOUR IN COOK'S RIVER.

little, and we began to unmoor. At eight o'clock we weighed and came to sail, with a light variable breeze. At nine o'clock the wind came to the Northward and Westward; and the Queen Charlotte being to the Northward of us, was enabled to lie out, but I could not accomplish it. The flood-tide making in, and finding we set very fast towards Passage Isle, we brought up, and being exceedingly anxious to get into the main river, began warping against the tide. The Queen Charlotte got clear out, and I made her a signal to anchor, which she obeyed. About eleven o'clock it began to blow very fresh from the North North West, with constant rain, and we were obliged again to bring up. At noon the weather grew moderate, and we endeavoured by every means to get out to sea, but found it a difficult matter to accomplish, owing to the uncertainty of the tide, and the wind continually shifting. However, at eight o'clock, having worked out as far as the outer rocks, a breeze sprung up from the Southward, with which we made all sail, and got out, though we passed very near a ledge of rocks to the Northward: when a-breast of that ledge, we were driven past it in a hurry by the flood-tide, which took us and carried us very fast to the Northward. Soon afterwards the breeze failed us, and I was afraid of coming too near some sunken rocks, situated to the Northward and Eastward of the North ledge; therefore run a warp out to check the ship. The breeze coming on again in a short time, we slipped the warp, and run further off, and at ten o'clock brought-to for the yaul, which I had sent to weigh the kedge. At eleven o'clock the boat came on board, and about the same time we joined the Queen Charlotte, and found she was nearly under way. During the night we had light airs,

and

110   A VOYAGE TO THE

CHAP. V.

1786.
July.
Wednes. 26.

Thursday 27.

and the tide carried us very faſt to the North Eaſt into a deep opening, which is formed by Anchor Point, and the land to the North Eaſt of Point Bede. Our depth of water was too much for anchoring, being upwards of ſixty fathoms; ſo that we were under the neceſſity of waiting for a breeze to puſh out again. At five o'clock in the morning a light breeze came on from the Eaſtward, with which we ſtood North North Weſt for Anchor Point, having got out of the opening with the ebb tide. The lead was kept conſtantly going, and we had ſoundings from forty-eight to thirty fathoms water, over a bottom of fine grey ſand.

At noon Point Bede bore South by Eaſt half Eaſt, and Anchor Point North 21° Weſt, diſtant from the neareſt land about five leagues. The latitude, by obſervation, was 59° 34′ North.

We ſtretched up the river, with light breezes from the Southward and Eaſtward, till half paſt five o'clock, when the flood-tide being ſpent, we came-to with the ſtream-anchor in twenty fathoms water, over a rocky bottom: Anchor Point bearing North 33° Eaſt, five miles diſtant; the Volcano Mount North 86° Weſt; the North land in ſight on the Weſtern ſhore, North 24° Weſt; and an appearance of an opening on the Weſt ſide, North 63° Weſt.

A large column of ſmoke iſſued from the ſummit of Mount Volcano, but no fiery eruption was to be ſeen; neither could we perceive any fires, or other ſigns of the coaſt being inhabited on either ſide the river, which was rather remarkable, as the adjacent country ſeemed pleaſant,

and

NORTH WEST COAST OF AMERICA.

and well sheltered from the inclemency of the weather. This inclined me to think that the Russians we found in Coal Harbour had been up the river and quarrelled with the natives; and I began to fear that our success in the river would be very small; however, I determined to stand on, and leave nothing unattempted towards attaining the principal object of our voyage. At ten o'clock we weighed and stood up the river with the flood and a light breeze from the Southward. The ebb making strong at eight o'clock in the morning, we could not stem it with a light breeze; therefore anchored in twenty-four fathoms, over a rocky bottom; Anchor Point bearing South, 30° East, distant five leagues; the Volcano Mount South West half West; the extremes of an island on the West shore, from North, 62° West, to North, 48° West, distant about five leagues. At the time we anchored, the tide run four miles an hour; the ebb setting from the North by East, and the flood from the South by West, and about half-tide it run nearly five miles an hour. Our latitude was 60° 9′ North, and we found 23° 15′ Easterly variation. The land on the Western side near the shore appearing very pleasant, and likely to be inhabited, I determined to stand over and look for anchorage. At four o'clock a point of land which contracts the river to the Westward bore North 54° West, five miles distant. We now had soundings from 20 to 25 fathoms of water over a rocky bottom; but after hauling round the point, we shoaled it, and at six o'clock, having thirteen fathoms water over a shingly bottom, we came-to with the best bower; the Northernmost land in sight on the West shore, bearing North 20° East, and the distance from the nearest land about five miles.

CHAP. V.

1786.
July.
Thursday 27.

Friday 28.

CHAP. VI.

Indians come to the Ships with Furs.—Shew a thieving Disposition.—Bring great Quantities of Salmon to barter.—Short Description of the Country near Trading Bay.—Climate.—Produce.—The Ships leave Trading Bay, and proceed down the River.—Requested by the Indians to join with them against the Russians.—Presents given at parting.—Leave Cook's River, and proceed towards Prince William's Sound.—Prevented from making it by contrary Winds.—Proceed along the Coast.—Disappointed in meeting with Cross Sound.

CHAP.
VI.
1786.
July.
Friday 28.

SOON after we anchored, two small canoes came off from the shore, nearly a-breast of the ship, and went along-side the Queen Charlotte. I afterwards learnt that they had nothing to barter, except a few dried salmon, which captain Dixon purchased for beads; and also made them a few presents, in order to convince them that our intentions were friendly, and that we wished to trade with them in a peaceable manner. They seemed to comprehend captain Dixon's meaning, and promised to bring furs the

Saturday 29. following day. About seven o'clock the next morning we had the pleasure of seeing two large canoes and several small ones pushing off from the shore. The large canoes contained about twenty people each; the small ones held but one, or at most two persons. When at some distance from us they joined in a song, which was continued for a

consider-

NORTH WEST COAST OF AMERICA.

considerable length of time; and afterwards came alongside, extending their arms as a token of their pacific intentions, and many of them held up green plants, probably for the same motive. Most of these Indians had their faces daubed entirely over with red oker and black lead, which gave them a very disgusting appearance; their noses and ears were in general ornamented with small blue beads or teeth, and they had a slit cut in the under lip, in a line parallel with the mouth, which was adorned in a similar manner. We procured from this party near twenty sea-otter skins, and a few cloaks made of the earless marmot skins sewed together very neatly. They traded in a fair open manner, and were very importunate with us to go on shore. I intreated one of them, who appeared to be a chief, to come on board, which he declined at first, unless I sent one of the sailors into his canoe as an hostage; but whilst I was speaking with him, one of his companions ventured on board, and presently afterwards the chief and several others followed his example; however, to convince them that they were perfectly safe, I sent one of my people into their boat, agreeably to the chief's request. After staying on board some time, and gratifying their curiosity with looking at the vessel, they left us and paddled on shore, seemingly well satisfied with their reception.

From this favourable beginning, I was inclined to think we could not change our situation for a better, therefore determined to keep it a few days; accordingly we sighted the best bower, and moored with it to the Southward, and the stream to the Northward. Our observation at noon gave 60° 49′ latitude.

ON the 30th we were visited by several canoes, from whom we purchased some good sea-otter skins, together with several marmot cloaks, racoons, and foxes; they also brought us plenty of excellent fresh salmon, which we obtained for beads and buttons. Our traffic for some days was much in the same state, and the behaviour of the natives was very quiet and peaceable; however, according to Indian custom, they made no scruple of thieving, and some that were on board the King George on the 3d August, gave us a specimen of their talents in that line, by stealing the hook from a block-strap, and a grindstone-handle, which being made of iron, was no doubt reckoned a prize. I did not however think it prudent to use violence with them for these trifling depredations, and contented myself with ordering a good look-out to be kept, to prevent their stealing any thing in future.

AN elderly chief went on board the Queen Charlotte, from whom captain Dixon gathered some information respecting the Russians. He clearly understood from the old man's pointing to the guns, and describing the explosion they made, as well as from other circumstances, that there had lately been a battle between the Russians and the natives, in which the Russians were worsted: the chief at the same time intimated, that they would not quarrel with us on that account, as he was certain we belonged to another nation, from the difference in our dress. How this quarrel originated we could not learn, but most probably it was occasioned by theft.

THE Indians, on leaving the ship, gave us to understand that their neighbourhood was drained of furs, but that they

they would go to procure more in the adjacent country. In the afternoon a strong gale of wind came on, which continued till the forenoon of the 5th, varying from South South East to South South West. A considerable sea set into the bay, that caused the ships to ride very heavy, but we found much more so at slack water than at any other time. This difference I imagine to be occasioned by our lying in a different tide to what there is in the stream; so that during the time of low water a sea rolls in; but as soon as the tide makes in the stream, it runs along the mouth of the bay, and breaks off the sea considerably. About ten o'clock in the forenoon, the weather growing moderate, one large canoe and several small ones came along-side, bringing us four good sea-otter skins, a few martins, racoons, and foxes, and plenty of fine salmon. The large canoe had been absent two days, to trade for furs in various parts of the river, and the people now gave us to understand that the adjoining country was entirely drained of skins, and that they could not procure any more. One of the Indians in the large canoe had a very good Nankin frock, and another a blue frock, which they wanted to sell: several of them had a number of small blue glass beads, which they seemed very fond of, but the frocks were held in very little estimation. These articles must doubtless have been procured from the Russians previous to their quarrel, and soon after they came into the river. I was inclined to believe the information we obtained from our visiters respecting the scarcity of furs in this part; as I had observed for some days past the canoes came from different quarters, and the few skins they brought were of an inferior quality; I therefore determined to quit Cook's River the first opportunity, and proceed

CHAP. VI.

1786.
August.
Saturday 5.

proceed to Prince William's Sound, where I expected to procure a good supply of fine furs.

AT noon the weather was very unsettled, with every appearance of an approaching gale, which prevented me from weighing. Towards evening a fresh gale came on from the Southward; and at nine o'clock, when the flood made, it blew very strong, which occasioned us to let go the small bower, and veer away on both cables, until we brought the small bower a-head. The gale continued till noon on the 7th; during which time no canoes came near us; but about two o'clock, the weather growing more moderate, two small canoes ventured off, from whom we purchased a sufficient quantity of salmon to serve the ship's company one day; but they brought no furs of any kind whatever. Towards evening two large canoes came off from the Eastern shore; but the weather then being very bad, they passed on, without calling along-side, and went on shore a-breast of the ships, where they hauled their canoes, and turned them bottom up, probably to answer the purpose of temporary habitations, as we soon afterwards saw a fire lighted near each of them. Notwithstanding the heavy gale of wind we recently had experienced, it raised no sea on the opposite beach; on the contrary, the water was so smooth, that a small boat might be able to land on any part of it with safety.

Monday 7.

WE still had fresh gales to the Southward, with thick hazy weather; this, however, did not prevent two small canoes from venturing along-side with a few salmon. In the afternoon of the 8th, two of the natives came on board, and I gave each of them a knife, a gimblet, and some

Tuesday 8.

some beads. They were totally at a loss what to make of the gimblets, till I pointed out their use, and taught them to bore a hole through a piece of wood, which at once discovered their value; and they admired the gimblets far beyond their other presents.

CHAP.
VI.
1786.
August.
Tuesday 8.

WHEN my visiters prepared to go on shore, it came on to blow very hard; on which I gave them to understand, that if they would stay on board till the gale was over, I would haul their canoes upon deck; to this proposal they readily agreed, but an old surly man in one of the canoes objected to it, and insisted on their leaving the ship, which they did, and after a good deal of difficulty got safe on shore. At eight o'clock the gale increased, and at nine it came on to blow so strong at South, that I judged it prudent to have the topgallant-masts got down upon deck, the topmasts struck close down to the rigging, and the lower yards kept aloft, ready for making some sail, should we be forced from our anchors. The water, however, continued more smooth than could have been expected; and the vessel being made snug, rode very easy. At eleven o'clock, when she tended to the flood, apprehending that our present scope of cable would be insufficient to ride her against both wind and tide, we wore away to one and a quarter cable on the best bower.

AT eight o'clock next morning, the weather appearing more settled, we began to sway up the topmasts; but whilst we were engaged in this business, it came on to blow very fresh, which determined me to keep all fast, as I did not judge it prudent to quit our situation till there was a probability of our clearing the river.

Wednes. 9.

CHAP.
VI.

1786.
August.
Wednes. 9.

THE heavy and continued gale of wind for some days past had raised no surf on the beach to the Westward of us, and I am inclined to think there never is much sea near the shore with any wind whatever. My reason for forming this conjecture is, that the natives have fixed wears for catching salmon in several places, which, should any sea set in shore, would certainly be washed away by the surf.

THE land to the Westward is prettily diversified with vallies and gently rising grounds, which in general are clothed with pines and shrubs. Many of the vales have small rills of water which discharge themselves into the sea, and in one of them were several houses and some stages on which the natives dry their salmon. These, contrasted with the mountains situated behind them, which are entirely covered with snow, compose a landscape at once beautiful and picturesque.

DURING the late stormy unsettled weather, the air had been mild and temperate, and I am inclined to think that the climate here is not so severe as has been generally supposed; for, in the course of our traffic with the natives, they frequently brought berries of several sorts, and in particular blackberries, equally fine with those met with in England.

BESIDES the various sorts of furs met with here, and which have already been enumerated, Cook's River produces native sulphur, ginseng, snake root, black lead, coal, together with the greatest abundance of fine salmon; and the natives behave quietly and barter fairly; so that a most profitable

profitable trade might doubtless be carried on here by any persons of sufficient enterprise to undertake it.

Towards midnight the gale subsided, and at three o'clock in the morning of the 10th a light breeze coming on from the North North East, we began to unmoor. At five o'clock we weighed, and came to sail with a moderate breeze at North East. Soon after we got under sail, the wind began to haul round to the South East; and finding that the ebb-tide set us in towards the South point of the bay we had just left (and which obtained the Name of Trading Bay), it became necessary to haul the wind close. Just as we got a-breast of the point, we were taken by a very rapid tide setting to the South West (which was a direction very different to what we expected); and there being little wind, and that little Southerly, we were not able to get out of the tide, though a very little push would have done it; for the South South East tide line was just without us. Immediately afterwards I saw a dry shoal bearing South West, right in the direction of the tide's course, and we were driving for it at the rate of five miles an hour. I presently saw that there was no other method of avoiding this shoal than by anchoring, and was glad to find we had clear ground; therefore anchored immediately in eleven fathoms water, over a bottom of fine dark sand inclining to mud. The Queen Charlotte came-to at the same time, about half a mile to the Westward of us.

The South Point of Trading Bay bore North 24° West, four miles distant; the East point of an island to the Southward of us, South 5° East, and the North East point of the shoal South 14° East, distant a quarter of a mile.

At

CHAP.
VI.
1786.
August.
Thursday 10.

At low water the shoal was dry for about a mile and a half, extending from North East to South West. It appeared to be a bank of black muddy sand, flat on every side, and the water so smooth all round, that if we had drifted on it, in all probability we should not have received any injury. However, as we had little wind, and fine clear weather, I sent my whale-boat to sound all round it. Within this shoal to the Westward the land appeared very high, and in many places covered with snow. Near the sea was a narrow slip of low land covered with pines, and there appeared some openings like harbours; but time would not admit of my sending the boat to examine them. I saw a rock from the mast-head, which is covered before high water in the direction of North half East, from the Eastern point of that island to the Southward of us, and forms part of a shoal that appears to stretch out two or three miles. A rock was also seen about half a mile from the South point of Trading Bay, which, together with the shoals, makes the navigation in this part of the river much more dangerous than it was supposed to be. Whilst we lay at anchor, several small canoes came off from a town near the South point of Trading Bay. In one of them was a man whom I had found very useful in procuring furs during our stay in the bay; on which account he was called " *the Factor*." I clearly understood from him, that the Russians frequented the West side of the island to the Southward, and that there is a passage betwixt that and the main; if so, I think it must be greatly incommoded with shoals, and dangerous on account of the rapidity of the tides. My friend the Factor brought nothing to dispose of except a few salmon. It seems, his principal motive in paying me this visit was, to

beg

beg our assistance against the Russians. He was very importunate with me to grant his request, intimating at the same time that he could presently assemble a large fleet of canoes, with which, assisted by our ships, they could easily get the better of their enemies. On my refusing his request, he seemed rather mortified; but to console him in some measure for this disappointment, I gave him a light horseman's cap, of which he was very proud; and his countrymen beheld him with such a mixture of admiration and envy, that I greatly question whether he will be able to keep it long in his possession. I also distributed a few trifles amongst the other Indians, and they returned on shore perfectly satisfied, notwithstanding I refused to espouse their cause against the Russians.

At one o'clock the whale-boat returned from sounding, and the officer who was in her informed me, that he found four and five fathoms water about half a mile from the shoal, and all round it near the same depth over a bottom of black muddy sand, the tide running at the rate of four miles an hour. Soon after four o'clock, the flood being nearly done, we weighed and stretched over for the Eastern shore, with a light breeze from the South South East. After getting about two miles to the Eastward, the water deepened so much, that we got no ground with sixty fathoms of line; but after passing the mid channel, we struck the ground in thirty-four fathoms water, over a shingly bottom, and the water shoaled gradually as we advanced towards the Eastern shore. About nine o'clock we anchored in sixteen fathoms water, over a shingly bottom, as I judged the ebb to have been done; but it run down near an hour longer than I expected. When at anchor, the South point of Trading Bay bore North 46° West. The extremes of the island on the Western shore South 65° West, and South 30' West, distant from the nearest land on the East shore about two leagues. Next morning at half past five o'clock, the flood-tide being done, we weighed and made sail with a light breeze at South South West, and carried soundings along shore about two leagues distant, from fifteen to twenty fathoms, over a shingly bottom. At eight o'clock, the North point of an island on the Western shore bore North 84° West, six leagues, and some rocks that are situated two miles from the Eastern shore, South 53° East, three leagues distant. These rocks make their appearance at all times of tide, yet are not noticed in captain Cook's chart of the river, but are in Mr. Edgar's, who was master of the Discovery; he I think has laid them down about a league too far to the Southward.

WE tacked at nine o'clock, and soon afterwards saw a number of canoes, which at first I concluded were traders coming off to the ship; but on looking at them through a glass, I perceived two Russian boats amongst them; they were about a league to the Northward of us, and appeared to be standing over for the island on the Western shore: just at this time the breeze from the South South West freshening, the boats set their sails, and pushed over for the island. They no doubt were the same party we met at Coal Harbour; and probably the Factor's intelligence, respecting their having a settlement on the West side of that island, was true.

HAVING

HAVING in general light variable winds, with calms by turns, we took the advantage of the tide in standing down the river, and by noon on the 13th were well clear of it. At that time the extremes of the Barren Islands bore South West and South, 38° West; Cape Elizabeth North, 80° West, distant about five leagues; and our distance from the nearest shore about three leagues. The land on which Cape Elizabeth is situated is an island, and in the straits formed by it and the back land there is good anchorage and shelter. Hereabouts would be a most desirable situation for carrying on a whale-fishery; the whales being on the coast, and close in shore, in vast numbers; and there being convenient and excellent harbours quite handy for the business. The Barren Islands, which are situated nearly in the midway between Point Banks and Cape Elizabeth, are very high and totally barren; they lie in a cluster, and appear to have good passages between them. With a fine breeze from the West South West we stood along-shore, at the distance of three leagues, steering East by North for Prince William's Sound. The lead was kept constantly going, but we got no ground with forty fathoms of line. At eight o'clock I changed the course to North East half East, in order to make the South West point of Montague Island; the Westernmost land in sight bearing West South West, and the Easternmost North by West, eight or nine leagues distant.

LIGHT variable winds, with intervening calms and hazy weather, prevented us from making any great progress towards the entrance into Prince William's Sound. At two o'clock in the afternoon of the 17th, having nearly a calm, and the current setting us directly off shore, we anchored

CHAP. VI.
1786.
August.
Thursday 17.

anchored in forty-three fathoms water, over a bottom of gravel mixed with small stones and shells. The extremes of Montague Island bore North, 45° East, and North, 9° East; the middle of the passage into Prince William's Sound North, 2° East; and our distance from the nearest land three or four miles. During the afternoon and night we had light airs, inclining to calm, with thick foggy weather.

Friday 18.

Next morning a moderate breeze sprung up from the West South West; but the fog was so thick, that we could not see any object half a cable's length from the ship. At six o'clock in the afternoon, the fog rather dispersing, we weighed and came to sail; but the day being so far spent, I did not think it prudent to stand in for the passage in the night; therefore stood to the Southward under an easy sail. We had soundings in forty-four fathoms water, with a bottom of grey sand; but at midnight, in standing to the North West, we struck no ground with ninety fathoms of line, and presently afterwards got no bottom with 106 fathoms. At nine o'clock

Saturday 19.

next morning, the fog clearing away over Montague Island, we saw the North East point bearing North, 39° East, four leagues distant; but light baffling winds prevented our making any great progress towards it. At four in the afternoon the extremes of Montague Island bore from North by East to East, the nearest part about four miles distant, and a rock which lies to the South West of the Green Isles, North, 11° East. A light breeze now sprung up at East, with which we steered North North East, and I began to conceive hopes that we should get into the passage before night came on; in this however I was disappointed; for as soon as we got the passage open, we took the current, and the wind growing

growing scant, it set us to leeward of the passage, and very fast towards some small islands and rocks which are situated at the South extreme of an island that forms the Western side of the passage: I therefore, at six o'clock, was under the necessity of tacking and standing to the South South East; and even then, with a three-knot breeze, and all the sail we could carry, for near three hours, we could barely keep clear of the rocks; indeed I could have anchored at this time, but we had eighty-four fathoms water, which I thought too great a depth to anchor in. During our ineffectual attempt to make the entrance, we had the boats a-head towing the ship, but all to no purpose; and I must own that it was rather a mortifying circumstance to be thrown out, after making ourselves almost sure of getting into the passage, as at one time we had every reason to expect, and had got all ready for anchoring. The wind continued variable, but generally in the Eastern and Northern boards, which was quite unfavourable to us, and we consequently plied to little advantage. At three o'clock in the afternoon of the 21st the South West point of Montague Island bore North West by North; having then a fresh breeze at East North East, I stood directly in for it, intending, if possible, to have luffed round it, and to have anchored in a sandy bay that lies just round the South West point. For some time every thing was in our favour, and I had hardly a doubt of gaining anchorage, until we brought the South West point to bear North by East, when the current took us on the weather-bow, and drove us bodily to leeward; so that there was not a possibility of our making the wished-for entrance. At four o'clock the extremes of Montague Island bore North, 4° East, and North, 45° East, distant

CHAP.
VI.

1786.
August.
Saturday 19.

Monday 21.

from

from the South West point three miles. A fresh gale coming on at North East, with heavy squalls and thick rainy weather, we tacked and stood to the South East by East. On sounding, we had twenty fathoms water, over a rocky bottom. Till the 24th the wind continued at North East, blowing fresh and in squalls, with thick rainy weather; so that I gave up all hopes of making Prince William's Sound by the South West passage, and determined to try for an entrance that leads into the Sound by Cape Hinchinbrooke. At five o'clock in the morning of the 24th, the wind shifting to East South East, I steered North East, in order to make the Eastern passage into the Sound; the weather thick and hazy. For some days past no land had appeared in sight; but this afternoon at four o'clock we saw land, which formed a high bluff point, bearing North, 46° West, about four leagues distant. The former heavy gales from the North East were now succeeded by light variable winds and thick foggy weather, which caused us to ply occasionally, though to little purpose, as it was totally impracticable, with such weather, to make our intended port.

AT eight o'clock in the evening of the 26th a light breeze came on from the South West, the fog dispersed, and we had clear, pleasant weather; so that I was in expectation of a settled South West wind; therefore steered North North East for the Eastern passage into Prince William's Sound.

TOWARDS midnight, the breeze freshening with thick dirty weather, we brought-to with the ship's head to the Southward; and at three o'clock, the fog clearing up, we we bore away to the Northward and made sail. Our favourable prospect however was but of short duration; for we again had variable winds and foggy weather to encounter with; on this, I sent my whale-boat on board the Queen Charlotte for captain Dixon, in order to consult him respecting our future proceedings. He came immediately on board the King George; and after fixing on King George's Sound for our winter quarters, we came to a resolution of quitting this part of the coast in a day or two, should the wind continue unfavourable, and endeavouring to make some harbour farther to the Southward. Indeed it was high time to come to a determination of this sort; the season for our business was far advanced, and much time had been spent to no purpose, owing to contrary winds and bad weather, a continuation of which, together with heavy gales of wind from the Westward, might soon be expected to set in with a continuance; it was therefore thought most prudent, should we be disappointed a short time longer, to make the best of our way to the Southward, and endeavour to get into Cross Sound, or the Bay of Islands; both of them being harbours seen by captain Cook during our last voyage. Having settled these points, captain Dixon returned on board his own vessel.

The sun breaking out just at noon, we had an opportunity of taking an observation, which gave 59° latitude, the longitude 146° 3′.

We sounded at four o'clock with 100 fathoms of line, but got no ground; the extremes of the land in sight
bore

CHAP. VI.

1786.
August.
Sunday 27.

bore from West half North to North North West half West, distant from the nearest part of it seven or eight leagues. At six o'clock the land in sight bore West by South and North East. The land to the North East appeared to be two low islands, which I conjectured were situated between Kayes Island and the land of Cape Hinchinbrooke; at the same time the points of an opening, which I took for the Eastern passage into Prince William's Sound, bore North West half North, and North North West, distant five or six leagues. Having a moderate breeze from the North East, and fine weather, we stood in towards the opening till eight o'clock, when the wind hauled to the North North East, which laid us off so much that we could not fetch in; therefore we tacked and stood to the Eastward under an easy sail, intending to try for the passage next morning. At two o'clock we wore, and steered North by West half West, with a breeze from the North East by North. At four o'clock, having a fresh gale at North East, and fine clear weather, I expected from the course we had been steering during the night that we should have had the small islands, seen by us the preceding evening, bearing about North by East, and distant about four miles; from which situation, with the North East wind we now had, we could have run into the passage with a large wind; but I was much surprised to see the small islands bearing North East by North, and distant about nine leagues; so much had the current driven us off shore during the night. However, we stood to the North North West under all the sail we could set; hoping, if the weather remained settled, that we might be able before night came on to get into the passage,

Monday 28.

passage, and anchor there; so that if the wind failed us, we might be able to work in to the Sound with the tide; but at seven o'clock it began to blow very fresh, with thick hazy weather, and every appearance of an approaching gale, the land entirely hid with a thick fog. Under these circumstances I did not think it prudent to run in for the passage; therefore at half past seven o'clock we tacked and stood to the South East. I now gave up all thoughts of getting into the Sound this season; therefore determined to quit this part of the coast immediately, and stand to the Southward, where there was a probability of meeting with more favourable weather.

WITH a fresh gale from the East North East, we steered South East by South, the weather still thick and foggy, attended with rain. During the night we frequently sounded with eighty fathoms of line, but got no bottom. The wind never fixed at one point for any length of time, but varied continually; sometimes blowing fresh and in squalls, with alternate calms and thick rainy weather.

ON the 4th of September, finding myself very indifferent, I sent for captain Dixon to come on board, intending, should my illness increase so as to prevent me from keeping the deck, for the Queen Charlotte to take the lead, and make for Cross Sound, from thence to Cape Edgecombe, and afterwards to King George's Sound, where we had before determined to winter, and build a shalop of about sixty or seventy tons burthen, if we were fortunate enough to get in before the winter season set in so

S   bad

CHAP.
VI.

1786.
September.

Tuesday 5.

bad as to prevent us from making the necessary preparations for effecting that purpose.

At eight o'clock in the morning of the 5th we saw the land making in two very high mountains, one of which bore North North West half West, and the other North North West half West, distant fourteen or fifteen leagues. These mountains we supposed to be Mount Saint Elias and Mount Fairweather, according to their situation in captain Cook's chart. We now had light variable airs, which caused us to ply occasionally, and retarded our progress very much. Our latitude at noon was 58° 16′ North, and the longitude 140° 3′.

Saturday 9.

In the afternoon, finding myself so ill as not to be able to keep the deck, I desired my first mate to speak the Queen Charlotte, and request captain Dixon to take the lead, which he accordingly did. In the forenoon of the 9th, Mount Fairweather was seen bearing East North East. This mountain is situated a little to the Northward and Eastward of Cross Sound. At noon, having a moderate breeze from the South East by East, with open cloudy weather, we stood in shore to the North East by East; the land in sight extending from East North East to North North East half East, and a low point North East half East, four or five leagues distant. Our latitude then was 57° 54′, and the longitude 137° 58′. At two o'clock, the wind being then at East South East, our course was changed to North East, in order to made Cross Sound; but in a few hours afterwards, being well in with it, captain Dixon hailed, and desired my first mate

to

to acquaint me, that he saw no appearance of a port in the situation laid down in captain Cook's chart for Cross Sound; but that what captain Cook took for an opening in the land, was nothing more than a deep valley with low land in it, which, at the considerable distance he was from the shore, might easily be mistaken for a deep opening, and consequently a good harbour might be expected.

CHAP. VII.

Fruitless Attempt to fall in with the Bay of Islands.—Proceed along the Coast towards King George's Sound.—Unsuccessful Attempt to make it.—Departure from the Coast.—Passage from thence to the Sandwich Islands.—Saint Maria la Gorta.—Arrive off Owhyhee.—Refreshments obtained.—Natives Propensity to Theft.—Plan of future Proceedings.—The Ships leave Owhyhee.—Pick up a Canoe with some Indians in Distress.—Anchor at Woahoo.

CHAP. VII.
1786.
September.
Saturday 9.

NOT falling in with Cross Sound, as was expected, and having no spare time to look for it in any other situation, we tacked at four o'clock, and stood to the Southward with a moderate breeze from the East South East, and dark unsettled looking weather: the land in sight extending from North North West to East South East, about four leagues distant from the nearest part.

Sunday 10.

THE wind continued moderate till four o'clock the next morning, when a strong gale came on from the North East, attended with heavy rain. At nine o'clock the wind shifted to East South East, the gale increasing with thick rainy weather, which obliged us to hand the topsails and reef the courses. Towards noon the gale gradually subsided, and at six o'clock we had a light breeze from the South South West, with a very heavy cross sea, which caused

caused the ship to labour exceedingly. During the night we had light variable winds with constant rain: this however was not of long continuance; for at noon on the 11th a heavy gale sprung up from the East South East; the rain still continuing without intermission

THE almost constant succession of bad weather we for some time past had experienced, induced me to think that the bad weather season was set in, and that our making a port on the coast would be very precarious; in that case we should be obliged to water, and spend the winter at the Sandwich Islands. Under this consideration, I judged it prudent to put the ship's company to an allowance of water at the rate of two quarts a man a day.

THE gale continued to blow from the Eastward and Southward, with very little intermission, till noon on the 13th; it then grew moderate. Our latitude then was 56° 37′, and the longitude 138° 31′. Having then a moderate breeze from the South by East, we steered East North East, in order to make the land near Cape Edgecombe. At nine o'clock the wind shifted to the South West, blowing fresh, with hazy weather.

AT midnight we hauled the wind to the Southward, and at five o'clock the next morning bore away and made sail, standing in for the land with a moderate breeze at South West. At six o'clock the land near Cape Edgecombe was seen bearing North East by North, and at eight the land in sight extended from North half West to North North East half East, distant from the nearest

CHAP.
VII.
1786.
September.
Thursday 14.

part four or five leagues. We now stood to the North by East, in order to gain the situation laid down by captain Cook for the Bay of Islands, where we had great hopes of making a good port; but after getting within two leagues of the land, no place could be discovered which had the appearance of a harbour, or even a safe bay: at the same time we could get no ground with eighty fathoms of line. Just before noon, nothing like a harbour making its appearance, and observing a ledge of rocks to the Northward of us stretching some distance from the shore, towards which a current was sweeping us very fast, captain Dixon (who still took the lead) thought it most prudent to haul off shore to the Westward; at the same time the wind backed a little to the Southward, which enabled us to clear the reef. We should not have been in much danger, had there been a commanding breeze; but we unfortunately had light winds, and a considerable swell rolling on towards the shore, against which the ship could scarcely steer or make any way. The latitude at noon was 57° 6' and 136° 40' longitude.

During the afternoon we had light variable winds and dark gloomy weather. At six o'clock the land in sight extended from North by East to South East half East, distant from the nearest shore three or four leagues. Towards evening the weather had a dirty unsettled appearance, and in the night a heavy gale of wind came on from the East South East, with thick rainy weather, which continued till ten o'clock the next forenoon, when the weather grew more moderate.

Friday 15.

WE

WE plied with variable winds till noon on the 16th, when seeing no probability of meeting with a harbour near Cape Edgecombe, we gave up all further thoughts of it, and determined to stand for King George's Sound.

CHAP. VII.
1786.
September.
Saturday 16.

A FRESH breeze now sprung up from the West South West, which brought with it clear weather. On the 18th at noon we were in 53° 46' latitude, and 134° 6' longitude; and at one o'clock the land was seen bearing East North East, fourteen leagues distant: at four, the land extended from North to East South East, and an appearance of a bay bore East by North. Having a fresh gale at North North West and clear weather, by six o'clock we were within two leagues of the shore, and had an opportunity of seeing that there was no appearance of a harbour, as we before had supposed, nor any sign of inhabitants.

Monday 18.

AT this time the Queen Charlotte being some distance a-head, wore and stood under our lee, and captain Dixon hailed, and acquainted me that he saw no appearance of a harbour or any inhabitants. The land in this situation is high, and breaks into abrupt cliffs which hang over the sea, and are washed by a very heavy surf. We now steered South with a fine gale at North West and clear weather; our distance from shore about two leagues. The wind still continuing favourable, we steered more to the Eastward, in order to keep well in with the coast.

ON the 21st, in latitude 50° 47', and 129° 28' longitude, we saw an island bearing North East by East half East, six or seven leagues distant; and at six o'clock in the

Thursday 21.

the afternoon the island bore North, 28° West, five leagues; at the same time another island appeared in sight, bearing North, 45° East, distant ten or eleven leagues.

Friday 22.

EARLY in the morning of the 22d we saw the land extending from North to North East, distant ten or eleven leagues. At noon the land extended from North West half North to North East by North; Woody Point bore North by West, three leagues, and a high rock detached from it North by West, a quarter West, two leagues distant. The land to the Southward and Eastward appeared to form a good bay, which we steered for with a fresh breeze from the North North West, in hopes of coming to anchor before night came on. As we drew near the shore I ordered the whale-boat to be lowered down, and sent her a-head to sound; but at half past two o'clock, seeing not the least appearance of shelter, I made the signal for the boat to come on board: at that time we were not more than three miles from shore, and had thirty-four fathoms water over a foul bottom. Immediately after the boat was hoisted up we stood along shore to the Eastward towards King George's Sound, the land extending from North North East half East to North West by West; Woody Point North West by North, three leagues, and the rocks off Woody Point North West half North, two leagues distant. The space between these rocks and Woody Point appears to be foul ground, as there are many rocks just shewing their heads above water, on which the sea frequently breaks. At seven o'clock we hauled off the land and stood South West by West, the wind then blowing fresh at North West by West; and

Saturday 23. and at daylight next morning wore ship and steered North

half

half East. The land at noon extending from East by South to West North West half West, we steered East North East, with a moderate breeze from the North West by North, and pleasant weather. Our latitude then was 49° 48', and the longitude 127° 8'. At two o'clock, seeing a canoe putting off from the shore, we shortened sail and brought-to for her to come up; she had two Indians in her, but we could not prevail on either of them to come on board: they had some fish which we bought, and I made them a few trifling presents; after which they left us and paddled for that part of the shore between Woody Point and King George's Sound. At five o'clock the North Point of the entrance into King George's Sound bore North, 73° East; the breakers that lie off that point East half North, three leagues distant: the Easternmost land in sight South, 73° East, distant eight or nine leagues, and the Westernmost land West by North half North, thirteen leagues distant. Having light winds and hazy weather, we found it impracticable to reach the Sound before night; therefore hauled to the South South East. In the course of the evening we frequently sounded, and had from fifty-four to sixty-two fathoms water over a muddy bottom. During the night we plied occasionally, with light variable winds and hazy weather. At six o'clock in the morning of the 24th the haze clearing away, we saw the land about the Sound, the North point of the entrance bearing North East by East, nine or ten leagues distant. The wind being still light, and frequently inclining to calm, our progress towards the Sound was very slow. At four o'clock in the afternoon of the 25th the North point of the entrance bore North, 61° East, three leagues distant: having a light breeze at South by East, we

CHAP. VII.
1786.
September.
Monday 25.

we steered East by South, expecting to gain the entrance; but at five o'clock the light breeze we had shifted to South East, and a current set us strongly to the North North West; so that it was impossible for us to fetch into the Sound; and night coming on, we tacked and stood to the South West by South. About six o'clock the wind began to freshen at South East, with every appearance of an approaching gale: therefore I thought it most advisable to get a little offing before it came on; as those gales from the South East, after blowing hard a while in that quarter, generally haul to the Southward, and blow with great violence; in which case the land of the Bay of Good Hope all becomes a lee and dangerous shore. At eight o'clock the horizon to the South and South East looked remarkably red and wild, with strong flashes of lightning in those boards. At ten the wind blew very fresh from the East South East, with thick weather and hard rain; at that time we wore and stood in shore to the North East, with an intention of keeping pretty near the entrance of the Sound, in order to be ready for pushing into it the next morning, should an opportunity offer; but at eleven o'clock the gale increased so fast upon us, that all hands were barely sufficient to make the ship snug enough for its reception. At midnight we wore and stood to the South by West; immediately afterwards an exceeding heavy gust of wind came on, which obliged us to clew the topsails down on the cap, the foresail (although a very small one, made purposely for a foul-weather sail) gave way at both clews, and both the foot and leech ropes broke short off; yet we fortunately got the sail made snug before it split, unbent it, and bent a new one. At three

Tuesday 26.

o'clock the wind shifted to the South East, and blew a
mere

NORTH WEST COAST OF AMERICA.

mere hurricane, which brought on a very heavy sea, and occasioned the ship to labour and strain exceedingly. It certainly was the most dreadful night I ever saw, and to add to the awful scene of a tremendous sea, loud thunder, fierce lightning, and **torrents of rain**, we had at each mast-head, and **at every yard-arm**, those meteors called by sailors *compasants*, which gave a light at least equal to the same number of lights hung aloft: besides those on the masts and yards, they were flying about on all parts of the rigging.

It is the generally received opinion of seafaring men, that when the compasant reaches the topgallant-mast-heads, the gale is at or near its height, and indeed we found it so; for about half past three, after a most violent gust of wind, which did not continue more than two or three minutes, the clouds began to break, and the weather became more moderate, the wind inclining to the South East by South. At six o'clock it fell almost calm, and we had a prodigious heavy sea from the South South East; soon afterwards we saw the land near the entrance into King George's Sound, bearing East North East, five or six leagues distant, on which we stood for it with a very light breeze at West, the weather looking unsettled, and a very heavy cross sea running. By two in the afternoon it grew nearly calm; and finding all our efforts to get into the Sound ineffectual, we hauled off shore to the Southward.

Light airs, with intervening calms, prevailed till four o'clock in the morning of the 27th, when a fresh gale sprung up at South East by East, attended with thick rainy

CHAP.
VII.
⎯⎯
1786.
September.
Wednes. 27.

rainy weather; we now stood to the North East by East; but the wind shifted every hour, so that there was not a possibility of keeping our course. At eight o'clock, having a moderate breeze at South West, we steered East North East; at the same time the land made its appearance through the haze, bearing from North North West to East North East. This breeze, however, was of short duration; for in the space of an hour it grew nearly calm, and continued light and variable till four in the afternoon, when a little breeze sprung up from the South West; but judging with so light a breeze that we could not reach the Sound before night (our distance from it being about six leagues), we stood to the South South East, with an intention of spending the night in standing off and on, and then, if an opportunity offered at daylight, to run into the Sound. During the former part of the night the wind blew fresh and in squalls, with frequent heavy showers of hail; this was succeeded by light variable winds and thick rainy weather. At six o'clock next morning we tacked and bore away to the North East, the weather hazy, and a prodigious heavy swell from the South West. The North point of the entrance into King George's Sound at eight o'clock bore North East half North, distant four leagues, and the Westernmost land in sight North West by North, six leagues distant. At nine it fell calm, and the heavy swell continuing from the South West, and a strong current setting to the North North East drove us very fast towards the shore, and some breakers that are situated to the Northward and Westward of the entrance into the Sound. At first I had some thoughts of getting our boats out to tow the ship's head round, and to keep her off shore; but the motion of the ship was so great,

Thursday 28.

NORTH WEST COAST OF AMERICA.

great, occasioned by the swell, that it would hardly have been possible to have hoisted them out without dashing them to pieces; indeed, if they had been out they could have had no effect on the ship against so heavy a swell rolling directly on shore. It continued calm till eleven o'clock, at which time we were very near the breakers, and the swell seeming to increase as we approached the shore, I was preparing to anchor with one of the bowers in sixty-four fathoms water, when a light breeze sprung up at South East; this was, in the situation we then were, almost directly from the entrance into the Sound; so that we could not make it, and had no alternative left but to get the ship's head off shore, and get an offing as well as we could.

CHAP. VII.
1786.
September.
Thursday 28.

At noon the breeze freshened at South East, and we stood to the South West; at the same time an exceeding heavy swell rolled in shore, which broke in a frightful surf on the rocks and breakers: the North point of the entrance into King George's Sound bore North, 65° West, four or five leagues distant; our distance from the breakers one mile and a half, and from the nearest land about three miles.

In the afternoon we had light baffling winds, with frequent squalls and heavy showers of hail and rain.

I now saw not the least probability of our getting into the Sound this season; the bad weather appeared to be set in for a continuance, our sails and rigging were much damaged, and the crews stood greatly in need of refreshment; under these circumstances, I came to a determination

CHAP. VII.
1786.
September.

nation of leaving the coast, and standing directly for the Sandwich Islands; and hailing the Queen Charlotte, I acquainted captain Dixon with my intention.

Friday 29.

AT eight o'clock in the morning of the 29th we steered South by West with a fresh Westerly breeze. Woody Point at that time bore North West half West, the Easternmost land in sight East by North, and the entrance of King George's Sound North, 50° East, eleven leagues distant.

Saturday 30.

THE breeze continued Westerly till the morning of the 30th, when it was succeeded by light variable winds, inclining to calm. The weather being clear and fine, the sailors hammocks and chests were got upon deck, and their clothes well aired; the ship was scraped clean between decks and aired with fires. In 46° 48' North latitude, and 131° 6' longitude, we found 19° Easterly variation.

October.
Monday 2.

Saturday 7.

ON the 7th October a strong gale of wind came on at South South West, with hazy weather and rain, which however was not of long duration, and the wind shifting to the South West, brought with it clear weather.

THE wind continued variable, chiefly in the Southern and Western boards, frequently blowing fresh and in squalls, with unsettled weather. On the 12th, in 38° 44' latitude, and 133° 16' longitude, the wind hauled to the Northward, and blew fresh from that quarter, till noon on the 14th, when, after a few hours calm, it shifted to the Southward and Eastward.

Thursday 12.

Saturday 14.

THE

THE scurvy beginning to make its appearnce on some of the people, the ship's company were served a pint of Port wine a-day instead of spirits.

CHAP. VII.
1786.
October.
Saturday 14.

WE proceeded towards the Sandwich Islands without meeting with any thing worthy of note. The wind hanging from South to South East, and being in general light and very variable between these points, rendered our progress tedious.

ON the 26th, in 32° 36′ latitude, and 143° 35′ longitude, we saw great numbers of tropic birds, one of which was in pursuit of a small land bird, very much like a snipe.

Thursday 26.

IN captain Cook's general chart the centre of an island, named Saint Maria la Gorta, is placed in 28° North latitude, and 149° 20′ West longitude. Our latitude at noon, on the 1st of November, was 28° 14′ North, and the longitude 148° 35′; in which situation, having fine clear weather, we certainly ought to have seen that island, but not the least appearance of land was to be seen from the mast-head; and the next forenoon we run directly over the spot where Saint Maria la Gorta should be situated; so that there is great reason to suppose no such place exists.

November.
Wednes. 1.

Thursday 2.

IN the morning of the 9th the wind blew very fresh and in squalls from the South East, attended with torrents of rain and fierce lightning. At nine o'clock it increased to a strong gale, with violent squalls, which obliged us to close-reef the topsails; but before that could be effected, the

Thursday 9.

the maintopsail was split; another was immediately bent and close-reefed. At three in the afternoon the wind hauled to South by West, and the weather grew more moderate.

Friday 10. During the 10th the wind varied from South South East to South by West, blowing fresh and in squalls, the weather dark and cloudy, with frequent heavy rains. Next Saturday 11. morning the wind gradually shifted to the Westward, and at eight o'clock we had a moderate breeze from the North West, the weather still thick and rainy; this continued till four in the afternoon, when we had a light breeze at North, with clear pleasant weather.

Sunday 12. At noon on the 12th the latitude was 21° 26′ and 152° 51′ longitude.

With a moderate breeze at North I steered South by West and South South West, in order to get to the Eastward of Owhyhee, so that if the wind inclined to the Southward we could easily run down the longitude.

Tuesday 14. On the 14th at noon, being in 20° 4′ latitude and 153° 47′ longitude, we steered West by South; and at five o'clock in the afternoon saw the land, which we presently found to be a high mountain on the island of Owhyhee, with some patches of snow on its summit, bearing West South West half West, near thirty leagues distant. Having Wednes. 15. light winds, we did not see the land till next day at noon, when Owhyhee again made its appearance, bearing South West half West, twelve or fourteen leagues distant. In Thursday 16. the morning of the 16th, with a fresh breeze at South East,

NORTH WEST COAST OF AMERICA.

East, we stood to the South West for Owhyhee, the North point bearing West by South, eleven or twelve leagues, and our distance from the nearest shore about five leagues. As we run along the coast several canoes came off to us, but they had nothing to dispose of except a few small fish: indeed the wind blew fresh, and there was so much sea running, that the natives could not with safety venture off with any thing to sell.

CHAP. VII.
1786.
November.
Thursday 16.

At noon, having a fresh breeze from the Eastward, we stood to the North West by North, about three miles distant from shore. About five o'clock the East end of Mowee bore North North West half West, nine or ten leagues distant. When night came on we could perceive large fires lighted in different parts of the country; most probably to inform the inhabitants in more distant parts of the island of our arrival. Early next morning, with a gentle breeze from the Eastward, we run along shore to the North West; and our distance from it being not more than three or four miles, a number of canoes were preparing to follow us. After approaching the North point of the island, we sounded in rounding the point, and had about sixteen fathoms water, over a bottom of white sand and beds of coral rock; our distance from the shore about two miles. No shelter was to be seen for ships to anchor under, and a very heavy swell set in shore, which is principally composed of steep black rocks, against which the surf beats with much violence. Here and there are fine little spots of white sandy beach, where the natives generally keep their canoes. The adjacent country is very pleasant, and there appeared to be several villages situated amidst fine groves of cocoa-nut trees,

Friday 17.

U As

CHAP.
VII.
1786.
November.
Friday 17.

As we run along with a gentle breeze within musquet-shot of the shore, the natives of both sexes were assembled on the beach in great numbers, waving pieces of their white cloth as a token of peace and friendship. Expecting to find good shelter in a bay situated on the West side of the island, and near a district called by the natives Toeyayaa, at eight o'clock I sent the whale-boat to sound, and look for a harbour. In the mean time, we stood off and on under an easy sail, which gave the natives an opportunity of bringing us the different produce of their island, which they presently did in great abundance; such as hogs, plantains, bread-fruit, taro, cocoa nuts, fowls, geese of a wild species, and great quantities of excellent salt: for these articles we bartered with nails, towes, and trinkets of different kinds; and so brisk a trade went forward, that in the course of four hours we purchased large hogs sufficient, when salted, to fill seven tierces, besides vast numbers of a smaller sort for daily consumption. Near two tons of vegetables, such as taro and bread-fruit, were also procured; and so amply did the natives supply us with those very useful articles, that we were obliged to turn vast quantities away for want of room to put them in. Indeed, it would not have been proper to purchase more of those kinds of vegetables than what would be sufficient for six or seven days consumption; for after that time they begin to decay very fast. We also got about one ton and a half of fine salt, and I immediately set twenty hands to kill and salt pork.

The Indians during the whole day traded very fairly; but some of the spectators, of whom we had great numbers of both sexes, shewed their usual inclination for
thieving;

thieving; and one man had dexterity enough in his profession to steal a boat-hook out of a boat along-side, though there was a boat-keeper in her, and another crept up the rudder chains, and stole the azimuth compass out of one of the cabin windows, and got clear off with it, notwithstanding a person was set to look after them over the stern. Many other trifling articles were stole from us in the course of the day; which is scarcely to be wondered at, as I do not think we had less than 250 canoes about the ship at once, which certainly contained more than 1000 people.

WHEN our trade was over, the natives entreated us to stay near the land, and in the morning they would bring us abundance of fine hogs. On my making them this promise, they parted with us in the most friendly manner, and paddled on shore.

AT five o'clock the boat returned, and the officer who was in her informed me, that in rowing into the bay which he had been to examine, he carried soundings from twenty to twenty-five fathoms water over a bottom of coral and sand, but that he could find no good anchorage or shelter for the ships: in consequence of which information I gave up the intention of proceeding further into the bay, and determined to stand off and on a day or two near our present situation, to procure a quantity of good hogs to salt for sea stock. We tacked occasionally during the night, and at eight o'clock in the morning of the 18th the North point of Owhyhee bore East by South four leagues, and the extremes of Mowee North by West, and North West by West, eight or nine leagues distant. With a light variable breeze we steered South East towards Owhyhee,

CHAP. VII.
1786.
November.
Saturday 18.

hee, and by noon were within three miles of the shore. Many of our yesterday's visiters now came along-side, bringing a number of fine hogs and plenty of vegetables, which we procured on the usual terms. At four o'clock it began to blow fresh from the South South West; and the natives having disposed of their cargoes, left the ships and went on shore. At six o'clock the North point of Owhyhee bore East by South, and our distance from the nearest land four leagues.

During the night we had light variable airs, and frequently calm, attended with strong lightning to the Westward.

Sunday 19.

In the forenoon of the 19th I went in my whale-boat on board the Queen Charlotte, to consult captain Dixon respecting our future proceedings. By this time we had purchased all the large hogs the natives had brought along-side, and probably pretty well drained this part of Owhyhee. The ships were very light, having such a quantity of water expended, and our rigging fore and aft stood much in need of repairing and overhauling; so that we thought it prudent to quit our present situation and proceed for King George's Bay, Woahoo, where we could lie well sheltered from the prevailing winds, and do every thing necessary both to the hulls and rigging of the ships: accordingly, at half past ten o'clock, with a light breeze at South South West, and very dirty unsettled-looking weather, we bore away to the Northward, intending to pass to the Eastward of Mowee, and then to run down for Woahoo. Towards noon the wind began to blow fresh from the West South West; and a few canoes which were

along-

along-side left us and paddled for the shore. The extremes of Mowee in sight, bore North by West half West, and West by North, distant four or five leagues.

AT two o'clock we had a fresh gale from the South West, on which I returned on board my own ship. The gale increasing, we close-reefed the topsails, and got down the topgallant yards. Being then within two leagues of Mowee, with the appearance of very bad weather, we edged off to the North East, in order to get a good offing before night came on. A little before dark we saw a canoe to the South West making after us, with a small mat up for a sail, and also paddling very hard: on this we brought to and picked her up. There were four men in the canoe, besides a quantity of provisions; such as potatoes, plantains, &c. It seems they belonged to the island of Mowee; and on our standing in for the East part of it, had put off with their little cargo, hoping to bring it to a good market; but after we bore away from the island, they found the weather so bad, with a strong wind directly against them, that they could not reach the shore; therefore bore up after us, set their little sail, and used every effort in their power to get up with the ship. I was greatly pleased that we were fortunate enough to get sight of them; for they must certainly have very soon perished, their canoe when they came along-side being almost full of water, and themselves so much spent with fatigue, that we were obliged to help them up the ship's side. We got all their things safe into the ship, hauled the canoe in upon deck, and made use of every method in our power to recover them, which had the wished-for good

good effect; and never were men more grateful than these poor Indians for the little favours we were so happy in shewing them.

When the canoe was got on board, we edged away again to the Eastward, and at seven o'clock hauled to the wind on the starboard tack, it then blowing strong from the South West, with thick rainy weather.

During the night we lay-to, and at four the next morning, having a fresh breeze at South South West, and clear weather, we wore and stood to the Westward.

At noon the South part of Mowee bore South half West, and the North point West, six leagues distant, the latitude by observation 20° 58′.

Light variable winds, chiefly in the Western board, with alternate calms, continued during the afternoon and night. At eight o'clock in the morning of the 21st we saw the island of Morotoi, the extremes bearing West by South half South, and South West by West, distant eight or nine leagues; the island Ranai also made its appearance, bearing from South West by South to South West half West, distant at least ten leagues; and Mowee about nine leagues distant. At two o'clock, being within three leagues of Mowee, we tacked and stood to the North North East with a moderate breeze from the North West; at that time the extremes of the island bore South East and West by South. The weather being very unsettled, no canoes ventured near us, but towards noon on the 22d, having

NORTH WEST COAST OF AMERICA.   151

having light winds and clear weather, a number of large
and small canoes from Mowee and Morotoi came along-
side with the various produce of those islands, which
consisted chiefly of a few small pigs, some sweet potatoes,
and sugar-cane. At one o'clock, finding that a strong
current was drawing us in very fast between the West end
of Mowee and the East end of Morotoi, we hauled off to
the North by West with a very light breeze from the
East North East. At four o'clock, having drawn a little
out, and got clear of the current, which sets strong to
the Southward between the islands, we edged away to the
North North West, the wind then blowing a light breeze
from the East South East.

CHAP.
VII.
1786.
November.
Wednes. 22.

TOWARDS sunset our visiters, after disposing of their
cargoes, took leave of us in a very friendly manner, and
pushed for the shore. The extremes of Mowee at that
time bore from South West to South East by East, four
leagues; and the extremes of Morotoi West half South
and West South West half South, five leagues distant.

IN the afternoon of the 23d, it then being nearly calm, Thursday 23.
with clear pleasant weather, the Indians that we picked
up off the East end of Mowee, took this opportunity of
going on shore. I endeavoured to prevail on them to stay
on board until the morning, that I might have an opportunity of standing close in shore, when they might have
gone with greater safety; but they chose to go away at this
time, and made light of the distance to the shore, though
it was not less than five leagues. These poor fellows did
not go away empty-handed; for besides the presents they
                6   had

had from me, almoſt every perſon on board gave them ſome little token of friendſhip; ſo that their misfortune turned out to great advantage.

The wind ſtill kept to the Southward, with unſettled weather. At noon on the 24th the Eaſt point of Mowee South by Eaſt half Eaſt, and the Weſternmoſt part in ſight South South Weſt half Weſt, diſtant ten leagues.

I already have obſerved that it was our intention on leaving Owhyhee to proceed immediately down for King George's Bay, Woahoo, and there to have done the neceſſary work of the ſhips as quick as poſſible; but on getting to the Northward of Mowee, I found the wind hang much to the Southward and Weſtward, and the weather very unſettled. The wind from thoſe points blows directly into King George's Bay; ſo that I judged it the ſafeſt method to keep the ſea to windward of the iſland until a true trade-wind ſet in with ſettled weather, and then puſh into the bay, which is exceedingly well ſheltered againſt the winds from Weſt by South, around by the North, to about Eaſt; but quite expoſed to the other winds, which ſeem to prevail a good deal at this time of the year. Accordingly we plied with variable winds till the morning of the 30th, without any material occurrence; at that time the wind ſeeming fixed to the Northward and Eaſtward, and the weather more ſettled than it had been for many days paſt, we bore away for Woahoo; the South point of which at noon bore South Weſt by Weſt, ſix leagues, and the North point Weſt by North, diſtant from the neareſt of the iſlands eight miles. At

four

four o'clock we hauled round Dick's Point, and at five came to anchor in King George's Bay with the best bower in twelve fathoms water, over a bottom of grey sand intermixed with small red specks, and moored with the stream-anchor in eleven fathoms. When moored, Point Dick bore East half South, one mile and a half; Point Rose West by South, six miles; and the bottom of the bay North West half North, two miles distant.

CHAP. VIII.

Visited by Taheeterre.—Pernicious Effects of Yava-root.—Transactions at Woahoo.—Wood purchased.—An Eatooa erected.—The Chiefs make Offerings to their Gods.—Meditate an Attack on the Ship.—Shewn the Effect of Fire-arms.—Two Indians embark for Atowi.—Take leave of Taheeterre.—Of an old Priest.—Departure from Woahoo.—Anchor in Wymoa Bay, Atowi.—An Excursion on Shore.

A FEW canoes came along-side soon after our arrival in the bay, but they brought scarcely any thing to sell; indeed there seem to be but few inhabitants in this bay, and those few are of no great consequence. I gave them to understand that we wanted water, and directed them to bring it to us, as they formerly had done: they would willingly have complied with my request, on account of the nails and beads which they were to have in exchange; but assured me that not only water, but every thing the island produced, was tabooed by the king's order.

FINDING things in this situation, I gave to a man, who appeared of the most consequence amongst our present visiters, a present for the king and another for my old acquaintance the priest, requesting him at the same time to inform his majesty that we wanted water and such refresh-

refreshments as the island afforded; and therefore I should be glad if he would immediately take off the taboo, that we might obtain a supply of those articles. At sunset the natives, at my request, left the ship and went on shore.

EARLY the next morning we had some canoes along-side, who brought us water and a few vegetables, notwithstanding the taboo. A number of large and small canoes came round Point Dick into the bay, and landed at the head of it; presently afterwards my old friend the priest paid us a visit, and came, according to his former custom, in a large double canoe, decorated with branches of the cocoanut-tree. After paddling round the ship with great solemnity, and running down every small canoe that came in his way, he came along-side; but before he entered the ship he enquired for me. On my appearing at the ship's side to receive him, he handed up a small pig, which at his coming on board he presented to me, as a token of peace and friendship. Indeed I have before observed this to be the usual practice at all the islands.

THE old man informed me, that in a short time the king (who had just arrived in the bay with a large fleet of canoes) would be on board to pay me a visit, and that when he returned again on shore the taboo would be taken off, and the natives at liberty to bring us every thing the island afforded. I made him a present, and also gave him one for the king, which I desired he would carry on shore and deliver with his own hand. The priest left us about ten o'clock, and returned again at eleven in his own canoe, accompanied by many others both large and small. In a very large canoe, paddled by sixteen stout men, was

the

the king himself, attended by many of the principal chiefs. When his canoe approached near the ship, all the rest paddled off to some distance, to make way for his majesty; who, after paddling three times round the ship in great state, came on board without the least appearance of fear, and would not suffer any of his retinue to follow him till he had got permission for their admittance, which I gave to eight or ten of the principal chiefs. The king brought me a few hogs and some vegetables by way of present; for which I made him a return that seemed to please him highly: most of his attendants likewise brought a few articles, which I received, and gave them in exchange such trifles as seemed to take their fancy, being desirous to establish myself on a friendly footing at this island, that our business might go regularly forward, and our wants be expeditiously supplied.

The king (whose name I before have observed is Taheeterre) is an exceedingly stout well-made man about fifty years old, and appears to be sensible, well disposed, and much esteemed by his subjects. He inquired whether we had been at Owhyhee; and on my answering him in the affirmative, he was very desirous of learning some particulars respecting that island and the king, with whom he seems to be at variance. But I could give him no other information than that the king was in good health, and that the island was in a very flourishing condition when we left it.

Taheeterre remained on board the greatest part of the day, and gave directions to the natives to bring us plenty of water, and every thing else that the island produced.

Towards

Towards evening he returned on shore, perfectly satisfied with his reception and the presents I had given him; and at sunset all the canoes left the ships.

WE soon begun to feel the good effects of Taheeterre's visit; the natives, now no longer under the influence of the taboo, brought us water very plentifully, and we procured a good supply of hogs and vegetables; so that I set a party to salt pork for sea-store; the boatswain and another set were employed about the rigging, and the carpenters in decking the long-boat.

ON the 3d Taheeterre paid me another visit attended as before, and brought his customary present of a few hogs, vegetables, and cocoa-nuts. Great numbers of canoes were about the ship, and multitudes of both sexes playing in the water, notwithstanding our distance from the shore. My friend the old priest was almost constantly on board, and, according to his usual custom, drank vast quantities of yava, which kept him in a most wretched condition; he seemed quite debilitated, and his body was entirely covered with a kind of leprous scurf. The old man had generally two attendants on board to chew the yava root for him, and he found them so much employment that their jaws were frequently tired, and he was obliged to hire some of the people along-side to chew for him at a bead for a mouthful. One of the yava-chewers, a very intelligent man, informed me, that to the Westward of Point Rose, in Queen Charlotte's Bay, there was an exceedingly snug harbour, where the ships might lie with safety. As we had a heavy swell setting into the bay round

Point

CHAP.
VIII.
1785.
December.
Sunday 3.

Point Dick, which caused the ship to roll very much, I determined, as soon as the carpenter had finished the long-boat, to send her down to examine it; and if it was found a safe situation, to remove the ships thither. The district near which the harbour lies is (as I understood) called by the natives Whyteetee, and the yava-chewer, whose name is Towanooha, and who I found was a man of considerable property on the island, offered to go in the boat when she was ready, and direct them to the place; which offer I readily accepted.

Monday 4.

We were favoured with another visit from his majesty on the 4th, and in addition to his usual present, he brought a large quantity of very fine mullet, which he told me were caught in a small salt lake at the head of the bay. He frequently ate with us, but I never could persuade him to touch either wine or spirits, nor did he ever use the yava, but always drunk water. He seemed greatly delighted with the attention paid to him; indeed his visits were by no means unacceptable; for he not only encouraged the natives to supply us freely with water and other necessaries, but at the same time kept them in good order; so that we were not in the least incommoded by the multitudes that were constantly about us. This afternoon our water was completed, having, in the space of three days, filled forty butts, besides a number of puncheons and brandy pieces; so eagerly did the natives pursue this profitable traffic.

We now begun to be in want of fuel, as a great deal was expended in heating water to scald hogs and various other

other purposes. On signifying our wants to the natives, they brought us a plentiful supply of excellent firewood, which we purchased for nails and buttons.

In the forenoon of the 5th, the carpenters having finished decking the long-boat, she was hoisted out, and some hands employed in rigging and getting her ready to go down to Queen Charlotte's Bay.

Numbers of sharks were about the ship, four or five of which we caught, and after taking out the livers they were given to the Indians, who thought them very acceptable presents, particularly the old priest, who got two of the largest, and having ordered them to be carefully lashed in his canoe, was going to send them on shore. On this occasion a very remarkable circumstance happened; just as the priest's canoe got a-stern of the ship, one of the sharks not being securely fastened, fell out of the canoe, and sunk to the bottom in eleven fathoms water; at the same time there were several large hungry ones swimming about, yet an Indian went down with a rope, slung the dead shark, and afterwards hauled him into his canoe, without any apparent fear of the others that surrounded him. I found that sharks were esteemed valuable, as they answer a variety of purposes; they salt the shark, and seem very fond of it, the skin serves for a cover to their drum-heads, and the teeth they fix in wooden instruments which they use as knives.

The natives continued to bring us wood, hogs, and vegetables, and vast numbers visited the ships to gratify their curiosity; those who had no canoes would swim from

the

the shore, though nearly two miles distant, and after staying all day in the water, swim away for the shore with as much composure as if they had only a few yards to go.

From the 7th to the 11th we had fresh gales from the North East and East North East, with frequent squalls and unsettled weather. A heavy swell set into the bay from the South East, which made the ship roll very deep.

During this interval, the surf running very high on the beach, few canoes ventured off, and some that attempted it were overset so often that they gave up their design; two or three canoes however got along-side in the afternoon of the 9th, with a little wood and some bread-fruit, which we purchased; and I made them some presents in addition, as a reward for their venturing off at so much risk. After disposing of their little cargoes they made for the shore; but not being able to land, were glad to return to the ship again, and take up their lodgings on board for the night.

The old priest was almost a constant visiter; sometimes indeed he would go on shore under the pretence of paying a morning visit to his majesty; but I soon found that his principal motive was to replenish his stock of yava, of which (as has already been observed) he consumed a great quantity.

By this time the long-boat was completed, and at eight o'clock in the morning of the 12th, the weather being moderate, I sent her under the direction of Mr. Hayward

to

to Queen Charlotte's Bay, to look at the harbour so much spoken of by the natives, and Towanooha, the yavachewer, accompanied him as a pilot.

TAHEETERRE paid me a visit this forenoon, and the surf on the shore still running very high, he came off in a single canoe, it being much safer in the surf than a double one. The king made use of a paddle himself, and when he came near the ship, observing her to roll very deep, he would not venture his canoe near her, but jumped into the water and swam along-side; we gave him a rope by which he got on board, but the motion of the ship disagreeing with him, he took leave of me in a very short time, jumped over-board, got into his canoe, and paddled for the shore.

My friend the priest now grew very restless and uneasy; on my enquiring the reason, he hinted that Taheeterre and his principal warriors were meditating some mischief against us, and taking me upon deck, he pointed to a large house on the top of a hill over the Eastern point of the bay which ascends from Point Dick: this house the old man assured me was building for an Eatooa, or God's house, wherein they were going to make great offerings to their different Eatooas (for almost every chief has his separate one), and to consult them on the event of an attack, which he assured me they intended to make on us if their oracles gave them encouragement. He appeared quite displeased with the king's conduct on this occasion, and desired we would be constantly on our guard against him.

Y   THOUGH

THOUGH this piece of information seemed rather improbable, yet I thought it prudent to be on our guard to prevent a surprise, and at the same time I ordered a constant watch to be kept on the cables, to prevent their being cut by the natives.

I HAD observed the natives building this house a day or two before the priest pointed it out to me, and had seen people constantly going up towards it loaded, probably with offerings to their different deities.

TOWARDS noon I could see, with the help of a glass, that the house was nearly finished, and the natives were covering it with red cloth.

As I had constantly treated the king and his attendants with great kindness and attention, I could scarcely give any credit to the old priest; although the hopes of possessing all the iron they might suppose we had on board might possibly tempt them to attack us: at any rate, I determined to admit Taheeterre on board as usual whenever he came, and to regulate my conduct by his behaviour. In the evening the priest left us and went on shore, promising to return the next day.

ON the 14th in the morning a vast number of canoes came to the ships, chiefly loaded with fire-wood; what hogs and vegetables we now procured being scarcely more than sufficient for a daily supply. Towards noon the king came off in a large double canoe, attended by a number of his principal chiefs, all of whom I admitted on board, and treated

treated with the usual freedom, but was well prepared for
an attack if they had attempted it; having all the loop-
holes in the combings of the hatches fore and aft opened, and
twelve or fifteen stand of arms below under the direction of
proper people, who very soon would have cleared the decks
if the Indians had offered us any violence; besides which,
I had centinels placed in different parts of the ship, and all
our great guns and swivels were pointed into the canoes
along-side, with lighted matches at hand. Taheeterre
could not help observing our situation, and spoke of it to
his attendants; notwithstanding which, he behaved in his
usual manner. After being on board some time, he was
very desirous to see the effects of our fire-arms, which I
shewed him, by discharging a pistol loaded with ball at a
hog that stood at some distance, and killed it on the spot.
The king and his attendants were startled at the report of
the pistol; but when they saw the hog lie dead, and the
blood running from the wound, they were both surprised
and terrified; and I have not the least doubt but this
instance of the fatal effects of our fire-arms made a deep
impression on their feelings, and prevented them from
attacking us.

The king staid on board near two hours, and after receiving a small present took his leave; informing me at
the same time, that he intended to leave the bay, and return to his residence at Whyteetee in the evening. I could
not help remarking, that immediately after Taheeterre left
the ship, all the canoes left us and paddled to the shore in
different parts of the bay, but the greatest number of
them landed in the Eastern part of it, where the king had
a temporary residence.

CHAP. VIII.

1786.
December.
Thursday 14.

Soon

CHAP.
VIII.

1786.
December.
Thursday 14.

Soon afterwards the old priest came on board, not in a large double canoe as usual, but in a small old crazy one that would scarcely swim, and appeared as if he had come off by stealth. The moment the old man got upon deck he began to tell me that the king was a great rascal, persisted in his former story, and begged me to watch him narrowly. After haranguing for a short time, he left me and went on board the Queen Charlotte, where he spent the remainder of the day. By this time our wooding business was completed, having purchased a quantity sufficient for at least six months consumption.

Friday 15.

Next morning at eight o'clock the long-boat came along-side, and Mr. Hayward informed me, that on going down to the place where his guide conducted him in Queen Charlotte's Bay, he found a small bay with very deep water, close to a sandy beach, where the natives generally landed with their canoes, but no place for a ship to ride in with safety; adjoining to the beach, in a beautiful valley, surrounded by fine groves of cocoanut-trees and a delightful country, there was a large town, where (as Towanooha informed him) the king generally resided, and the district round it was called Whyteetee. According to Mr. Hayward's account, there were very few canoes in the bay; neither did he see any great number of inhabitants; so that we may reasonably suppose they were come into the bay where we lay, led either by business or curiosity.

Not a single native came near the ships for two days, and their canoes were hauled out of sight, but we could perceive vast numbers of the inhabitants about the house

on

on the hill. During this time our people were busily employed about the rigging, and getting the ship ready for sea.

At daylight in the morning of the 17th the old priest, attended by his yava-chewer Towanooha, came on board. The old man seemed quite enraged at the king's recent conduct; he told me that the king and all his principal chiefs had been making offerings to their gods, and consulting them; but that the gods were good for nothing, and that the king and his adherents were no better than villains, for intending to do us any mischief, after the many presents they had received from both ships. I thanked my old friend for his intelligence, and told him that we should be constantly on our guard.

For some days past I had been strongly importuned by Towanooha, and a very fine young man of the first consequence in the island, who was a constant companion of the king's, to take them along with me to Atoui; and indeed Taheeterre had more than once urged me to take them; but I never thought they were in earnest until this forenoon, when the young chief, whose name is Paapaaa, came on board, and joined his entreaties with those of Towanooha in so very pressing a manner, that I promised to take them on board; and they returned on shore in order to prepare themselves for the passage. The yava-chewer, being now as it were a gentleman passenger, no longer considered himself as a servant, but took to drinking yava heartily, and laid in a plentiful stock of that root.

In

CHAP.
VIII.
1786.
December.
Sunday 17.

In the afternoon we had a fresh gale from the East North East, with frequent squalls, which prevented any canoes coming near us. Towards evening I observed the natives uncovering and pulling to pieces their new-built house on the hill; and about eight o'clock several large houses were on fire along shore near the bay; but as we had no Indians on board, I could not learn whether they were set on fire by accident or design, till the

Monday 18.

next morning, when the old priest and our two passengers coming on board, I enquired the reason of the fires we had seen on shore the preceding evening; and was given to understand, that they were Eatooa's, or houses belonging to gods with whom the chiefs were displeased; therefore out of revenge they had burnt gods and houses both together. In the forenoon a great number of large and small canoes came off and brought us a tolerable supply of various sorts of vegetables and a few hogs. Since our water was completed, having expended several casks, I directed the natives to bring us a further supply, which they very soon did in great abundance. The king also, with his retinue, paid me a visit; at his first coming on board he seemed rather shy, but upon the whole he conducted himself nearly in his usual manner. On my taking notice of the red house on the hill he appeared a good deal confused, and waving that conversation, begun to talk about his two countymen who were going with me to Atoui. He seemed very much interested in Paapaaa's welfare; he particularly requested me to take care of him and treat him well, and if we stopped at Atoui, he begged that I would leave him under the care of Taaao, who it seems is brother to Taheeterre, and a relation of Paapaaa's. The two passengers asked

asked me for a few trifles to leave amongst their friends before they set off, which I readily gave, and also made the king a present; on which he took leave of me for the last time, and after taking a very affecting one of his countrymen, particularly of Paapaaa, he quitted the ship and went on shore; the other canoes remained along-side to dispose of their cargoes, and we procured a supply of good hogs, which enabled me to set the salters to work again. In the afternoon the rigging was set up, the sails bent, and every thing ready for sea.

In the night the Queen Charlotte parted her bower-cable and brought up with the other bower. I sent a boat the next morning to assist them in creeping for the end of their cable, which was fortunately hooked in a short time, and the anchor was recovered before noon. On examining the cable, some were of opinion that it had been cut by the natives, and it certainly bore that appearance a good deal.

At four o'clock we began to unmoor, as I proposed getting to sea with the breeze that usually blows out of the bay in the night, but in a short time we found the stream-cable gone about three fathoms from the hause; as we lay in ten fathoms water, this part could never have been at the ground, and we never had rode the least strain by it; so that I was convinced it must have been cut by the Indians. We had a buoy on the anchor; therefore I sent the long-boat to weigh it, and we begun to heave a-head on the best bower: just as we had got a stay-peak the best bower also parted four fathoms from the anchor;

on this we immediately let go the small bower, and brought up for the night. The Queen Charlotte having weighed, and standing out of the bay, we made the signal to anchor, on which she stretched in the bay, and came close by us. At daylight the next morning we warped to the buoy of the best bower, and weighed the anchor, and at the same time weighed the small bower and got under sail with a light breeze from the North East.

The old priest was still on board along with my new passengers, and we were followed by several canoes; but towards noon the friendly old man took his leave, and I made him a present, with which he was highly pleased; he then went on board the Queen Charlotte, to take leave of captain Dixon, and soon afterwards left the ships, accompanied by the other canoes, and paddled for the shore. At noon the extremes of Woahoo bore West by North half North, and North East half North, distant from the nearest part of the island about three leagues. On getting in the bower-cable that had parted, we found it a good deal rubbed by the coral sand, of which the bottom where we anchored is chiefly composed; and on examining the place where it parted, I was of opinion that it had been cut with a knife, until the cable was opened, when I found all the yarns cut in the same manner, and no doubt by rubbing on the coral sand.

The best situation for anchoring in King George's Bay is near the middle of it, and about a mile from the reef; where there are six and seven fathoms water, over a bottom of dark sand entirely free from coral; but as the inconvenience

nience of our situation was not discovered till we were
leaving the place, we had no opportunity of changing it
for a more eligible one.

WE stood to the South West with a light Easterly breeze till night, when it grew nearly calm, and next morning the wind hauled to the Northward and Westward. At noon the extremes of Woahoo bore from North by West half West to North East three quarters East, six leagues distant. The wind freshened during the night, and at eight o'clock next morning blew a strong gale at North North East, with dark rainy weather. Soon afterwards the island of Atoui made its appearance, bearing North West by West, seven or eight leagues distant. Towards noon the weather grew more moderate; and being then within seven miles of Atoui, we stood on for Wymoa Bay, and at two o'clock anchored in thirty-five fathoms water, over a bottom of fine black and grey sand. As I knew the bank to be very steep, and the wind blowing fresh, I was afraid our anchor would start off; to prevent which we wore away to a cable and a half, and then the ship lay in forty-eight fathoms water over the same bottom; one cable's length astern there was one hundred fathoms, and a little further we found no ground with the deep sea line. Soon afterwards the Queen Charlotte let go her anchor a little within the King George, but by checking the cable too soon, she dragged it off the bank and could not get it to catch again with a whole cable out; therefore got her head off shore, hove their anchor up, and made sail; but finding they could not get up to us before night came on, they stretched well in, and anchored about a mile and a half to the Westward of the village of Wymoa and a fresh-water river, and opposite a large grove of cocoanut-trees that lie near the Western point of the bay.

THE King George lay to the Eastward of Wymoa; that town and the river bearing North by West, the East point of the bay bore East by South a quarter South, and the West point North West by West half West, our distance from the nearest shore about two miles.

SEVERAL canoes came off soon after our arrival, bringing abundance of fine taro. I enquired for the king and my old friend Abbenooe, and was informed that they, together with most of the principal chiefs belonging to the island, were at Apoonoo, a town situated towards the North East part of the island, where the king usually resides; but the natives told me the king and his retinue would shortly be down at Wymoa. I desired the natives to bring a supply of hogs, which they promised to do on the morrow; and indeed I had no reason to complain of their want of punctuality; for at daylight the next morning we were surrounded by canoes, which brought a number of very fine hogs for salting, and great plenty of taro, sweet potatoes, cocoa-nuts, and sugar-cane; and on my asking for water, they presently got into the method of supplying us, and brought off great plenty of excellent water.

NEXT morning at eight o'clock I went on shore to Wymoa, accompanied by my two passengers and one of the sailors, with an intention of walking round the Western point of the island, in hopes of finding a well-sheltered

sheltered bay for the ships to ride in. After getting on shore, I was received by a vast multitude of the inhabitants in the most friendly manner, and presently we were joined by a few people of some consequence, who offered to accompany us in our walk, which I readily accepted, and found them of great service in keeping the crowd at a distance, though they did not gather round us with a mischievous intention, but on the contrary, to render us any little service in their power. After walking two or three miles along the shore, we sat down to take a little refreshment. During our short repast, a chief named Tiaana (who I understood was brother to the king) joined us, and pressed me very much to walk back to Wymoa and eat with him there. As I was very anxious to find out a good bay for the ships, I declined this friendly request, but promised to call on him at my return, on which he took his leave with many professions of friendship, and we continued our walk along shore.

By three o'clock we got to the North West point of the island, and I found all that part of the coast open and exposed, with a very heavy surf rolling in on the beaches. Being disappointed in my search for a harbour, I begun to think of returning on board; but after we had walked four or five miles, I found it would be impracticable for us to reach Wymoa before night came on; at this time we were not far from a comfortable house belonging to Abbenooe; therefore I determined to take up my lodging in it for the night, and my companions were glad to embrace the same opportunity, as they were greatly fatigued with their walk. We arrived at the house about sunset, and one of Abbenooe's men, who had joined us in the

CHAP. VIII.
1786.
December.
Sunday 24.

course of the afternoon, gave directions for a hog and a dog to be immediately killed and dressed for our suppers, together with a large quantity of taro. The house was well lighted up with torches made of dry rushes, and at eight o'clock supper being ready, it was served up in great order, and I think few people ever ate a heartier supper than we did. My friend's man acted as master of the ceremonies, and served the provisions to each person; and after our feast was ended, he ordered the remains to be taken care of, as he told me it was for us to eat before we set out in the morning. We got up next morning at daylight, and finished the remains of the preceding evening's repast. Previous to our quitting the house, there were near an hundred women about it, most of them with children in their arms; they were very inquisitive to know my name, which they pronounced *Po pote*, and such of the infants as could speak were taught by their mothers to call on *Po pote*: on this I distributed some trifles amongst them, with which they appeared highly satisfied.

Monday 25.

WE walked towards Wymoa, and reached the shore a-breast of the Queen Charlotte about nine o'clock. I desired my companions to walk down to Wymoa; and being very anxious to get on board, I took a canoe and went on board the Queen Charlotte, where I found my own whale-boat, and got on board the King George towards noon.

DURING my absence they had carried on a brisk trade for provisions, and I had the pleasure of seeing the decks full of fine hogs for salting.

Being now well assured that Atoui afforded no place for the ships to ride in equal to Wymoa Bay, I determined to keep our situation a short time, for the purpose of salting pork for sea-store, and afterwards to proceed to Oneehow for a supply of yams, and to remain there till the proper season for the prosecution of our voyage to the coast of America.

CHAP.
VIII.

1786.
December.
Monday 25.

CHAP. IX.

Variety of Refreshments procured.—Visited by the King.—Presents given and received.—Deplorable Situation of an old Warrior.—Ceremony of the Tabooara.—A remarkably large Shark caught.—Grateful Behaviour of Neeheowhooa.—Arrival at Oneehow.—Obliged to cut the Cables in a Gale of Wind.—Leave three Invalids on Shore.—Anchor again in Yam Bay.—The Sick return on board.—Leave Oneehow, and arrive at Atoui.—Remarkable Circumstance of a Woman with a Puppy at her Breast.—Chiefs exercise with Spears.—House built for Captain Portlock.—The Ships leave Atoui and arrive at Oneehow.—Recover the King George's Anchors.—Attempt on the Life of an Atoui Chief.—Departure from the Sandwich Islands.

IN the morning of the 25th Tyaana, the chief whom I saw on shore, came off in a large double canoe, and brought me a present of some hogs and vegetables, which I received, and made him a return that pleased him very much. He informed me that the king, accompanied by Abbenooe and a number of other principal chiefs, would be down in a day or two, and in the mean time we should be plentifully supplied with every thing the island produced. After many professions of friendship Tyaana took his leave and returned on shore. Soon afterwards I sent the whale-boat on shore to Wymoa for the sailor I left behind

behind along with Paapaaa and Towanoha; my man returned with the boat, but the other two chose to remain on shore a day or two amongst their new friends, and I understood they were greatly caressed by the natives in general.

BESIDES hogs and vegetables, the natives brought bass and grass rope to barter, which we purchased, as it was likely to prove useful for various purposes. The natives, finding we encouraged this traffic, were very busy on shore manufacturing rope, which they did very expeditiously, and brought off whole coils made of green rushes and grass; this we bought for the purpose of rounding the cables, and the bass for running rigging.

THE natives continued to bring us an abundant supply of fine hogs, fruit, and roots, and a large party were constantly employed in killing and salting pork for sea-store. In the forenoon of the 28th we observed a number of canoes come round the Eastern point of the bay, and soon afterwards my good friend Abbenooe came on board, but so much reduced, and so covered with a white scurf, from the immoderate use of the yava, that I scarcely knew him. He brought two canoes loaded with different kinds of provisions, as a present for the two ships: after staying a short time with me, he went on board the Queen Charlotte with the present he intended for captain Dixon; and returning again in the evening, took up his lodgings with us.

ON the 29th the wind blew very fresh from the East North East, with frequent heavy squalls from the land, which

which prevented the king from coming off to the ships; but the weather growing moderate towards night, Abbenooe went on shore early the next morning, and returned at nine o'clock, in company with Taaao and most of the principal chiefs belonging to the island. His majesty brought me a very handsome present, consisting of hogs, taro, cocoa-nuts, and plantains, together with cloth, mats, and several elegant feathered cloaks; all which he insisted on my receiving: accordingly they were got into the ship, and I made him an ample return.

Paapaaa and Towanoha being now on board, I took an opportunity of introducing them to the king, agreeably to Taheeterre's request: previous to this, I gave them a few trifling articles which they presented to him, and were received with great affability and kindness, and he assured me that they should be under his immediate protection.

According to my expectation, I found that Abbenooe was a man highly esteemed by the king, who consulted him on every occasion.

Taaao appears to be about forty-five years old, stout and well made, and seemed the best disposed man that we had met with amongst the islands. He offered me his friendship in the most earnest manner, and assured me that we should be well supplied with every thing this and the adjacent islands afforded: he requested Abbenooe to remain on board, in order to prevent any disputes arising between our people and the natives in the course of their traffic.

The

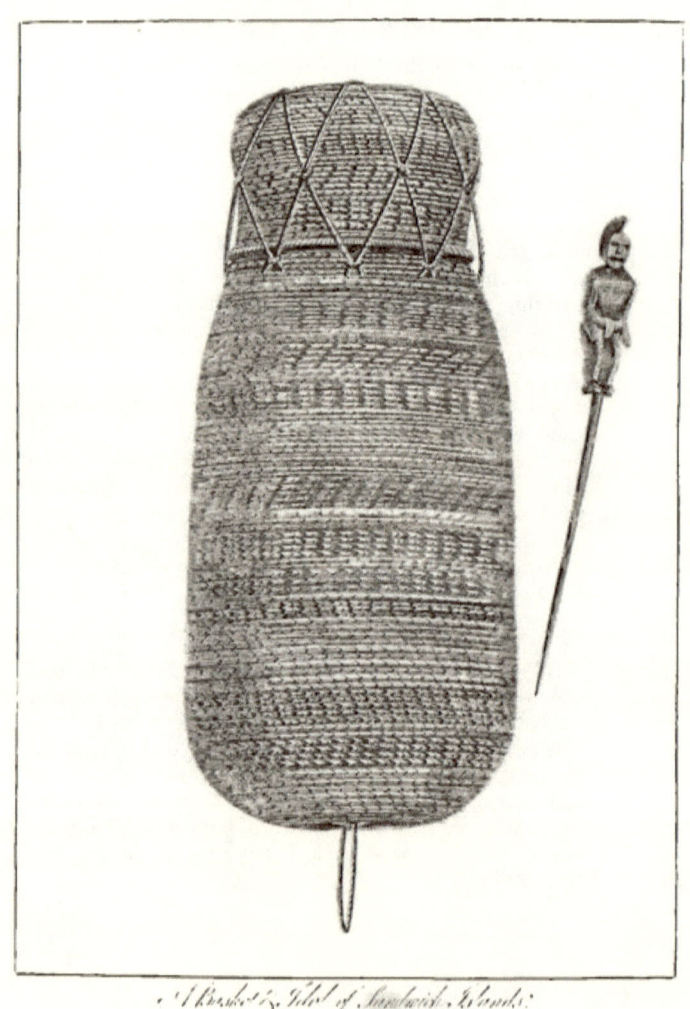

A Basket & Idol of Sandwich Islands.

The king and his retinue staid on board about two hours, and gratified their curiosity in looking at different parts of the ship, which they seemed greatly to admire. After taking leave of me they went on board the Queen Charlotte, where they stopped a short time, and then returned on shore. Abbenooe attended his majesty to see him safely landed, and afterwards came on board for the night; and as he constantly took up his abode with us, I had ordered a cot to be hung for him in the cabin, which pleased him so much that he never slept out of it.

VAST numbers of canoes came off on the 31st, bringing hogs and vegetables as usual; the king also paid me a visit, accompanied by an elderly man named Neeheowhooa, who I understood was his uncle, and a person of the first consequence. This old chief has, it seems, in his time, been one of the greatest warriors that Atoui, or any of the islands could boast of, and has been greatly instrumental in settling them under their present kings Taheeterre and Taaao; indeed his very appearance bespoke the hardy veteran; his body was almost covered with scars, and he was quite a cripple; and to add to his distressing situation, he had entirely lost one eye, and the other was in a weak state, occasioned by some wounds he lately had received in battle, and which were beyond their art to heal. Taaao appeared very unhappy on account of his uncle's situation, and perhaps thinking that we could perform wonders, begged of us to cure him. I recommended him to the care of my surgeon, who washed his wounds, applied dressings to them, and gave him some fresh ones, which he was directed to make use of once a-day. Neeheowhooa seemed perfectly to understand the surgeon's instructions,

CHAP.
IX.

1786.
December.
Sunday 31.

tions, and promised to follow them in the most punctual manner. After remaining on board a few hours, Taaao and his uncle left us, highly pleased with the treatment they had received.

1787.
January.
Monday 1.

THE next morning scarcely any canoes were to be seen, though the weather was very fine: on my asking Abbenooe the reason, he told me they were detained on account of a tabooara being laid on by the king. The tabooara it seems is a kind of tax which the king imposes on the property of those subjects whose plantations are near at hand, and consists of a certain portion of their various produce. At Abbenooe's request, I attended him on shore to see the ceremony, and indeed I could not but admire the order and regularity with which the natives conducted themselves on this occasion: men, women, and even children, paid their contributions with cheerfulness and good-will; some brought hogs, others taro, bread-fruit, and indeed every thing the island produced; all which were placed in separate heaps.

TAAAO and most of the principal chiefs attended to see the tabooara punctually complied with, and when it was finished, the whole was divided into two parcels, which the king told me were a present for the two ships, and desired me to send boats on shore to carry them off. I was greatly pleased with the king's generous method of proceeding, and determined he should not be a loser by his liberality, though I happened to have nothing on shore that I thought a suitable return for so noble a present. After taking a very friendly leave of me, the king retired to a house situated a little to the Eastward of the river,

NORTH WEST COAST OF AMERICA.   179

river, where he resides when at this part of the island; CHAP. IX.
and I went off in the long-boat, accompanied by my
friend Abbenooe. Before night we had got the whole of   1787.
our present on board, and the tabooara being over, the   January.
canoes came about the ships as usual.   Monday 1.

On the 2d and 3d the wind blew very fresh at East by Tuesday 2.
North, with frequent squalls; during which time we had Wednes. 3.
but little intercourse with the natives, and our stock of
vegetables was nearly expended: however, Abbenooe, ever
anxious to supply our wants, went on shore to procure a
supply of hogs and roots, ready to come off when the
weather grew moderate, and early in the morning of the
4th he returned on board, and informed me that he had Thursday 4.
got a number of hogs and vegetables ready for us. The
weather being now pretty moderate, I sent the long-boat
on shore at eight o'clock, and soon afterwards followed
myself in the whale-boat, accompanied by Abbenooe.
The sea being very smooth, we landed with the boat on a
beach a-breast of the village of Wymoa; and whilst the
people were getting the hogs and other provisions into the
long-boat, we walked two or three miles up a valley,
which leads from Wymoa towards the mountains. This
valley abounds with taro, which is planted in trenches that
contain about six inches depth of water; the taro-grounds
are divided at convenient distances by raised foot-paths,
which, as well as the trenches, are made of stones in a
very regular manner, and must have cost the natives an
infinite deal of time and trouble. Abbenooe conducted
me to a large new house belonging to him, situated at
some distance up the valley, and very well built after their
manner; here we sat down a little while, and after taking

A a 2   some

some refreshment, returned to Wymoa. By this time they had got every thing into the long-boat, and we took a passage in her on board. During my absence they had purchased a number of fine hogs, and great plenty of taro, potatoes, &c. so that we again begun to kill and salt pork for sea-store.

In the afternoon we caught a shark, so very large that it was obliged to be hoisted out of the water with a tackle; it measured thirteen feet and a half in length, and eight feet and a half in circumference, and the liver six feet; its mouth was so large, that it admitted the head of a puncheon with ease. On the shark being opened, there were found forty-eight young ones in her, each about eight inches long, two entire turtle weighing about sixty pounds each, besides several small pigs, and a large quantity of bones. The liver was kept for oil, and I gave the fish to the natives, who seemed to regard it as an inestimable treasure.

Taaao paid me another visit on the 5th, accompanied by his eldest son, named Taaevee, a very fine boy about twelve years of age. The king told me that he intended this as a farewel visit, as he intended to return to Apoonoo very shortly, but that Abbenooe should remain on board and accompany us down to Oneehow, which island and its produce he pressed me very much to accept of as a present, and desired Abbenooe to take care that the natives supplied us well with yams, without taking any thing in return; but I begged (if he would not permit them to sell the produce of the island) that they might be suffered to receive something for their trouble in digging and bringing off

off the yams to us; which at length he reluctantly assented to, and after receiving a present that seemed to please him highly, he took leave of me in the most friendly manner, as did his son and the attending chiefs; to each of whom, on parting, I gave a small present, and they went on shore with the greatest appearance of satisfaction.

Amongst the persons of consequence who attended Taaao on his farewel visit, was his uncle Neehcowhooa: his wounds were getting better, and he seemed quite at a loss how to express his gratitude and thankfulness; he begged permission to come on board every day to have them dressed, and seemed to think they would soon be healed. After attending his nephew on shore, he returned with a large double canoe full of hogs, for a present to the surgeon and myself, as a token of his gratitude. I took the hogs on board, but we declined receiving them as a present, though it was with some difficulty I prevailed on the old warrior to receive any thing in exchange. I desired him to come daily on board to have his wounds dressed, which pleased him very much, and he went on shore highly satisfied with the treatment he received.

On the 7th the king in a large double canoe, attended by several others, left the bay and set off for Apoonoo. Abbenooe still remained on board the King George, and we found him a most useful person: if ever any little dispute arose in our traffic with the natives, he always settled it to general satisfaction.

We

CHAP.
IX.
1787.
January.
Monday 8.

WE still were furnished with a few hogs and vegetables, and the natives brought us a plentiful supply of fire-wood, some of which made very good handspikes and capstan-bars; and as we began to run short of these articles, the carpenter set about making some. Not many canoes making their appearance to-day, I supposed a number of the natives had gone to their respective homes, having disposed of the articles they had brought for sale, and satisfied their curiosity.

Tuesday 9.

PLEASANT weather, with light variable winds from East North East; the anchor-end of the best bower cable being much worn, we yesterday cut about nine fathoms of it off, and this day were employed in rounding it with grass rope; a few hogs were purchased, and some fire-wood; several hands employed in sawing up and stowing the wood away. But few hogs brought to-day; I supposed that we had bought nearly all the natives wished to part with, and should for the future think ourselves well off in procuring a sufficiency for our present use. The canoes belonging to the bay constantly attended us; their principal cargoes consisted of cocoa-nuts, very fine sugar-cane, and bass, and grass-rope.

Wednes. 10.

EMPLOYED purchasing wood and bass-ropes, and getting all clear for sea; at seven o'clock, up topgallant-masts and yards; and at eight hove up and came to sail with a light breeze from the Northward. Between nine and ten it fell quite calm; at eleven a gentle breeze sprung up from the Westward, with which we run in and anchored again in Wymoa Bay. I think a number more canoes must have come into the

bay

bay during the night; for we had more about us now than I have seen since our arrival in the bay. We bought a few very good hogs; but the chief of their remaining merchandife feems to be now confined to what we term curiofities; fuch as their country cloth, mats, fpears, and various other articles.

On the 11th, employed in preparing for failing; dark cloudy weather and rain. At fix o'clock, with a frefh breeze from the North Eaft, we weighed and came to fail; Queen Charlotte and the long-boat in company. After clearing the bay, made fail for the South point of Onee-how; our diftance from the neareft fhore about three leagues; my firft officer, who had been dangeroufly ill, now recovered, and does duty again.

From the 12th to the 16th nothing particular occurred, when we came to anchor in Yam Bay with the beft bower, in fifteen fathoms water, over a bottom of coarfe fand. When moored, the following bearings were taken; namely, the North point of the bay 26° Eaft, diftant three or four miles, and the end of the reef that runs from that point North, 15° Eaft; the higheft part of the South Head run over the low land of the bay South, 37° Eaft; the South points of the bay, 15° Eaft, diftant three or four miles; the ifland of Tahoora South, 43° Weft; the ifland of Onechow North, 25° Eaft; and the bottom of the bay North, 60° Eaft, diftance about a mile and a half. We found a very heavy fwell rolling into the bay, which caufed fuch a furf on the beach as made it very dangerous for the natives to come off with any thing. Queen Charlotte not in fight; went on fhore to defire the natives to bring us off a fupply of yams; the furf ftill continued fo heavy on
the

CHAP.
IX.
1787.
January.
Tuesday 16.

the shore, that the natives could have no intercourse with us, and is very different to what we found it when we were here before; as then I safely landed with our whale-boat, and she might have remained on the beach without any danger of filling. At that time there was no Westerly swell, and the true trade-wind prevailed, which is by no means the case at this time. Towards noon the weather cleared up a little, when some canoes came off with a few yams, just sufficient for a present supply.

Wednes. 17.

On the 17th about ten o'clock I went on shore with the whale-boat, accompanied by Abbenooe; and as the surf ran even too great for canoes, we were obliged to row in under the reef, where we found a place that the boat could lie at her anchor with safety; and we went into a canoe to go on shore, but were overset by the surf before we reached it, and were obliged to swim for it. After landing, we walked about seven miles to the Northward along the hills, at some little distance from the beach; but in our walk I observed the coast all along to be very foul, and no place equal to Yam Bay to ride in. The country seemed very poorly cultivated, and Abbenooe told me, that since we took our stock of yams in, the people have in a great measure neglected the island, barely planting enough for their own use; and that some had entirely left the island, and taken up their future residence at Atoui. Towards evening we returned on board. The Queen Charlotte not in sight.

Thursday 18.

On the 18th and 19th the carpenter employed in caulking the sides, the people working up junk, and the armourer at the forge. The surf on the beach appearing
not

not very high, I gave the first watch leave to go on shore; they went on shore in our own boats, and had canoes to take them on shore from the boats; notwithstanding which, they were overset, and some of them would undoubtedly have been drowned, had not the natives swam into the surf and got them safe on shore. In the evening the whale-boat returned, having from the South seen the Queen Charlotte at a considerable distance.

This day several of my people had liberty to go on shore; all of whom returned except three, who were in a very poor state of health, and whom I thought of letting remain a few days till they got better; and Abbenooe had provided a comfortable house for their reception, and ordered them to be supplied with every refreshment the island afforded. Presently after, a heavy gale coming on, obliged me to cut our cables and run out of the bay, followed by the long-boat. We were under the necessity of leaving our three invalids on shore; but they were perfectly safe, and taken proper care of. Abbenooe and several others of the Indians were on board at the time, and went to sea with us; after getting a little offing we steered to the Northward, meaning, if the Westerly winds continued, to go through between Atoui and Oneehow, and join the Queen Charlotte, who I supposed was still to the Eastward of Oneehow, not having an opportunity of getting down to the bay.

From the 21st to the 26th kept beating off and on about Oneehow and Atoui, without being able to come to anchor till the 26th in the South point of Yam Bay. Our Indian visiters very impatient to get on shore again,

B b which

which the heavy surf still running prevented. The Queen Charlotte came to anchor about two miles to the Southward of us.

Saturday 27.

A HEAVY sea continuing, made it difficult for any canoes to get to us; at last a few ventured off from Yam Bay; one of them called along-side the long-boat, which I had sent into the bay on the 22d, to endeavour to get in the ends of the cables if he found it practicable, and lie at them till I should arrive with the ship. They brought me a letter from the officer, acquainting me, that on his arrival in the bay the slip-buoy of the best bower was gone, and that after getting hold of the slip-buoy rope of the stream-cable, before they had well got it taught, it parted, being chafed off by the motion of the rope against the coral sand. In their canoes also came our three invalids, who had been on board the long-boat ever since their anchorage in the bay. These people had been very well treated by the natives during their stay on shore; and in consequence of their not seeing the ship return so soon as they expected, the Indians supposed we had gone to Wymoa to remain, and were just at the time when the long-boat made her appearance in the bay, about taking them to Atoui in some of their canoes to join the ship; but on the long-boat's arrival they sent them immediately on board her, and brought with them the slip-buoy of the best bower-cable, and the buoy of the stream-anchor, both of which broke a-drift and drove on shore during the night after we cut out, at which time it blew very strong from the South West, with a very heavy sea. Abbenooe went on shore with an intention of procuring a stock of yams for us, and to get them at the first opportunity;

the weather continued still so bad that we could not make any trial for our anchor.

CHAP. IX.
1787.
January.

FROM the 28th to the 30th the weather still so very squally, that we could not attempt getting our anchors, and not thinking it safe to lie in our present situation, we weighed and came to sail; the Queen Charlotte and the long-boat in company, stood to the Southward to clear the island of Oneehow; and as the wind still lay to the Northward and Westward, which prevented us doing any thing towards recovering our anchors, I meant to anchor and get a fresh supply of provisions.

Sunday 28.

ON the 31st came to anchor in Wymoa Bay with the small bower in twenty-nine fathoms water, over a bottom of fine muddy black sand. When moored, we lay nearly abreast of the river and the town of Wymoa, from which we immediately had a sufficient supply of provisions of different kinds.

Wednes. 31.

VARIOUSLY employed on board. Abbenooe dispatched a messenger to the king to acquaint him of our arrival.

February.
Thursday 1.

ON the 2d, 3d, and 4th, employed in working up junks, painting the ship, and other necessary jobs.

Friday 2.

A GENTLE breeze from the South West, with fine weather. I gave the second watch leave to go on shore: a number of Abbenooe's people attended them by his order, to prevent quarrels between the seamen and the natives, and to furnish them with provisions. His orders were punctually attended to. In the evening, when the people returned, I found not a theft had been attempted, but they had

Monday 5.

B b 2

been

CHAP. IX.
1787.
February.
Monday 5.

been treated with every luxury the island afforded, and that in a most friendly manner. A remarkable circumstance, related by Mr. Goulding, a volunteer in the service, shews the great regard the natives have for their dogs: in walking a considerable way along the shore, he met with an Indian and his wife; she had two puppies, one at each breast: the oddity of the circumstance induced him to endeavour to purchase one of them, which the woman could not, by all his persuasions or temptations, be induced to part with; but the sight of some nails had such powerful attractions upon the man, that he insisted upon her parting with one of them; at last, with every sign of real sorrow she did, giving it at the same time an affectionate embrace. Although he was at this time a considerable way from the ship, the woman would not part with him till they arrived where the boat was lying to take him on board, and just upon his quitting the shore she very earnestly intreated to have it once more before they parted; upon his complying with which, she immediately placed it at the breast, and after some time returned it to him again.

This day, at my request, two chiefs that were on board from Wymoa exercised with their spears; the dexterity and astonishing expertness shewn by them wonderfully surprised every one on board; one of them, whose name was Na-maa-te-e-rae, that is, blind of one eye, is a well-made man of about five feet six inches high, his skin much affected by his immoderate drinking of yava; and though he appears to be a person of very little property, is yet much respected, and his company courted by all the principal men of the island. I suppose the attention paid him proceeds from his having been, and still remaining, a great warrior; the loss of his eye, one informed me, he met with in battle by a stone flung from a sling; but this accident does not prevent him from being a most expert warrior; his manner of exercising gave us sufficient proofs to the contrary. He took his stand about three or four yards from the cabin-door, unarmed; the other person stood at about eight or ten yards distance from him, provided with five spears; upon the signal being given for commencing action, a spear was thrown with the utmost force at Na-maa-te-e-rae, which he avoided by a motion of the body, and caught it as it passed him by the middle: with this spear he parried the rest without the least apparent concern; he then returned the spears to his adversary, and armed himself with a Pa-ho-a; they were again thrown at him, and again parried with the same ease. One of the spears struck a considerable way into the bulk-head of the cabin, and the barbed part was broken off in endeavouring to get it out. The remarkable coolness he shewed at the time the spears were cast at him, proved at once his courage and expertness. All who were spectators of the fight shuddered at the danger he seemed exposed to, and were astonished to see with what ease he parried every thing that was cast at him.

This day I gave the third watch leave to go on shore; the rest of the people variously employed; moderate breezes and fine weather. Being on shore myself, with my old friend Abbenooe, I observed in the village of Wymoa, about three hundred yards from the beach, a string of four or five houses, tolerably large, in very good order, without inhabitants; on my asking Abbenooe the reason of their being tabooed, he informed me that they were houses built

built for the king, whenever he honoured Wymoa with a visit, and that no persons whatever were allowed the use of them in his absence; he likewise informed me, that the king had given him directions to build me a house on a clear spot just to the Westward of these houses, and that he had brought me to this place for me to point out a situation to my own liking. For some time I declined accepting the favour, but my friend's earnest intreaty made me at last consent to gratify his generosity, and I fixed on a spot. No sooner had I given my consent than workmen were immediately employed; some were sent to fetch wood from the country, others to bring a kind of long grass for thatching; all of which orders were received with the greatest satisfaction, every one wishing to exert himself to the utmost, and delighted with the idea of having their friend Po-poo-te amongst them. Near the spot I fixed on I procured a large flat stone, on which I etched the initials of my name, the country I serve, and the year of our Lord; I explained as well as I could the meaning of this to my friend, who appeared much pleased with it: I desired he would cause the stone to be placed in the centre of the house. One very great inconvenience attends their houses, which is their want of windows; the extreme hot weather they have so much of makes it very uncomfortable and close; but they seem to think it a matter of no consequence to guard against any thing but the rains and cold. When they find it too warm, they directly go into the water to cool themselves, it being a matter of indifference to them whether it is night or day. I requested of my friend, in the building of my house, I might have windows in it, one at each end, one on each side the door, and one at the back, for the benefit of both

light

NORTH WEST COAST OF AMERICA.

light and air. He said it should be done as I desired; and every thing being settled to general satisfaction respecting the building, we proceeded up the valley, attended by a number of the natives of both sexes, young and old, who behaved with the greatest hospitality and friendship, pressing me earnestly to go into every house we came to, and partake of the best fare in their power to give; and numbers of the mothers bringing me their children to ho-ne, that is salute them, by touching noses; my compliance with which seemed to give them infinite satisfaction; and I can safely affirm it gave me equally as much: I was delighted to see so much happiness in the faces of hundreds of the Indians whom we had formerly so much reason to think were a treacherous people. This excursion gave me a fresh opportunity of admiring the amazing ingenuity and industry of the natives in laying out their taro and sugar-cane grounds; the greatest part of which are made upon the banks of the river, with exceeding good causeways made with stones and earth, leading up the valleys and to each plantation; the taro-beds are in general a quarter of a mile over, dammed in, and they have a place in one part of the bank, that serves as a gateway. When the rains commence, which is in the winter season, the river swells with the torrents from the mountains, and overflows their taro-beds; and when the rains are over, and the rivers decrease, the dams are stopped up, and the water kept in to nourish the taro and sugar-cane during the dry season; the water in the beds is generally about one foot and a half, or two feet, over a muddy bottom; the sugar-cane generally in less water, grows very large and fine, and is a great article of food with the natives, particularly the lower class; the taro

CHAP. IX.

1787.
February.
Tuesday 6.

also

also grows frequently as large as a man's head, and is esteemed the best bread-kind they have; they frequently make a pudding of it, which they keep till it becomes a little sour, and then they are very fond of it, preferring it to every thing else. The Indians that were a little while at sea with me almost fretted themselves to death when their stock of po-e was exhausted, which was very soon done, from the immoderate quantity they ate of it. I have seen my friend Abbenooe eat near two quarts of it at a meal, besides a quantity of fish or pork. While we were walking among these taro-beds a number of the natives were in them, gathering it and sugar-cane to supply the ships; they were up to their middle in water. After gratifying my curiosity amongst the plantations, my friend accompanied me to a large house situated under the hills on the West side the valley, and about two or three miles from the sea-beach. I found this house to be very large, commodious, and clean, with a new mat on the floor; on the left side of the door was a wooden image of a tolerably large size, seated in a chair, which nearly resembled one of our armed chairs; there was a grass-plat all round the image, and a small railing made of wood; beside the chairs were several to-e's and other small articles. My friend informed me that this house had been built with the to-e I had given him upon my first calling at Oneehow, and that the other articles were presents that I had made him at different periods, and that the image was in commemoration of my having been amongst them. Few people were admitted into this house. Amongst other articles in it were several drums; one in particular was very large, the head of which was made out of the skin of the large shark I have already mentioned; and

and I was told these drums were dedicated to their gods. We had some refreshments; such as pork, salted fish, taro, plantains, and cocoa-nuts, and then returned to the beach. The long-boat being in shore to take off some provisions of different kinds that were collected by a taa-boo-a-ra, or general tax laid on the natives by the king; I ordered the officer in her to remain at anchor a little distance from the beach until some of the things came down; and during the whole time had great reason to be well satisfied with the natives who attended, some in canoes, others swimming about. I went off in the long-boat, accompanied by Abbenooe and some other chiefs, who were highly delighted with the sail to the ship, as there happened to be a very brisk breeze; the method of steering with the rudder took much of their attention; and Abbenooe took a spell at the helm, and said that he would try to steer their canoe in the same way. On my arrival on board I found every thing in good order. It is not in my power to give half the praises that are due to these people, from the king to the tow-tow; their attention and unwearied industry in supplying us with every thing in their power was beyond example; their hospitality and generosity were unbounded; and their eagerness to do us acts of kindness was amazing. I hope, by the help of their own ingenuity, they will be enabled, from their observations upon our methods of sailing, building, &c. to bring these articles among themselves to much greater advantage than they are at present. My friend Abbenooe's attachments to both ships companies was singular; in general he slept on board the King George, where I had a cot hung up for him in the cabin, with which he was very much pleased; the old man had some falls before he was used to it, by getting in at one side

side and rolling out at the other; but he always got up again with the greatest good nature, and in a very little time surmounted that difficulty.

Wednes. 7.   On the 7th the people were employed in getting provisions, which Abbenooe informed me he had got ready for the boats. About ten o'clock the boats returned well loaden with hogs and other provisions.

Thursday 8.   This day the king arrived in the bay, attended by several large canoes; he came on board, and appeared very well pleased at the friendly intercourse that subsisted between his subjects and us. Our people always went on shore unarmed, which prevented the natives having any apprehensions of danger, and created a mutual confidence in each other. The king staid on board a few hours, and I then attended him on board the Queen Charlotte, to see captain Dixon.

Friday 9.   From the 9th to the 12th nothing particular occurred. Light winds from the Westward, with clear pleasant weather. The swell from South West still continuing, led me to think that we should have the wind again from that quarter; and not wishing to ride out another Western gale in our present situation, I determined the first opportunity to weigh and get out of the bay. About ten o'clock the wind hauled to the West North West, with which we weighed and stood out of the bay: the Queen Charlotte in company. At nine o'clock, the Queen Charlotte being a considerable way a-stern, we wore ship and hove-to, with the ship's head to the Northward, to give her an opportunity of joining us. Three canoes came off with provisions.

After

After having sold their cargoes, they took their leave of us; as did our faithful friend, who left his son on board, wishing to go with us. The Queen Charlotte in company. From this day to the 16th nothing particular occurred.

CHAP. IX.
1787.
February.

EARLY on the 16th our old friend Abbenooe came off from the East point of Atoui in a large double canoe, and brought us a fine hog and some taro. I made him a present, with which he was satisfied, and immediately went on board the Queen Charlotte; and on his leaving her, I bore away to the Westward, intending to run for Oneehow, to make a trial for the recovery of our anchors left there. Should I succeed, I meant then, if possible, to return to Wymoa Bay, and endeavour to get the Queen Charlotte's small bower. I should, if there had been any dependence on the weather, have tried for her's first; but as the anchors at Oneehow were the greatest object, and there was the most likely probability of getting them (lying in shoal-water, and the best bower having a buoy on it), I was glad to embrace the first spurt of good weather, with an Easterly wind, to make the trial; as a Northerly, Southerly, or Westerly wind create such a swell, that it would make it impossible to do any thing of that kind. At six o'clock we brought-to with the main-topsail to the mast. My reason for taking this step was, that in case the breeze should fail, and prevent us from proceeding to Oneehow, we might be near Wymoa in the morning; from whence there was a probability of procuring some vegetables. When we brought-to, the extremes of Atoui bore about North and North West, about seven miles distance, until daylight, when the appearance of the wind being settled to the Eastward, we bore away, and made sail for Oneehow.

Friday 16.

how. Served half a pound of bread *per* man, and a pound and a half of fresh pork. At noon the extremes of Oneehow bore West South West; distance from South-head about five leagues. The clouds to the Westward flying from South South West, and a swell from the South West, induced me to bring-to, and wait until these appearances of an approaching Westerly wind subsided. I think we may with great truth affirm, that during the time we were among these islands we had more disagreeable weather and cross winds, than was experienced in the Resolution and Discovery during their whole voyage, which was upwards of four years.

Saturday 17. MODERATE breezes from the East South East and South East. About two o'clock passed the South-head of Oneehow, and run towards Yam Bay; and at five anchored with the small bower in twenty-nine fathoms, over fine white sand; the Queen Charlotte anchoring at the same time a little to the Southward. The weather continuing fine, all hands were up, and began to look for our anchors; both of which, in the course of the day, were recovered, and got on board.

Sunday 18. ABOUT two o'clock in the morning began to unmoor, got the kedge on board, and began heaving in the bower cable. The weather beginning to look unsettled, with a swell continuing from the Westward, led me to think we should very soon have bad weather, and a Westerly wind. Experience had sufficiently taught me that we could not ride in this Bay with the wind any way to the Westward of North or South, without imminent danger. At five weighed and made sail: the Queen Charlotte in company. Stood to the Westward until we got a convenient distance from the land, which was when we lost hearing the surf, and then Northward. During the night steered from North West to North East, with a moderate breeze. The wind chopping suddenly round to the South West, with rain and every appearance of bad weather, induced me to haul to the North West, under the three topsails, till daylight, which was about six o'clock; bore away to the North East at seven; saw the West part of Atoui, bearing East by South, distant eight leagues; and at half past seven saw the West part of Oneehow, bearing South, distant seven or eight leagues. About ten the weather cleared up, and the wind light and unsettled, from East South East to South. At noon a moderate breeze; the island of Atoui bearing from East to South East by South, distant from the nearest part about six leagues; our course about East for the North side of Atoui; latitude 22° 29′ North. During the time of working for our anchors I employed some hands in procuring yams, salt, and water, which the natives brought us off in small quantities, and before we got under sail I think we had purchased yams enough for three or four days. I cannot too highly commend the behaviour of both the ships companies during the whole of the voyage to this time; sometimss trifling differences have arisen; but I think I may venture to say there never were less among such a number of people; their attention and unwearied industry during the time of getting our anchors, without the least murmuring or backwardness, delighted me, although they had scarce time to swallow a mouthful of victuals.

198   A VOYAGE TO THE

CHAP.
IX.
1787.
February.
Monday 19.

At one o'clock a fine breeze from the South; steering East by South, along the North side of Atoui. I was in hopes that as we drew near the North side of the islands we should have canoes off with hogs and vegetables. We had pretty well drained the South side. As to Oneehow, I believe were the hogs all collected together, they would not amount to a dozen; and I was afraid we should fall very short of a supply of yams, as my old friend Abbenooe informed me, that since the stock we before carried from the islands, they have neglected cultivating the land. Indeed his information agreed with my own observations while on shore; for I walked over a great deal of ground lying entirely waste. It appeared to me that a number of the natives that formerly inhabited this island have quitted it to reside at Atoui; probably the iron which they procured from us formerly, enabled them to purchase possessions in Atoui; as Oneehow is but a poor spot, abounding in scarce any thing but yams, potatoes, sugar-cane, and the sweet root, with a very trifling quantity of wood: whereas Atoui is amply provided with many articles of provisions, particularly the taro, which the natives prefer to yams or potatoes; and I am sensible that none of them will live at Oneehow that can procure a sufficiency to reside at Atoui. During our run along the North and West parts of Atoui, we saw no appearance of any harbour. Latitude 22° 14′ North.

Wednes. 28.

From the 20th to this day the people variously employed on board, repairing the rigging, &c. standing off and on for a favourable wind to take us to Wymoa Bay; where we anchored this day with the small bower in
thirty-

thirty-seven fathoms water; black muddy sand; the East
point of the bay bearing East three quarters South, and the
West point North West by South; the river's mouth North
half West, and the valley that runs up from the village of
Wymoa North East half East; our distance from the
shore about two miles. Made an attempt for the Queen
Charlotte's anchor without success. No canoes coming to
us this evening, made me send the whale-boat in shore to
purchase some taro.

CHAP.
IX.

1787.
February.
Wednes. 28.

LIGHT variable winds, with pleasant weather; the
people employed in procuring provisions; most of the
canoes having left the bay with the greatest part of the
chiefs, and gone to Apoonoo. This day a man of some
little consequence, named No-ho-mi-te-hi-tee, who had
been very often on board, and rendered us a good deal of
assistance in procuring provisions, pressed me very much to
take him into the ship with us. The man appeared so very
earnest in his solicitations, that at last I consented to his
going in the ship, and meant to have given him a trip to
the North West coast; and at our next touching at these
islands, either to have left him there or brought him to
England. He informed me, that he had collected a number of little articles, which he made a present of to his
father, a very old man, almost worn out with age. But
Poo-a-re-a-re, one of the king's messengers, who rules
with unbounded sway when the king and principal
chiefs are from the island, knowing the old man was possessed of a great many articles, went to him and demanded
all his treasure, consisting of a few to-es, beads, rings,
and various little articles which his son had given him.
The old man denied having any thing; for he had
taken

March.
Thursday 1.

taken care not to lodge them in his house, but had deposited them in a hole in the ground at a convenient distance from the house. The messenger still persisted in his telling him where they were, and the old man continuing obstinate, the messenger caught hold of him by the throat, and threatened that if he would not deliver up his goods he would murder him; and indeed he had nearly strangled him before he would shew him where his treasure was deposited. At last the old man was obliged to discover all, which was immediately taken away by the messenger. No-ho-mi-te-hi-tee landed with his canoe just at the time, and saw his father in this situation, but did not interfere; perhaps not for want of courage, but dreading to lay hands on a messenger of the king's, who are held in great esteem. He left his father to get out of the affair, and came on board as before related. Being pretty late in the evening, and knowing we never allowed any of them to come on board in the night, he took good care to call frequently out for Po-pootee, in a most piteous tone, to let me know it was he, and that he wanted to come on board, which he did. He then told me his sorrowful tale, and wanted me to punish the messenger for his ill behaviour; but had I been inclined to do it, I could not; for he never after that put himself into my power. No-ho-mi-te-hi-tee in a few days after that, being tired of living on salt provisions, left me; and I had no opportunity of seeing the king or Abbenooe before I left the islands, to inquire what was done about it. From this time to the 3d, employed in getting provisions, when we weighed and came to sail (Queen Charlotte in company), and stood out of the bay, with an intention to proceed immediately to the coast, leaving for the second time these friendly islands.

CHAP. X.

Passage from the Sandwich Islands to the Coast of America. —Good Effects of Beer made of the Sweet Root.—Arrival at Montague Island.—Anchor in Hanning's Bay. —Boats sent on a trading Expedition.—Meet with a Vessel from Bengal.—Their distressing Situation.—Refreshments sent to the Nootka.—Plan of future Proceedings.—Visited by a powerful Tribe of Indians.—Their Propensity to Theft.—Departure from Montague Island. —The Ships separate.—Arrival of the King George in Hinchinbrooke Cove.

WE now proceeded for the coast a second time, and till the 19th nothing of material consequence occurred. Latitude 26° 2′ North. This day, concluding myself about twenty-five or thirty leagues to the Eastward of the Resolution and Discovery's track towards the coast, and nearly in the latitude that the islands of Saint Maria la Gorta are laid down, having a strong gale with very thick weather, I did not think it prudent to run during the night; therefore at six o'clock handed the foresail and brought-to under close-reefed maintopsail, mizen-stay-sail, and foretopmast-stay-sail; ship's head to the South West. Queen Charlotte brought-to close under our lee quarter. During the night it continued to blow very hard, with heavy squalls from the South South East.

CHAP. X.

1786.
March.
Monday 19.

D d FROM

CHAP. X.

1787.
April.
Thursday 12.

FROM this time to the 12th of April we kept our course for the coast; latitude 52° 46' North. Both ships companies were very well, except the carpenter of the Queen Charlotte, who had been a long time troubled with a lingering complaint; and Richard Greenhult, one of my quartermasters, who had been very ill at the islands, had recovered amazingly, and was now out of danger.

THE method of brewing the sweet root having already been taken notice of, at this time I shall only observe, that three quarts of molasses were put into six gallons of beer, in addition to a pint of essence of malt; and after being a short time in bottles, it was nothing inferior to the finest cyder. Richard Greenhult had a bottle given him daily, and it was found of infinite service to him; indeed its good effects were almost instantaneous; and it certainly is a most excellent and valuable medicine; for the poor man was so reduced with an almost continual spitting and vomiting of blood, that at one time my surgeon was of opinion he could not live many days.

Monday 16.

WE kept standing to the North West, with fresh breezes in the Southern and Western boards. On the 16th, the water being much coloured, we tried for soundings, but got no bottom with 140 fathoms of line. Our latitude at that time was 58° 10' North, and 147° 18' longitude. In our last passage to the coast, in nearly the same latitude, and 2° 15' longitude to the Westward of our present situation, we struck soundings in seventy fathoms water, which inclines me to think, that after getting to the Eastward of that longitude, though in the same latitude, the

water

water deepens very much; and to the Westward of that longitude, and in the same latitude, it shoals, especially on drawing towards Cape Greville, or the Isle Saint Hermogenes. At three o'clock in the afternoon we saw a seal, and passed several patches of the sea-leek, and pieces of drift-wood, but got no soundings with 150 fathoms of line.

CHAP. X.
1787.
April.
Monday 16.

Our latitude at noon on the 17th, by double altitudes, was 57° 54'; at the same time the latitude, by account, was 58° 25': this difference I paid no regard to; as there was a probability that neither the watch or the altitudes were to be depended on; but on speaking captain Dixon, I found he had got an altitude by his time-piece when it was very near noon, which gave the latitude 57° 50'; so that we must have been set by a current during the last twenty-four hours, thirty-five miles to the Southward. Indeed the last year, when we were about this coast, we found almost a constant current setting to the Southward. Towards evening, judging that we were not more than ten leagues from the South West point of Montague Island, I hauled the wind to the Westward, under an easy sail, in order to wait for daylight to run in for the land; but in this I was disappointed; for soon after midnight it began to rain, and the weather grew very thick. About three o'clock in the morning the weather cleared a little; and being very anxious to make the land, we bore away with the wind at South by West, and steered North West by West. This however was of short continuance; for in less than an hour the weather again became very thick, and the wind began to blow very fresh at South; on which we hauled to the wind, and sounded with 150 fathoms line, but

Tuesday 17.

Wednes. 18.

CHAP.
X.
1787.
April.
Wednes. 18.

Monday 23.

but got no bottom. We now had a succession of fresh gales and thick dirty weather, which caused us to ply occasionally: as I did not think it prudent, under such circumstances, to stand in for the land. Strong gales, attended with thick hazy weather, continued with very little intermission till the 23d. On that day at noon, being in 59° 11′ latitude, and 148° 15′ longitude, we had soundings in seventy-six fathoms water, over a muddy bottom, with small black specks and black stone; and at two o'clock the land made its appearance through the haze, intirely covered with snow, bearing from North North West to West by South, about eight leagues distant: but soon afterwards the weather grew thick, which prevented me from getting a good sight of the land, so as to be certain of our exact situation. The fog rather dispersing at four o'clock, we again saw the land bearing West by South, which at first I took for the South West point of Montague Island; but presently afterwards land was seen bearing North North East, which I immediately knew to be the point just mentioned; and the land bearing to the Westward to be the land to the Westward of the passage into Prince William's Sound. We continued standing on to the North West till seven o'clock, when we wore and stood to the Eastward. Just at this time the weather cleared up, and gave us a good sight of the land, and passage into the Sound; the middle of which bore North North East, about eight leagues distant.

Tuesday 24.

DURING the night we stood to the Eastward under an easy sail, and at daylight the next morning we stood in for the South West point of Montague Island with a light breeze at North West, under all the sail we could make.

At eight o'clock having a fine breeze at West South West, we steered North for the entrance; the East side of which bore North by East, and the West side North, distant from each point five or six leagues. At nine o'clock the West point of Montague Island bore North East one fourth North, five leagues distant, and the middle of the passage North half East. I now judged that we were in about thirty-five fathoms water, and on sounding we had thirty-four fathoms over a bottom of sand and shells. I have found from experience, that in going off in the same direction the water deepens gradually, and in about fifty fathoms there is a muddy sandy bottom; but on crossing that direction either to the Eastward or Westward, the water deepens very quick into eighty, and upwards of one hundred fathoms. The wind failing us a little, the whale-boat was sent a-head to tow. At noon, the extremes of Montague Island in sight bore East by South five miles, and North by East four leagues, our distance from the nearest shore about three miles. On sounding, we had sixteen fathoms water over a rocky bottom. Our observation gave 59° 50′ latitude, and, according to the bearings and distance of the South West Point of Montague Island, I made its latitude to the 59° 47′, which I am certain is right within a mile or two. In Captain Cook's chart that point is situated in the latitude of 59° 36′, which is eleven miles too much to the Southward; but as he had no opportunity of getting an observation near it, and trusted to his ship's run, he might easily make a mistake of eleven miles. Mr. Edgar in his chart has placed it very near the truth. According to good observations taken of the sun and moon on board both ships a short time before we made the land, and brought forward by the

CHAP. X.
1787.
April.
Tuesday 24.

the ships run, we agreed to a mile with the longitude, which Captain Cook has laid the South West point down in.

It may not be amiss to observe, that all ships coming into this harbour ought to keep the shore of Montague Island on board as close as they can; for if they get off into the channel, and over towards the West shore, they will soon bring sixty, seventy, and eighty fathoms water, and that depth too close in shore for anchoring.

Towards one o'clock an appearance of a good bay or harbour presented itself on the Montague Island shore, towards which I directed my course. This bay is situated five or six leagues within the South West point of Montague Island, and nearly a-breast on the island that forms the West side of the Channel. At two o'clock the whale-boat was sent to sound and examine the bay. In the space of an hour she returned, and the officer who was in her reported that the ships could ride in it with safety. On this I hauled in for it, and anchored at four o'clock in twenty fathoms water over a muddy bottom. We moored with the best bower in twenty-one fathoms over the same bottom. In running into the bay just off the South point, we had seven and eight fathoms water over a bottom of black mud and sand. This bank appeared to run nearly across the mouth of the bay, and, after passing it, we deepened the water to twenty-one fathoms, in which depth we anchored. When moored, the South point of the bay bore South West by South two miles and a half, and the North point North North West half West, two miles distant, our distance from the nearest shore about

one

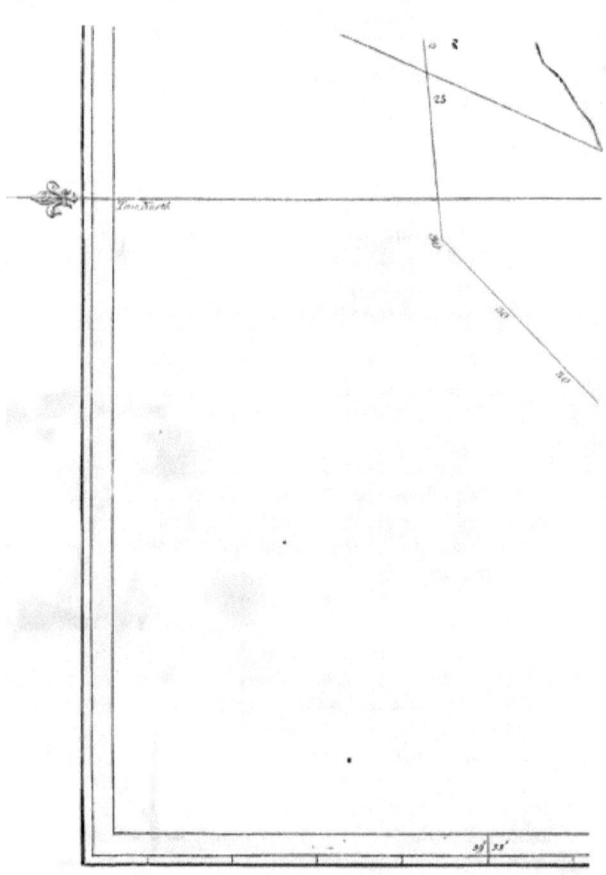

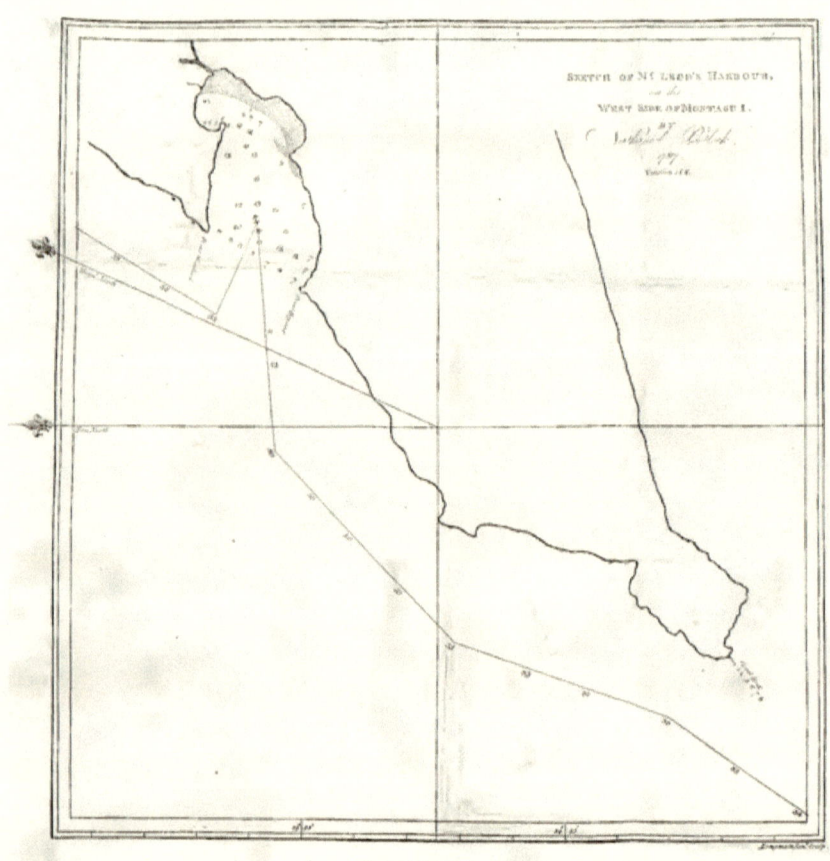

one mile. On looking round the bay, I thought I could perceive it to take a short turn round a point nearly at the bottom, on which I went accompanied by Captain Dixon to examine it. We carried good and regular soundings to the said point, and found that a ship could lie in four and a half and five fathoms water, with the South point of the bay just shut in with this point at about a cable's length from the shore. The inner point may be taken close on board, as it is quite bold; the bottom of the bay is flat.

BEFORE I left the ship we were visited by five canoes, some with one man in, and others with two; but I was rather surprised to find that they had not the skin of any animal among them. They had many beads of various sorts, particularly some small green and some yellow ones, which they seemed to value very much; and I observed they were of the same kind with those we saw in Cook's River the last summer. Our visitors frequently repeated the word *Nootka*, pointing at the same time up the Sound. Never having either at this place or in Cook's River heard the natives make use of this word before, I was induced to think that they had been taught the word by some visitors who had recently been at Nootka, and I was presently convinced that there had lately been some people trading with them; for, on my asking after the sea otter skin, I was given to understand that they had sold all their skins to a Thomas Molloy, who I could understand had left the Sound. This piece of information, however incorrect it might be, gave me small hopes of our being able to do any thing in Prince William's Sound; however, I thought it was but right to try for it, and

only

CHAP. X.

1787.
April.
Tuesday 24.

only to wait in this place for an opportunity of proceeding up. Towards evening our visitors left us, and paddled out of the bay, after stealing several fishing-lines that were hanging overboard. The only wind to which this bay is exposed is at South West, and with that wind a vessel may run before it into the harbour, leaving the North point on the larboard hand. After hauling close round, and bringing that point on with the South point of the bay, a ship may anchor and run a hauser to the trees to steady with; in which situation there are four and a half and five fathoms water over a soft muddy bottom.

Wednes. 25.

On the 25th we got some water off for present use, and the seine was hauled, but without success. Part of the ship's company were sent on shore on the 26th to gather shell-fish, which were the only refreshment this place was known to afford. The only space to walk in was along the beach, the adjacent country being entirely covered with snow. There were plenty of wild geese and ducks about, but so very shy, that we could not get within shot of them. In a walk I took along the beach I saw the remains of two Indian huts, and a quantity of wood that had been cut down with edge-tools. The cuts in the wood were so large and fair, as to convince me they were made by tools of a different kind to those used by the Indians: I therefore concluded that the Russians had visited this place the last autumn, not supposing that the people of any other nation had been in these seas.

No Indians coming near us, I determined to leave this bay the first opportunity. Accordingly, at four o'clock in the morning of the 27th, having a light breeze from
the

the South South West, we unmoored, and hove short, ready for getting out of the bay, and proceeding up the Sound. But about five the weather grew very thick, and the wind shifted to the North East, which induced me to veer away, and steady the ship with the kedge. During the 28th we had light variable winds, with calms by turns; but next morning at three o'clock the weather again grew favourable, and a breeze springing up at East, we unmoored ship, weighed, and sailed out of the bay. I was in hopes, that after getting out, we should take the flood-tide, and be enabled to get some leagues up the channel; but we found the tide very faint, and the wind directly against us. Indeed, I have reason to think that the flood-tide hardly ever has any strength in this situation; but the ebb is much stronger, owing to the great freshes that are always running out. At seven o'clock, finding we got no ground, we bore up, and run into the bay again, and anchored nearly in our former situation.

IMMEDIATELY after anchoring, I set off, accompanied by Captain Dixon in his whale-boat, in quest of Indians, and to examine the coast of Montague Island up towards the Sound. As we rowed along, we found a bold shore, with anchorage in thirty fathoms water over a muddy bottom, about a mile from the land. After rowing about five leagues from the ships, we came to a deep wide bay where vessels may safely ride at anchor, in from twenty to ten fathoms water over a muddy bottom. In ten fathoms the situation is near the bottom of the bay, and about half a mile from the shore; but the best anchorage seems to be nearest the South side, and no nearer the land than in ten or twelve fathoms water. We landed on the North shore,

CHAP. X.

1787.
April.
Sunday 29.

shore, and walked a considerable distance, but could not perceive the least trace of any inhabitants. Whilst the people were dressing some pork and mussels for dinner, I went in my whale-boat round the North point of the bay, and could perceive the coast of this island towards Prince William's Sound for six or seven leagues, without any appearance of an harbour, or even a safe bay. I returned into the bay again, and after taking some refreshment, we proceeded towards the ships, where we arrived about nine o'clock, without seeing any Indians during the whole day. Having still light variable winds, chiefly from the Northward, I sent the whale-boat in the morning of the 30th to sound from the ship across the channel, and along the coast of an island which makes the West side of the Channel. The weather was very fine and pleasant, but still no Indians came near us. Towards evening the boat returned from sounding; they had, very soon after quitting the bay, fifty and sixty fathoms water over a muddy bottom, and in the mid channel, no ground, with all their line, which was seventy fathoms. Close over to the island there were forty and fifty fathoms water within a cable's length of the rocks and beach; and they carried the same kind of soundings as far as the North extreme of the island, when, the day being far advanced, they sounded no further. Short round this North point, in the direction of North West and West North West, the officer who went in the boat informed me was a deep sound, in which were the appearances of good harbours. As I was desirous of examining every place where there was a probability of meeting with inhabitants, I set off early the next morning with the whale-boats, accompanied by Captain Dixon, to look into this Sound; but, previous to our setting

Monday 30.

May.
Tuesday 1.

setting off, I left orders with Mr. M'Leod to move the ships up the channel as far as the Green Isles, if an opportunity offered, and there to wait my return. By ten o'clock we got round the North point of the island, which I distinguished by the name of Mulgrave Island, and found the land take a quick turn to the West and West North West. We rowed into the Sound about eight or ten leagues, and the land to the Westward and Southward of us appeared like islands lying between us and the sea. To the Northward also the land appeared detached and in islands, and the high land to the North West was certainly those mountains which from Cook's River are seen to the East and North East. During this excursion we saw neither inhabitants, huts, or the least traces of any, although it appeared a very eligible situation, being very near the sea-side, and well sheltered from the inclemency of the weather. Towards noon we rowed into and landed in a small cove where we took some refreshment. Shortly afterwards, I observed the clouds to rise from the South West, and being anxious to join my ship, and proceed up the Sound with the first favourable wind, we set off towards them. After getting out of the Sound, we found a fresh breeze from the Southward, with which we stretched over for Montague Island with sails and oars, and about eight o'clock in the evening saw the ships lying in the bay examined by us on the 29th April, and which was named Hanning's Bay, after the worthy family of the Hannings, who are strenuous supporters of our present voyage.

We got on board about ten o'clock, where I found every thing in good order. My first mate informed me, that

CHAP. X.
1787.
May.
Tuesday 1.

that about four hours after we left the ship, a breeze sprung up from the South West, of which, agreeably to my order, he took advantage, and proceeded thus far, where he anchored, in consequence of the wind's failing, and the ebb tide making down. I found the ships in a very good situation in the bay, riding by their bowers in twenty-one fathoms water over a muddy bottom, and steadied with their kedges. The Southernmost point of the bay bore South South West half West three miles, the North point North half East one mile, and the bottom of the bay East by South one mile and a half distant. During the night we had light variable winds, with calms by turns; but at nine o'clock the next morning a fine little breeze springing up from the Westward, we weighed, and stood out of Hanning's Bay, and after clearing the North point of it, stood up the channel towards Prince William's Sound. At noon I sent the whale-boat a-head, and in shore, to sound, and the ships run along shore about one mile and a half distant from Montague Island, in forty fathoms water; the whale-boat carried from thirty to thirty-five fathoms water over a muddy bottom. The wind growing scant, I ordered the whale-boat a-head to tow the ship. However, at two o'clock a fine breeze came on from the South South West, with which we continued running up the channel, and had soundings from thirty-five to twenty fathoms water over a muddy bottom, until we drew near the Green Islands, when the water shoaled, and we frequently had seven and eight fathoms over a rocky and sometimes a shelly bottom. At six o'clock we passed three beds of kelp, which we avoided, as it was near them we had the shoal water, and at this time it was dead low water. After running two or three leagues above

these

Wednes. 2.

these shoals on the Montague side, there appeared several small islands situated near the shore, and some rocks, which are covered at high water, lying to the Northward of them, and about two miles from the shore, stretching along nearly as high as the upper end of Montague Island. However, night coming on, and there appearing a good channel between the two Westernmost rocks, with a probability of finding good anchorage within them, and the place very likely to be well inhabited, I was induced by these circumstances to push in. Accordingly I sent the whale-boat a-head to sound, and we carried in from seventeen to twelve fathoms water, until we got some distance within the rocks. The water then, as we approached the shore, began to shoal very quick, and we came to anchor in ten fathoms over a bottom of black sand. Presently afterwards, observing a patch of kelp at a very small distance from the ship, I sent a boat to sound on it, and they found only three fathoms water over a rocky bottom. The shoal was about a ship's length from East to West, and nearly the same breadth, with nine or ten fathoms water all round it. As our present station was by no means a safe one, I went in the whale-boat to sound beyond a point that lay to the Southward, round which promised good shelter. Immediately on passing the shoal just mentioned, I found the water to deepen as we rowed towards the point from ten to twenty-two fathoms over a muddy bottom. After finding safe anchorage for the ships, I went on board, got under way directly, and run in round the point, when we anchored in twenty-one fathoms water over a muddy bottom, and moored with the stream anchor to the North East in fourteen fathoms. When moored, a small island, forming the Southernmost part

CHAP.
X.

1787.
May.
Wednes. 2.

of the bay, bore South West half a mile, the Northernmost point of the bay, North West three quarters North, three miles and a half, and the bottom of the bay North East by East two miles distant. The Westernmost of the two rocks that we passed in between was just to be seen above water, and bore West three quarters South more than a mile distant, and the Easternmost rock was covered, it being then about two thirds flood. It would not be prudent for any ship to run through this passage in thick weather; but when the weather is clear, it is tolerably safe with a good look-out, the lead going, and keeping nearly in the mid channel.

Thursday 3.

EARLY the next morning the carpenter was sent on shore to cut down some trees for sawing into plank, and I went myself up the bay to sound and examine it. I found a most excellent port land-locked, with seven fathoms water over a muddy bottom, about one cable's length from the nearest shore; but to my great surprise I could not meet with a single Indian, or the least traces of any having been there recently, although the place seemed very likely to be inhabited; so that, finding my search fruitless, I returned on board. In the afternoon the long-boat was hoisted out, and a party was employed in fitting her for a trading expedition up the Sound.

Friday 4.

ABOUT four o'clock in the morning of the 4th, the wind blowing fresh from the North West, with an increasing sea, which caused the ships to ride heavy, I came to the resolution of running into the harbour. Accordingly we unmoored and got under way; but soon after getting within the first point, the wind failed us, and we were

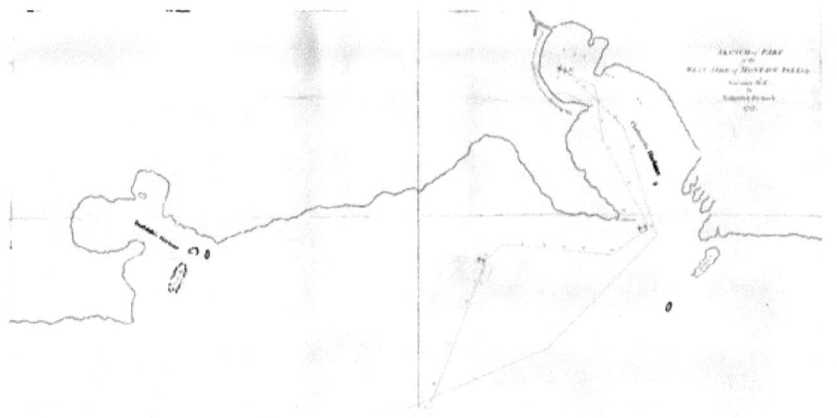

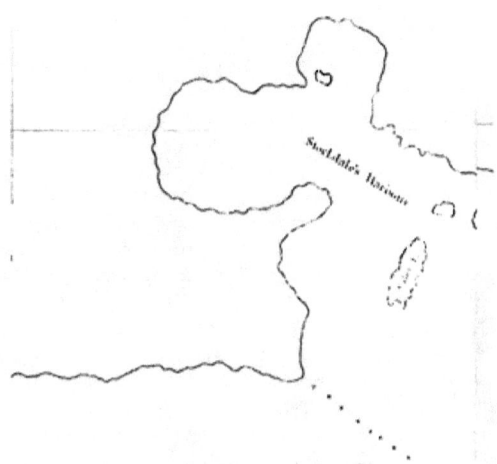

were obliged to warp in. In heaving up our stream anchor, the stock broke close to the shank, and as it was an iron stock, the anchor was rendered useless. This accident was likely to prove a very unlucky one, as I had spared Captain Dixon an anchor in the room of one which he lost at Atoui; so that I now had not a small one to steady the ship with except a kedge, which would not hold with the least wind. By three o'clock, having warped the ship into a good birth, we anchored with the best bower in seven fathoms and a half water over a muddy bottom, and moored with a hawser made fast to the North shore. When moored, we lay in five fathoms at low water. The people were employed in getting my long-boat and the whale-boat belonging to each ship ready for going up the Sound on a trading expedition, under the direction of Captain Dixon; and in the mean time I proposed staying with the ships, in order to have them hauled on shore, for the purpose of cleaning and paying their bottoms. We could also fill our water, and do many other necessary works, this harbour being a very convenient one for all our various employments.

NEXT morning at daylight the boats set out on their expedition, and by five o'clock were out of sight clear of the harbour. Our various operations now began. I sent a large party to clear away the stones on a part of the beach, where I intended to lay the ship. At ten o'clock we began to haul her in, and by noon she was placed. Some hands were employed in cutting pine branches to bream with. The cooper was sent on shore, with two assistants, to brew spruce beer, and others were busied in the hold. In the afternoon the starboard-side of the ship was

was cleaned, and paid with a coat of tar, chalk, and train-oil, well boiled together. The sheathing-worm had entered in some places, but not so much as I could have expected.

Sunday 6. WHEN last at the Sandwich Islands I bought a double canoe, which was now fitted up, and I sent her with two of the people into an adjacent creek, to catch crabs and pick muscles; they being the only refreshment, the decoction of spruce excepted, in our power to obtain: the seine had been hauled repeatedly, but without success. Towards noon I had the pleasure of seeing an Indian come into the harbour in a single canoe; he presently came along-side, but brought nothing to barter, except a little porpoise-blubber, which he seemed to consider as a dainty. I made our visiter a present which pleased him very much, and at the same time endeavoured to make him comprehend what kind of trade we wanted. He seemed to understand me, and left the ship, well satisfied with his reception; so that I had hopes he would bring others to us with some trade. Great numbers of wild geese and ducks were flying about; but they appeared very shy: indeed I did not chuse to fire at them, fearing that the report of fire-arms might prevent any Indians from coming into the harbour.

Monday 7. BY noon on the 7th the larboard side of the ship was finished; and at high water we attempted to heave her off, but she did not fleet; on which, I ordered some salt water, that we had under the cables in the main-hold, to be started, to lighten her against the night-tide; being pretty certain of her fleeting then; as I had observed the night-

night-tides to be considerably higher than those in the daytime. During this time the people were all busily employed in watering and wooding; both of which being found close to the beach, made it very convenient; and the cooper brewing spruce beer: to a puncheon of beer three gallons and a half of molasses were added; it was afterwards worked with prepared yeast, and we succeeded in the first brewing, which is not generally the case.

Next morning at three o'clock, being high water, and a high tide, we hove the ship off, and laid her in her former station. The Queen Charlotte took our place on the beach; and as the tide fell they begun cleaning and breaming: her sheathing was something worm-eaten, but every thing else in good order. Captain Dixon was apprehensive that a part of her false keel was knocked off by a shock they received at sea, which was supposed to be against a whale; but I found all secure.

In the forenoon of the 8th we were visited by three of the natives in two canoes, but they brought nothing to sell, except two river otter-skins and two seal-skins, which I bought, and made them a present besides; so that they went away highly satisfied. These Indians mentioned the word *Nootka* very frequently; and every time it was repeated they pointed up the Sound: they also mentioned the name of Thomas Molloy. I found they were acquainted with the use of fire-arms, and I rather suppose they have gained that knowledge from the Russians. From several circumstances, I was inclined to think that our late visiters belonged to the party we saw in the first harbour we anchored in.

CHAP.
X.

1787.
May.
Thursday 10.

EARLY in the morning of the 10th captain Dixon returned with the boats from Snug Corner Cove. During this excursion they had purchased about thirty-six sea otter skins of different qualities, and a few other furs; the chief part were procured near Cape Hinchinbrooke, to which place they first went, and afterwards proceeded towards Snug Corner Cove; as the Indians gave them to understand there was a vessel in that neighbourhood. The natives spoke several English words very plainly, and pointed out to captain Dixon the place where this vessel lay. In consequence of this information he set off, attended by some of the Indians in their canoes, to the place they directed him to, and in the evening of the 8th arrived on board. He found her to be the snow Nootka, captain John Meares, from Bengal. Captain Meares had left that place in March 1786, and arrived in Prince William's Sound some time in October, where he wintered, and had buried great part of his ship's company, who died of the scurvy, and the survivors were in a very weak sickly state. Captain Dixon brought me a letter from captain Meares, in which he pointed out his wants and his distressing situation; most earnestly begging my assistance; as without it he despaired of getting his vessel from her present station. I read this letter with great concern, and determined to give them every assistance in my power whenever an opportunity offered of conveying it to them.

It has already been observed that the Nootka wintered in Prince William's Sound. Another vessel belonging to the same owners left it just before the Nootka's arrival. Both these ships, I learned from captain Dixon, had given such great prices in barter for skins, that the value of our cargo was greatly reduced. The only articles the natives would

would even look at were green and red beads, and unwrought iron, in pieces nearly two feet long; but hatchets, howels, saws, adzes, brass pans, pewter basins, and tin kettles, would not be taken in barter even for fish; so that all we could depend on in our trade with the natives at this place, was pieces of iron and a few beads. I therefore ordered a tent to be erected on shore for the armourers, and they were busily employed in working up iron into towes about eighteen inches long, and spearheads, near two feet in length; these being articles the Indians were very fond of. About eight o'clock, being on shore giving directions about the armourers tent, I was informed from the ship, that they saw a boat about the entrance of the bay, plying into the harbour: conjecturing it to be the Nootka's, I went immediately on board, and sent my whale-boat out to her assistance. At ten o'clock my boat returned with the Nootka's long-boat in tow: their assistance was very acceptable; for the long-boat's crew were almost worn out with wet and cold, and were in a very weak condition. Captain Meares came in the boat himself, and from him I received some further account of their distressing situation during the winter; and indeed it must have been a very dreadful one; for before the winter broke up the captain and a Mr. Ross, his chief mate, were the only two persons capable of dragging the dead bodies from the ship over the ice, and burying them in the snow on shore. Nay, there was not a single person on board who was not deeply affected with the scurvy. I learned from captain Meares, that on his arrival in the Sound he could not for a long time purchase one single skin; they being all disposed of to his consort, the Sea

Otter,

CHAP. X.
1787.
May.
Thursday 10.

Otter, commanded by a Mr. Tipping, who, as well as himself, was a lieutenant in the English navy. Both these ships had traded with unwrought iron and small transparent beads, the same kind as those we saw amongst the natives in Cook's Bay, who no doubt had got them from captain Tipping; as he was in the Sound at the very time we were in Cook's River. Captain Meares also informed me, that several other ships have at different times been trading on the coast from India and China, a circumstance that we had no idea of at the time we left England, and in all probability will hurt our traffic so much, that instead of four thousand sea-otter skins, which I at one time expected to procure, I shall be very happy if in the course of the season we can purchase a thousand between both ships. I understand that he expected a ship to arrive at King George's Sound early in June next; it therefore became necessary that the King George and Queen Charlotte should separate; and Captain Dixon and myself agreed for the Queen Charlotte to push on directly for King George's Sound, in order to get the start of that vessel, if possible; and the King George to remain in and about Prince William's Sound. I also resolved to dispatch my long-boat on a trading expedition to Cook's River, under the direction of Mr. Hayward, my third mate, and Mr. Hill, with six good and trusty men, in whom I could place entire confidence. I appointed Hinchinbrooke Cove as a place of rendezvous for the long-boat, and for her to be with me by the 20th of June; if she did not join me by that time, I was to wait for her till the 20th of July, but no longer. Afterwards I directed Mr. Hayward to procure a passage for himself and the people to China

China from this Sound, if he should find any ship in it bound that way; if not, to proceed immediately to Kodiac, and procure a passage to Europe by way of Asia.

TOWARDS evening the wind blew strong and in squalls. As we were riding chiefly by the shore-hauser, I was afraid of its parting; therefore let the small bower go under-foot; but next morning, the weather growing moderate, it was hove up again. All hands were busily employed in wooding, watering, brewing, and working in the hold. The Queen Charlotte having finished cleaning, breaming, and paying, hauled off the beach into her former station. In the afternoon we completed our water, having filled forty butts, two brandy-pieces, and nineteen puncheons.

AT five o'clock captain Meares took leave of us, and proceeded on towards his ship with as many refreshments of various kinds as the boat could well carry. We spared him some flour, loaf-sugar, molasses, Sandwich Island pork, gin, brandy, and cheese, and two good seamen, to assist in navigating his ship to China; at which place he was to return them: their names were George Willis and Thomas Dixon, both of whom went on board the Nootka, agreeably to their own requests, and not from any entreaty whatever. Besides the above articles, I furnished captain Meares with 150 cocoa-nuts, which I had great hopes would help to recover his people.

MOST

CHAP.
X.
1787.
May.
Saturday 12.

MOST of our necessary business being now completed, the armourers forges and the brewing utensils were brought on board, and every thing was got in readiness for sailing. At six o'clock in the afternoon the long-boat set off for Cook's River, her crew in good spirits, and well found for a six weeks cruise. In the evening four canoes came along-side, but they brought no trade; and after staying a short time, paddled away for the shore.

Sunday 13.

IN the afternoon of the 13th we were visited by two large Indian boats, containing about forty men, women, and children; a number of small canoes attended them. They brought only two very indifferent skins and a few fish, which I bought, and made their chief, whose name I understood was Shee-na-waa, a handsome present. Shee-na-waa I found was chief of the most powerful tribe in the Sound; they were audacious thieves, and, what was very remarkable, even the little boys were furnished with small hooked sticks for the purpose of picking pockets. Our visiters remained about the ship till near six o'clock, when they left us and went out of the harbour. At this time the Queen Charlotte's boat was about two miles without the harbour with a fishing party; and the Indian boats immediately joined her. Being rather uneasy for fear of their pillaging the boat, I kept a look-out on them with my glass, and presently perceived a struggle between the two parties; on this I immediately set off in my whale-boat, she being always ready armed; and leaving directions with my mate to follow in the yaul, pushed out towards them with all speed. The Indians no sooner saw

the

the boat round the point than they took to their paddles and went off as fast as they were able. I rowed out and joined the Charlotte's boat, and found the Indians had taken away all their fishing-lines, and were just forcing their anchor out of the boat when I hove in sight. On enquiry I found captain Dixon's people had no fire-arms in the boat; which was very unlucky, as even the sight of a musket will prevent the Indians from attempting any violence; so thoroughly have the Russians taught them by experience the fatal effects of fire-arms. Captain Meares told me (and he had his information from the Russians whom he saw at Kodiac, where he touched on his way hither) that a party of them, since our visit in the Resolution, had wintered in the Sound, and (according to their description of the place) in the very harbour we now were at anchor in, where they had a battle with the natives, who were beaten off; but seven Russians lost their lives in the skirmish. Captain Meares likewise touched at Oonaska, and proceeding from thence along the coast, he passed the Schumagin Isles. When he came as far as what captain Cook calls Whitsuntide Bay, he took it for the entrance into Cook's River, and finding an opening, he stood into it, and did not find out his mistake for some time: at length meeting with some Russians, they informed him that the strait he then was in led into Cook's River, and that all the land between the Isle Saint Hermogenes and the strait was the island of Kodiac. On receiving this information, captain Meares stood on, and got into Cook's River near Smoaky Bay; b t was prevented by bad weather from proceeding much further. During his short stay in the river, he procured only

two

two sea-otter skins; the natives about Cape Douglas and Mount Saint Augustin being in the Russian interest.

Every thing being now ready for sea, we weighed anchor at daylight in the morning of the 14th, and with a light breeze from the North East, proceeded out of the harbour; and after getting out of the bay, hauled up towards Prince William's Sound. During the former part of the day we had light variable winds, so that the boats were sent a-head to tow the ship; at three in the afternoon a fine breeze came on from the South West, with which we stood over for Hinchinbrooke Cove. At six o'clock I sent my whale-boat on board for captain Dixon; and this appearing a good opportunity for his getting out of the Sound, we determined on separating, and each ship to adopt the plan that has already been mentioned. Soon afterwards captain Dixon returned on board, and we took leave of each other; the Queen Charlotte shaped her course out of the Sound, and I bent mine for Hinchinbrooke Cove. At nine o'clock the South West breeze failed us, and we had light winds about North East, right down the Cove. At that time we were close to some rocks that lie at the entrance, and in fifty fathoms water; and upon this the boats were sent a-head, and we stood over for the South shore of the Cove. The wind continued scant all night, and that little was directly against us; so that we could barely hold our own. I would have anchored within half a mile of the shore, but we had near fifty fathoms water; so that it was necessary to keep under way and wait for a breeze; and at six o'clock next morning

morning a fine breeze sprung up from the South South West, with which we run up; and observing a point well up in an arm of the cove, that promised good shelter round it, I sent the whale-boat to examine and found the place; and following with the ship, I presently saw that there was an excellent harbour round the point; therefore stood in, and at eight o'clock came to anchor with the best bower in seven fathoms water, over a muddy bottom, and moored with the small bower.

CHAP. X.
1787.
May.
Monday 14.

CHAP. XI.

Indians visit the Ship with Sea Otter Skins.—Boats sent on a trading Expedition.—Plundered by the Indians.—Return of the Boats.—Arrival of the Nootka.—Assist in getting her ready for Sea.—Long-boat sent to Cook's River.—Departure of the Nootka.—Long-boat's Return.—Sent a second Time.—Visited by different Tribes of Indians.—Various Employments carried on.—Abundance of Salmon, Herrings, and Crabs.—Arrival of the Long-boat.—Departure from Port Etches.

THOUGH our situation was a very eligible one, yet I found, on sounding around the ship, that we could have a still better birth, by lying higher up the harbour; I therefore determined to shift about a cable's length further in; but the people being greatly fatigued by towing the vessel all the preceding night, I deferred my design for the present, and gave them leave to take some rest.

In the course of the day several canoes came along-side, from whom I purchased ten or twelve good sea-otter skins. Several parts of the harbour appearing likely to afford some fish, we hauled the seine frequently, but met with no success. In the morning of the 16th we hove up the small bower, and after hauling the ship within shore of the best bower, let it go again in five fathoms water

over

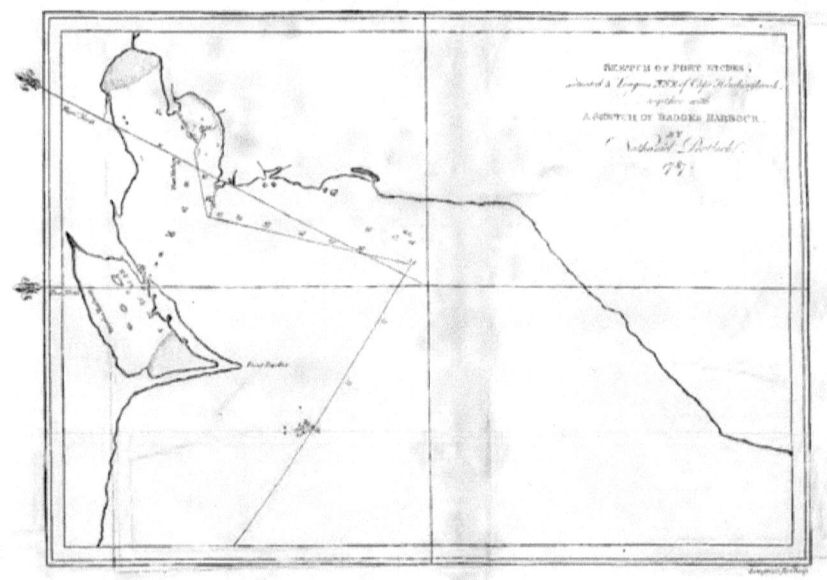

over a muddy bottom, and moored the ship head and stern. When moored, we had the Sound open to the South West between two points of land, about half a point of the compass: through which space we could see any thing that passed in or out of the Sound by Cape Hinchinbrooke passage. The land all around us had a dreary appearance, being covered with snow five or six feet deep, quite down to high water mark; so that the only space where we could walk was on the beach after the tide had fallen. At the head of the harbour were two fine fresh-water rivulets, likely to produce plenty of salmon at a proper season. A few of the natives came along-side with some good sea-otter skins, and a small quantity of fish, for which we were obliged to pay extravagantly.

In the morning of the 18th I went in the whale-boat to examine an arm trending to the Eastward above our present harbour. After passing the upper point, I found the arm soon terminated in a flat shore, with shoal water at some distance from the head of it. I then rowed along the North shore, and discovered an arm leading in between two points, not more than a quarter of a mile distant from each other. I stood in for the entrance, and had five and six fathoms water over a muddy bottom between the two points. The passage now widened considerably, and branched out in opposite directions; one arm leading nearly South West, and the other North East. I went up the South West arm, and carried five and six fathoms water over a muddy bottom for more than two miles; it then grew flat at a considerable distance from the head. After sounding this arm, I returned with an intention of sounding the other; but on getting a sight of the ship, I observed the ensign flying, which was a signal for canoes

being

being along-fide: I therefore deferred founding, and rowed immediately for the ship, where I arrived about noon, and purchased a few good skins from the natives. On my inquiring for salmon, they gave me to understand that there was none at present; but that when the snow melted from the hills, there would be plenty.

Sunday 20. As the articles we had to barter with did not seem to be held in great estimation, I determined to dispatch the whale-boat and yaul, under the direction of Mr. Cressleman the second mate and Mr. Bryant, on board the Nootka, to request of captain Meares some articles of trade which I wanted, and knew he could well spare; at the same time they were to trade with the natives up the Sound if any opportunity offered. I intended to have gone myself, or sent Mr. M'Leod on this business; but he had been so frequently laid up with a complaint in the bladder, that I could neither trust him with the care of the ship for any length of time, or send him out with the boats, for fear of his complaint returning at a time when he might be particularly wanted. In the forenoon we had fresh gales from the Eastward, but the weather growing moderate about two o'clock, I sent the boats off to proceed up the Sound. We now had no boat left by the ship, nor any other way of getting on shore but in the Sandwich Island canoe; and she being very dangerous for any who did not understand how to manage her, it became necessary to contrive some safer kind of conveyance. Accordingly the carpenter, assisted by the cooper and three other hands, begun to build a punt of twelve feet long, six feet wide, and about three feet deep. This plan was first suggested by the carpenter, and I approved of it very much, as the punt

NORTH WEST COAST OF AMERICA.

punt could not fail to be useful in wooding and watering whilst the boats were absent.

NEXT morning several canoes came along-side with a trading party; they brought thirteen very good sea-otter skins and a few indifferent ones. The harbour affording very fine crabs and mussels, I sent a number of the people to procure some, and they returned in the evening with a good quantity of each. The weather being moderate, our operations on shore went briskly forward; one party were employed in cutting wood, another in sawing plank, and the carpenter, with his assistants, were busy about the punt.

IN the afternoon of the 22d two canoes visited us and brought a few good skins. If I understood them right, the adjacent country was called Tacklaecimuke, and that it was principally inhabited by a tribe, the name of whose chief was Nootuck, and the name of another chief belonging to the same tribe was Coocha.

THREE canoes belonging to Nootuck's tribe came to the ship on the 23d, but brought nothing to sell, except a few halibut. Indeed, most of the sea-otter skins we have procured since our arrival here were green, and recently taken from the animal; so that we were obliged to stretch and dress them ourselves.

ON the 24th we had strong gales from the East by South with rain, which prevented any canoes from coming near us. In the afternoon, the carpenter and his party launched the punt, and came on board in her.

IN

CHAP.
XI.

1787.
May.
Friday 25.

IN the forenoon of the 25th the whale-boat returned from the Sound: they had parted with the yaul just off the North point of the bay. Mr. Cresleman brought none of the things I sent for to the Nootka except a compass; the other articles, captain Meares assured me I should have on his joining me near Cape Hinchinbrooke, which he proposed doing as soon as possible.

Saturday 26.

IN the forenoon of the 26th we had a very heavy gale of wind from the Eastward, and the yaul not making her appearance, it gave me great uneasiness, as her crew were not only quite exposed to the weather, but might probably be driven out of the Sound and all perish. Neither could I send the whale-boat to look for and assist them, without running a great risk of losing her crew likewise. At six o'clock the gale increasing to a violent degree, with constant rain and sleet, the top-gallant masts were got down upon deck, and the topmasts struck close to the rigging. The wind continued blowing very strong till six o'clock in the afternoon

Sunday 27.

of the 27th, when the weather growing rather moderate, I dispatched the whale-boat in search of the yaul, with proper refreshments for her crew, if they were fortunate enough to meet with her. At nine o'clock both boats came along-side, and the yaul's crew were in a much better state than I expected to see them, though they must have suffered very much. The whale-boat met the yaul at the entrance of the bay, making an effort to get in; but it must have been a fruitless one, had they not met and taken them in tow; for the boats were scarcely got along-side before it begun to rain and blow as violently as before.

Wednes. 30.

From this to the 30th, the weather was so strong, that our operations on shore were greatly retarded, and scarcely any business was carried on. During this interval, we had

4   only

NORTH WEST COAST OF AMERICA.   231

only three canoes along-side, with cod and halibut, suffi- CHAP.
cient to serve the ship's company one day, and a few to-   XI.
lerably good sea-otter skins. On the 30th the weather   1787.
growing moderate, the people were sent on shore to cut   May.
wood and bring off water for present use.   Wednes. 30.

On the 4th June the weather appearing settled, I dis-   June.
patched the whale-boat and yaul on a trading expedition, Monday 4.
under the direction of Messrs. Cresleman and Bryant. I
at first intended to have sent them round Cape Hinchinbrooke, and on toward Kayes Island; but on second consideration I judged it would answer my purpose best to
send them up an opening situated between that we lay in,
and Snug Corner Cove, by which means they would stand
a chance of obtaining part of the trade intended for the
Nootka; but by going on the other side, they were likely
to meet only with Indians coming to the King George. In
the evening I sent a few hands in the canoe to procure
some crabs, and in two hours they returned with a good
quantity of fine ones. Just as night came on, a few Indians came along-side, bringing some halibut and cod, but
no furs.

Early the next morning I sent the carpenter with a   Tuesday 5.
party of men over to the North shore to cut some sticks
for spare topmasts, a mizen-mast, and a main-yard; another party were employed sawing boards, the cooper
brewing spruce beer, and the remainder of the ship's company were clearing the gun-room and airing the sails;
some of which had got wet during the late bad weather.

On

CHAP.
XI.
1787.
June.
Wednef. 6.

ON the 6th, the weather being fine, I sent the boatswain with four of the people to dig a piece of ground for a garden on a small island situated in the entrance of the cove, and which I named Garden Island. After the ground was ready, we sowed variety of seeds in it, such as cabbage, onion, Scotch kale, radish, savoy, purslane, thyme, celery, spinach, cauliflower, turnip, mustard, rape and cress, with peas, beans, French beans, and lettuce, besides oats and barley. The soil being tolerably good, it would be rather extraordinary if, among so great a variety, nothing should come to perfection. In the afternoon of the 7th a small open canoe, with five Indians in it, came along-side, from whom I bought two good sea-otter skins, and a large quantity of fine cod.

Thursday 7.

AT ten o'clock in the evening the whale-boat and yaul returned from their expedition with a few very good skins, which they purchased of a chief, whose name was Sheenaawa, and whom I conjecture to be the same person that paid us a visit at Montague Island. I intended them for a longer trip, but it seems they unluckily got into a large flat bay, where the boats grounded, and before they could extricate themselves from the shoals, the tide ebbed, and left them dry for near two miles round. Sheenaawa and his tribe, which consisted of near two hundred men, saw their situation, and paid them a visit, most of them armed with spears and knives. The boats crews at first were greatly alarmed at their situation; but their fears rather subsisted when they found that plunder was what the Indians wanted. This they endeavoured to prevent, but at the same time kept their plunderers in good temper, which was the most prudent method the people could possibly have taken; for had they acted in any other manner, and strove to have prevented them from stealing by force of arms, not a man in either boat could have escaped the vengeance of their numerous opponents. This plundering party obtained an excellent booty in their own estimation. They stole most of the trading articles, two musquets, two pistols, and some of the people's clothes; and what old Sheenawaa seemed to regard as a thing of inestimable value, was Mr. Cresfleman's quadrant, which he seized together with his ephemeris and requisite tables. It was at this time that they purchased the skins I have just mentioned, Sheenaawa's people affecting to traffic as a sort of introduction to their depredations. During this short expedition our people had an opportunity of seeing that the land on which Cape Hinchinbrooke is situated is an island.

In the afternoon of the 9th, being at Garden Island, I saw the Nootka turning in towards the port, and immediately sent the whale-boat and yaul to her assistance. At seven o'clock she anchored just without the King George. Two canoes came along-side in the morning of the 10th with only one sea-otter skin. The Indians appeared rather shy on seeing the Nootka, which I cannot account for in any other way than their having fired at some of the natives just before they left Sutherland's Cove, and, as I was given to understand, wounded one of them. In the forenoon captain Meares came on board the King George, and requested me to send my carpenter on board his vessel to examine her masts, pumps, and sides; which request I complied with, although he had much work to do on the ship's account. Towards evening I went on shore to visit our different parties at work, and had an account from the carpenter

carpenter of the situation he found the Nootka in: her masts and yards were in good order, but the sides in many parts were dangerously open, and her pumps in a very bad condition, not having a spear, or lower box that would fit either pump, nor even a pump-break fit to work with. The next day captain Meares requested me to let my carpenter work on board the Nootka a few days, in order to put her in a condition fit for sea, which I readily complied with; and thinking the leaks in her sides and the pumps the most material objects, I recommended him to have them put in order first. The carpenter accordingly went on board, and presently sent me word that they had no oakum; on this I gave him directions to make use of our own, and by the time he had finished, he expended near two hundred weight. The pump geer that wanted armourers work was sent on board the King George, and I set the armourer to work about it immediately. I also sent a party on shore to cut wood for the Nootka, and the punt was employed in carrying it on board; and whenever the weather permitted, the cooper was employed in making spruce essence for her use.

In the forenoon the long-boat arrived from Cook's River, and had met with tolerable success; Messrs. Hayward and Hill assuring me that much more business might be done in another trip. As soon as the boat was cleared, I ordered her to be fitted out with provisions, and an assortment of trade for a second expedition. Mr. Hayward informed me, that on their arrival in Cook's River, soon after getting above Point Bede, they fell in with a party of Kodiac Indians, who they supposed were hunting on account of the Russians; but they saw none of the Russian party,

party, and the inhabitants of Cook's River behaved in a very friendly manner. The long-boat, being provided with provisions and articles for trade, sailed again for Cook's River early in the morning of the 12th, with positive orders to return by the 20th July; and the same crew that went in her the first trip, were volunteers to go a second time. In the forenoon we saw several canoes, one of which went along-side the Nootka, but the rest kept at a distance, seeming afraid to come near.

CHAP. XI.
1787. June.
Tuesday 12.

Our seamen and artificers were engaged in various employments for the Nootka till the 15th, when a very strong gale coming on from the Eastward with violent gusts of wind from the vallies, and constant heavy rain, prevented any work from being carried on. During this interval not one canoe appeared in the Cove. The weather becoming moderate on the 16th, our people resumed their various employments, and by the 17th had put the Nootka in a condition fit for sea. Several canoes visited us, bringing a few indifferent skins, and some fine halibut. For some time past the weather had in general been very wet, which affected the health of the sailors very much, and many of them were laid up with fevers and violent colds. The Nootka being ready for sailing, I sent my whale-boat in the morning of the 19th to assist them in getting under way, and at one o'clock she stood out of the Cove. Our spruce-beer was now in good order, and daily served out to the ship's company; and I had the pleasure to find the sick people get considerably better.

Friday 15.

Saturday 16.
Sunday 17.

Tuesday 19.

The surrounding country now wore a different aspect from what it did on our first arrival: the heavy rains had

H h 2   melted

melted most of the snow, and every thing seemed to promise the speedy approach of summer. The surgeon, and those people who had lately been ill, took a walk on shore on the 20th, and gathered a good quantity of water-cresses, which they found growing near the fresh-water rivulets. We caught plenty of flounders along-side with hook and line: these, with crabs, which were now very fine, proved an excellent change from salt provisions. Some of the people in fishing along-side for flounders caught several cod and halibut. On this I sent the canoe on the 22d out some distance into the bay to try for them, and they soon returned with a load of fine halibut and cod. This success induced me to send her out frequently with a fishing party, and they caught considerably more than what was sufficient for daily consumption; so that I ordered the remainder to be salted for sea store. In the afternoon a party of Indians visited us, from whom I bought some good sea-otter skins. They pointed towards the South West, and gave me to understand that we might procure plenty of good furs from that quarter. This piece of information determined me to send the boats on another expedition, and in the afternoon of the 24th I dispatched the whale-boat and yaul on a trip to the South West part of the Sound with provisions for a month, and a proper assortment of trade. All the remaining part of the ship's company that could be spared had leave given to recreate themselves on shore. Some of them ascended the highest hills in the neighbourhood, on the sides of which they found good quantities of snake-root, and a variety of flowers in full bloom. About eight o'clock in the evening I observed two Indian boats and several canoes come into the bay: they all landed on a sandy beach, which

NORTH WEST COAST OF AMERICA.

which bore West South West from the ship, and about three miles and a half distant.

NEXT morning at five o'clock our new visiters came along-side in one of their large boats; the party consisted of about twenty-five men, women, and children. Their chief appeared to be a well-disposed man, rather low in stature, with a long beard, and seemed about sixty years of age: he was entirely disabled on one side, probably by a paralytic stroke. The old man made me a present of a good skin, but had little to sell except a few salmon, which we bought of him. I made the chief, whose name I understood was Taatucktellingnuke, a present, and one to each of those who seemed to be of consequence; I also distributed some trinkets among the women and children.

TAATUCKTELLINGNUKE gave me to understand that the country he came from was called Cheeneecock, and situated in the South West part of the Sound. Our new friends staid along-side during the whole day, and went on shore in the evening, perfectly well satisfied. I found the whole of this party very friendly and well disposed; and indeed most of those who had visited us were so; particularly the natives belonging to Tacklaccimute, who I am inclined to think inhabit Comptroller's Bay, and the Shucklamute people, who take up their abode in the North side of Montague Island.

I LEARNED from my late visiters that the country where Sheenawaa and his tribe take up their residence, is called Taaticklagmute; that they were the most powerful tribe
about

about the Sound, and hated by all their neighbours, with whom they were continually at variance. Old Shenawaa, since his plundering our boats, had never appeared in the harbour; but some of his people sometimes brought us a few sea-otter skins, which they had obtained either by plunder or barter; for I understood that his country does not produce any of the sea-otter; but they have abundance of river-otter. Tacklaccimute, Shucklamute, and Wallaamute, are the countries that afford the sea-otter. This last-mentioned place, from every information I have been able to obtain, is situated considerably beyond Comptroller's Bay to the Eastward; and we have seen none of the inhabitants; but the Indians that have traded with us, frequently brought skins which they said came from that country; and I always observed that none of those skins were marked, as is the usual custom when they are intended for sale, but made up into cloaks, and worn by the people, to defend them from the inclemency of the weather.

SHEENAWAA (whose rapacious disposition has already been noticed), whilst the Nootka wintered in Sutherland's Cove, sent frequent messages, intimating that he intended to come and cut them off. These messages, or rather threats, were always delivered to an Indian girl that an officer belonging to the Nootka had purchased on their first arrival in the Sound. This girl made her escape from the Nootka towards the latter part of the winter, and probably gave the Indians an account of her weak and defenceless situation; for there is hardly a doubt, from the number of men that Sheenawaa had with him at the time of the affair with our boats, that he then meditated an attack on the Nootka; but very bad weather coming on immediately afterwards, probably frustrated his design.

CHAP. XI.
1787.
June.
Monday 25.

THE party who were daily sent out to fish for cod and halibut had their hooks and lines often broken by large ground-sharks; several of these were killed, but they were of no use, their livers yielding scarcely any oil.

TAATUCKTELLINGNUKE paid me a visit on the 26th, and was particularly anxious to take one or two of our people with him on shore to spend the night, offering at the same time to leave some of his people on board as hostages till their return. I complied with this singular request, and gave two of the people leave to accompany him on shore; he left three of his tribe on board, being desirous to convince me that he intended no harm.

Tuesday 26.

EARLY the next morning the friendly old chief came on board in one of his boats, and brought our people with him. After we had exchanged hostages, I made the old man and his companions some trifling presents, and they went on shore highly pleased.

Wednes. 27.

I FOUND that these Indians lodged in temporary huts, composed only of a few sticks and a little bark; the principal part of their food was fish; by way of variety they ate the inner rind of the pine-bark dried; but their greatest luxury was a kind of rock-weed covered with the spawn of some fish or other, of which they gather and eat great quantities: they also eat the inner rind of the angelica and hemloc roots, which, though poison to us, by constant

Saturday 30.

IN hauling the seine on the 30th, we caught a large quantity of herrings and some salmon; the herrings, though small, were very good, and two hogsheads of them were salted for sea-store.

July.
Sunday 1.

OLD Taatucktellingnuke took leave of me on the 1st of July, and with his tribe left the harbour and paddled towards Montague Island.

Friday 6.

AT noon on the 6th the whale-boat and yaul returned from their expedition without the least success, not having seen a single canoe during their trip. Their route was from our harbour towards Montague Island, and from thence over to the South West part of the Sound; having my directions, if they found it could be done without much risk, to look into an opening that is supposed to lead from the Sound into Cook's River, through the river Turnagain. On getting over on the South West shore, they met with great quantities of drift-ice, coming, as they supposed, out of that opening, and at the same time heard a constant jumbling noise resembling the breaking up of ice in a large river. Foggy weather now coming on, the officer who had charge of the boats did not think it prudent to venture in with them, but spent the night near that situation, and the morning being still foggy, he directed his course to the North, and came back by Snug Corner Cove, without (as I have before observed) meeting with any Indians whatever.

BEING now convinced that little or nothing could be done by sending the boats on another expedition, and expecting the long-boat's return in a few days, after which I intended to get to sea as quick as possible; I set all hands to work in getting the ship ready; a large party were sent on shore to cut wood, and others were employed about the rigging.

WE daily caught large quantities of salmon, but the unsettled state of the weather not permitting us to cure them on board, I sent the boatswain with a party on shore to build a kind of house to smoke them in. On the 9th the house was finished, and the boatswain with his party were employed in smoking salmon; there was sufficient room to hang six hundred fish up conveniently; and seven fires being constantly burning, they were cured very well. In the forenoon one canoe came along-side with two very good frocks made of sea-otter skins. The people gave me to understand that they had been to Wallaamute, and purchased the frocks at that place, which I had no reason to doubt; as I recollected seeing them about the ship near a month before this time, since which they never made their appearance until now.

THE seine was frequently hauled on the 11th, and not less than 2000 salmon were caught at each haul; the weather, however, preventing us from curing them so well as could have been wished, we kept only a sufficient quantity for present use, and let the rest escape. The salmon were now in such numbers along the shores, that any quantity whatever might be caught with the greatest ease.

During

During the 12th and 13th the wind blew very strong and in violent gusts from the Eastward, with constant heavy rain, which prevented any work from going forward. Towards afternoon on the 14th, the weather growing moderate, the people resumed their different employments.

In the morning of the 21st I went in the whale-boat into a small bay about three miles from the ship, on the South side of the harbour, where some days before I discovered a quantity of fine watercresses. The weather being tolerably fine, I took the carpenter (who lately had been very ill) and a few others in the boat along with me, that they might have a walk, and receive some refreshment from the watercresses. This little excursion had a wonderfully good effect on every one. We sat down on the grass, and made a hearty dinner of fried pork and salmon, and, by way of sallad, had an abundance of watercresses; we likewise gathered a sufficient quantity to serve every person on board. Behind the beach where we landed is a fresh-water lake, that empties itself into the bay by a small river at the Northern part of the beach, in which there was abundance of salmon. Just above the beach, between the bay and the lake, there was a piece of wild wheat, about two hundred yards long and five yards wide, growing at least two feet high, among which we found the watercresses. This wheat with proper care might certainly be made an useful article of food. On the edge of the lake I saw the track of an animal which greatly resembled that of the moose-deer. We returned on board in the evening without seeing any Indians.

At ten o'clock in the morning of the 22d, the long-boat appearing in sight, I sent the whale-boat to her assistance if it should be necessary; at noon she came alongside, and I found all the crew in good health. In this trip they had experienced a great deal of very bad weather, and had not met with such good success as we expected; their purchases being about forty prime skins and a number of inferior ones. They fell in with numbers of the Kodiac Indians, who always behaved in the most friendly manner, as did all the inhabitants of the river. During this expedition they were up about a league above Trading Bay, on the opposite shore, where they found good and safe anchorage for shipping, and a greater number of inhabitants than in any other part of the river.

Having clear pleasant weather on the 23d, the powder was sent to Garden Island to be dried and sifted, and the cooper was employed in repairing the casks which were defective: a party were employed in getting fire-wood on board, and others in getting the ship ready for sea. In the afternoon of the 24th our wooding and watering was completed, and every thing from the shore was got on board. We lopped off all the branches off the highest tree on Garden Island, and fixed a staff about ten feet long at the top, with a wooden vane on it, and near the bottom was inscribed the ship's name, with the year and day of the month. Every thing being ready for sea at six o'clock, we unmoored and hove short on the best bower; but it being then calm, we could not proceed out of the port. However, at two o'clock the next morning a breeze sprung up from the Eastward, with which we weighed and got under sail, and by four, being clear of the Cove, the boats were hoisted in.

CHAP. XII.

Range along the Coast of Montague Island.—Short Account of Prince William's Sound.—Description of the Inhabitants. — Their Persons. — Manners. — Dress.—Diseases.—Ornaments.—Food.—Cookery.—Situation for a Settlement.—Produce.—Weapons.—Hunting Implements.—Specimen of their Language.—Proceed along the Coast.—Anchor in Portlock's Harbour.—Intercourse with the Natives.—Long-boat sent on a trading Expedition.—Visited by a distant Tribe of Indians.

CHAP. XII.
1787.
July.
Wednes. 25.

ON quitting the harbour (which obtained the name of Port Etches) I at first intended to stand out of the Sound by way of Cape Hinchinbrooke; but on opening that passage, the weather looked very thick and dirty to the South East; so that I came to the resolution of pushing for the passage on the West side of Montague Island; knowing that with a Southerly wind we might get good and safe anchorage in that passage; but should we be taken on the Eastern side of Montague Island, with a Southerly or South East wind, which in general brings dirty weather with it, we probably might be thrown into a very dangerous situation. I therefore shaped a course for the North point of Montague Island, with a fresh breeze at East North East. At seven o'clock we passed two bays, situated on the North East point of the island, both of which are noticed in Mr. Edgar's chart. In the afternoon

noon we had light variable winds inclining to calm; and at four o'clock the bay we first anchored in on coming up this passage bore South half West, four leagues distant. I was very desirous to make that bay before night came on, as the weather began to look very unsettled; but the wind now shifted to South South West, which was directly against us. At seven o'clock the wind freshened, and brought with it very thick rainy weather; so that we could scarcely see the land, though not more than five miles from it. Not liking the appearance of the weather, I stood over for a passage between Foot Island and the land to the Westward of it. Through this passage our long-boat had generally sailed in going to and returning from Cook's River; and they had named it the Prince of Wales's Passage. As Mr. Hayward informed me there was good anchorage in it, I was very desirous of getting in before worse weather came on; therefore, with a fresh breeze from the South South West, I stood directly for it; but on opening the passage at eight o'clock, I found the wind blowing directly down it, and a strong tide setting against us; so that we were obliged to spend the night in plying between Montague and Foot Island.

We plied occasionally till noon on the 26th, when a light breeze coming on from the Northward, we stood down the channel. At four o'clock the wind hauled round to the South West; Hanning's Bay at that time being under our lee, we bore up and run for it; and at seven o'clock came to anchor in that Bay in sixteen fathoms water, over a bottom of coarse sand. We weighed anchor again at eight o'clock next morning, and the wind being light, the boats were sent a-head to tow the ship.

At

CHAP. XII.

1787.
July.
Friday 27.

At noon a fresh breeze came on from the South South West; which being directly against us, we stood in again, and at one o'clock came to anchor near our former situation. There being no probability of our getting out to sea that afternoon, I went on shore, accompanied by Messrs. Hayward, Hill, and Bryant, in the whale-boat and yawl; and near a fresh-water creek which lies in the Southern part of the bay, we hauled the seine, and caught a quantity of salmon sufficient to load both the boats, and afterwards returned on board.

Saturday 28.
Sunday 29.

DURING the 28th the wind continued to blow fresh from the South South West, which kept us at anchor; but at seven o'clock the next morning a light breeze springing up from the Northward, we weighed, and with the boats a-head towed out of the bay. The wind presently shifted to the Southward, which greatly retarded our progress, and at six o'clock in the afternoon the ebb-tide being done, we anchored in the South bay in twenty-four fathoms water, over a bottom of muddy sand.

Monday 30.

AT four o'clock next morning a light breeze coming on from the Eastward, we weighed and got under sail. At six o'clock, however, the ebb being done, and the wind hauling to the Southward, we were obliged to anchor in twenty-one fathoms water, over a black sandy bottom; the South point of the bay bearing South three quarters West, two miles, and the South point of some low land lying off the entrance into the Prince of Wales's Passage West by South, three leagues distant. In this situation it was low-water at 6" 45", the moon 15ᵈ 14ʰ old. Soon after we arrived in the bay, three of our old acquaintance

quaintance from Cheeneecock came along-side in two canoes; they were out on a hunting expedition, and had three very good sea-otter skins, which I bought, and made them a trifling present. At noon we weighed and came to sail with a light breeze from the South South East. At four o'clock the South West point of Montague Island bore South East, two leagues distant: being then about two miles from shore, we sounded in sixty-three fathoms water, over a muddy bottom. At seven o'clock, observing that we began to lose ground very fast, although there was a two-knot breeze from the West South West, with which we stood to the South South East, we prepared for anchoring, and soon afterwards came-to in sixty-five fathoms water, over a muddy bottom, with the kedge and a hauser; the South West point of Montague Island bearing East three quarters South, five miles, and the North point of Foot Island North by East, four or five leagues distant. I suppose the flood to have made soon after six o'clock, and come from the South East half South, at the rate of three miles an hour: it set directly towards the entrance of the Prince of Wales's Passage. At nine o'clock the tide made still stronger, and though we had our sails set, with a gentle breeze from the Northward, the kedge came home; on this, we bent another hauser, and veered it to the better end, which rode the ship; the tide now going at the rate of three miles and an half an hour. The flood being done at one in the morning, we weighed and came to sail: presently afterwards a fine breeze sprung up from the West South West, with which we steered to the Southward; and at four o'clock were well clear of the land, the South West point of Montague Island bearing North North East half East, three leagues,

and

CHAP. XII.
1787.
July.
Tuesday 31.

and the Westernmost land in sight West half South, sixteen or seventeen leagues distant.

As we are now taking our leave of Prince William's Sound, though the publication of captain Cook's and other voyages hath obviated the necessity of a copious description of the natives, their manners, customs, &c. and the produce of their country, yet a few particulars may be selected from what hath hitherto come under general observation, which may afford the reader satisfaction; as they are the result of very close attention and minute remarks on their behaviour and general conduct.

These people are for the most part short in stature, and square-made men; their faces, men and women, are in general flat and round, with high cheek-bones and flattish noses; their teeth are very good and white; eyes dark, quick of sight; their smell very good, and which they quicken, by smelling at the snake-root parched. As to their complexions, they are generally lighter than the Southern Indians, and some of their women I have seen with rosy cheeks; their hair is black and straight, and they are fond of having it long: but on the death of a friend they cut it short, to denote them to be in mourning; nor have I ever observed that they have any other way to mark their sorrow and concern for their relations. The men have generally bad ill-shaped legs, which I attributed to their sitting in one constant position in their canoes. They seem possessed of as great a share of pride and vanity as Europeans; for they often paint the face and hands, their ears and noses bored, and the underlip slit. In the hole in the nose they hang an ornament (as they deem it) made of bone

bone or ivory two or three inches long. At the ears they mostly wear beads hanging down to the shoulder, and in the slit in the lip they have a bone or ivory instrument fitted with holes in it, from which they hang beads as low as the chin. These holes in the lip disfigure them very much, some of them having it as large as their mouth. But with all this fancied finery they are remarkably filthy in their persons, and not frequently shifting their garments, they are generally very lousy; and in times of scarcity those vermin probably serve them as an article of food; for I have seen them pick and eat to the number of a dozen or more; and they are not very small. Their clothing consists wholly of the skins of animals and birds. I must do them the justice to say, that we in general found them very friendly; and they appear so remarkably tender and affectionate to their women and children, that you cannot please them more than in making them small presents: but carry your attention to their women no farther, for nothing gives them greater displeasure than taking liberties with them. Another very prevalent inclination is that of thieving; which is by no means peculiar to them, but is equally to be seen in all other Indians, not only from strangers, but from one another. I have frequently, in the course of my trading with them, seen them steal from one another, and on being detected, they will give up the articles they have stolen with a laugh, and immediately appear as unconcerned as if nothing had happened amiss. I am sure that with them thieving with dexterity is rather thought a grace than a disgrace; and the complete thief is a clever fellow, but the bungling pilferer is less admired. You may generally know the man who comes as a professed thief, for his face will be all

CHAP.
XII.
1787.
July.
Tuesday 31.

all daubed with paint; and whilst you may be viewing the curious figure he cuts with his painted face, you may be sure that his hands are not idle, if there is any thing near him worth stealing: and whenever you see the arm slipt from out the sleeve of the frock of skins which they always wear, you may be well assured that the person is intent on thieving; and they always conceal the articles they have stolen under their frock, until they have an opportunity of stowing them away in their canoes; but notwithstanding our knowing the professed thief, and all our vigilance, they frequently stole little things from us, but of no consequence. During our intercourse with them they grew less addicted to thieving, in consequence of my sometimes appearing a little angry with them, and taking some pains to convince them of the impropriety of their behaviour. Upon the whole, they appear a good kind of people, and I am convinced in a little time, provided a settlement of sufficient strength were established, would be an industrious set of people in hunting and procuring the sea-otter and other skins for sale to the settlers. The weaker tribes, I think, are frequently robbed and plundered by the stronger, and prevented from hunting, which would not be the case, were there a proper settlement established in some convenient place, for that would give protection to the whole of the inhabitants of this Sound: and indeed I believe from this to King George's Sound they are by no means so numerous as was in general supposed, therefore not so dangerous to settlers. I think this Sound, and as far as Comptrollers Bay, would not muster three hundred fighting men; and Cook's River, according to Mr. Hill's observation, could not muster much above that number; and the whole of these people stand so much in awe of fire-

arms,

arms, that a few men well provided would be perfectly secure; and were I to advise a place for wintering at and forming a settlement, it should be the West harbour of Port Etches. It hath several advantages over any place I have seen on the coast; one of them is, that it lies so near the sea, that in all probability it would be one of the last places that would freeze, and one of the first in which the ice would break up. In the next place, you would be much sheltered by the high land lying to the Eastward and Northward from the bleak winds in the winter, and you have all the Southern aspect open over the low land, which lies to the Southward of you: which land in a little time might be turned to very useful purposes in raising articles of food for the settlers. You might see from this situation the passage from the sea, and a great part of the Sound. The country around, after the snow leaves it, which is about the middle of June, is pleasant enough; the weather is at times, long before that period, very fine and pleasant, and at other times exceedingly boisterous, with constant rain, which washes in a short time great quantities of the snow away, soon leaves the lower parts clear, and you immediately perceive the vegetables coming forth.

THIS country abounds in trees of the pine kind, some very large, a good quantity of alder, a kind of hazel, but not larger than will do for making hand-spikes. The fruit bushes are in great abundance, such as bilberry bushes, raspberry bushes, strawberries, alderberry bushes, and currant bushes red and black. The vegetables are water-cresses, wild celery, sour dock, shepherds purse, angelica, hemloc, and wild peas. We did not see any wild onions in Cook's River. Besides the above-mentioned vegetables, they have the wild onion; unfortunately none of our seed that was sown on the little island came to any thing; I am much afraid the greatest part of it was spoiled from age, being before we left England near a twelvemonth old. I sowed some in different parts about the country; perhaps some of it might thrive. The berries were none of them on our sailing fit for gathering, but would in a little time be quite ripe; and I am sure any quantity of them might be gathered for a winter's stock. We made use of the alder buds when they were tender as greens, and when boiled they eat very well. All hands partook of them one day for dinner; but they had a strange effect; not a person on board but what was physicked in a most extraordinary degree. On some it acted as an emetic as well as a purge; it kept us going for about thirty-six hours, when it stopped, leaving us all somewhat lighter than we were. This bout prevented me from sending the boats on a trading expedition two days longer than I intended. The buds of the young black currant bushes we made use of as tea, with the pine-tops mixed, which drank very pleasant.

The articles of food of the inhabitants are fish and animals of all kinds, of which they eat very heartily when they have it in their power; they eat the vegetables which the country affords, and the inner bark of the pine tree, which in the spring of the year must be of infinite service in recovering them from the scurvy; with which disease I am apt to think they are much afflicted during the winter; having seen many of them with swollen legs and sores, which I am pretty certain proceeded from that disease: as the summer advanced we saw little of those appearances. They never practise the method of smoking their

their provisions, and, for want of salt, have no other way of curing their winter stock of fish than drying it in the sun; their fresh fish they generally roast, by running some sticks through to spread it, and clapping it up before the fire. Their animal food they generally dress in baskets or wooden vessels, by putting to it red hot stones until the victuals are dressed enough; and it is surprising how quick they dress their provisions in this way.

During the summer season they lead a strange wandering life, and the shelter they live under in bad weather, when from home, is either their canoes or small sheds, made of a few sticks covered with a little bark; their winter habitations are also very ill made and inconvenient; those I have seen are not more than from four to six feet high, about ten feet long, and about eight feet broad, built with thick plank, and the crevices filled up with dry moss; and in those houses they generally stow very thick. The method they use in making plank is, to split the trees with wooden or stone wedges; and I have seen a plank twenty or twenty-five feet long, split from a tree by their method.

Their weapons for war are spears of sixteen or eighteen feet long, headed with iron; bows and arrows, and long knives; all of which they are amazingly dexterous in using. Their fishing implements are wooden hooks, with lines made of a small kind of rockweed, which grows to a considerable length, and will hold a good strain, if kept clear of hinks, and properly moistened. With these hooks and lines they catch halibut and cod; salmon they catch in wiers, or spear them; and herring I believe they catch with small nets: the implements with which they kill the sea-otter and other amphibious animals are harpoons made with bone, with two or more barbs; with a staff of about six or eight feet long, on which is fastened a skin or large bladder well blown, as a buoy; and darts of about three or four feet long, which they throw with a wooden instrument of about a foot long.

I OMITTED in its proper place to mention, that at the South part of the little bay where we found the water-cresses, we saw a tree with an inscription on it; the characters, some were of opinion, were Greek; but for my own part I could not make out what most of them were; they were badly cut. It appeared to me as if the inscription had been made in the latter part of the last year, and I am of opinion by a man who some time after the Nootka's arrival left her; this man is a native of one of the islands in the Mediterranean; and it should seem was drove from the Nootka by bad usage, and I believe is still among the Indians.

IN regard to the dialect of these people, it may be proper to introduce a few specimens, though it appeared to be such a confused, unintelligible jargon, that it was not without some difficulty that we could collect these instances:

Nootuch	-	*a principal chief's name of Tack-lacumute, a friendly tribe about Comptrollers Bay, the best traders about the Sound, and bring most sea-otter skins.*
Cocha	-	*a chief of ditto.*
Nus-cook-weelick		*a ditto of Montague Island, called by the natives Shuk'ake; a friendly tribe. This chief changed names with me.*
Nesqueluck	-	*a ditto ditto ditto.*
Abayack	-	*a ditto ditto ditto.*

Sha-newten

Sha-newten	-	to sleep.
Waallamute	-	a country to the E. N. E. of Port Etches.
Ishkaa	-	to get up after sleeping.
Kaa-naa	-	to take.
Taa-koo	-	to bring.
Nelltoolee	-	a toe or iron.
Yaa-mack	-	beads.
Congaamack	-	a marmot's skin.
Onaakaa	-	snow.
Pha-nee-cook	-	a tribe to the South West part of Prince William's Sound; a friendly tribe.
Cau-nuck	-	fire.
Muck	-	water.
Taa-tuck-tell-ingnuke		chief of Cha-nee-cock, a country to the South West of Prince William's Sound; a friendly tribe; not many skins.
She-ne-waa		chief of Taa tick-lag-mute, a country to the West North West from Port Etches; a very troublesome tribe; abundance of river-otter, but few sea-otter skins.
Gau-luck		shore.
Naa-taakie	-	snow, according to Shee-na-waa's tribe.
Naa-go-wack-tooke		wood.
Cus-kuck, or Nus-kuck		chief.
Coo-lin		ten.
Naa-nuck	-	twenty.
Auckluck	-	wind.
Maajack		sun.
Ingite	-	ground on shore.
Caapuckaa		river otter.
Taakenooke	-	let me look at it.
Seerme	-	rain.
Chilha		a child.
Ugaanuck	-	a woman.
Yaagala	-	good, or handsome.
Naatunafuck	-	sea-otter.
Naatunamoughtaa		young sea-otter.
Luckluck		a bear.
Yauna	-	yonder.
Yautka	-	gone away.
Chetleugh		no no.
Peeduck	-	all gone, I have no more.
Peeduck Naatunafuck		I have no more sea-otter skins.
Lawle	-	friendship. At the same time they extend their arms, and repeat the word Lawle frequently; and to signify that you are a friend, you must do the same.

CHAP.
XII.

1787.
July.
Tuesday 31.

AFTER getting well clear of the passage into Prince William's Sound, we steered East South East, with a light breeze from the Westward and pleasant weather; but the wind afterwards hauling to the Southward, we steered to the East by North.

August.
Friday 3.

THE 3d August being remarkably fine, the sailors hammocks were got upon deck; the ship was scraped fore and aft, and sprinkled with vinegar, and well aired with fires.

Saturday 4.

THE mean result of several observed distances of the sun and moon taken on the 4th gave 138° 20′ longitude; The latitude at that time was 57° 12′ North. At three o'clock we saw the land, bearing North by West, and more than twenty leagues distant, which we took for Mount Fairweather. The wind now shifted to the Eastward, and continued some time from that quarter, which prevented us from making any great progress towards Cape Edgecombe. However, as we could fetch something to the Eastward and Southward of Mount Fairweather, I determined to try for a port near the situation in which captain Cook places Cross Sound, although we were not fortunate enough to fall in with that place last season. At

Sunday 5.

four o'clock in the afternoon of the 5th Mount Fairweather bore North 10° West, near twenty leagues distant. This mountain, or rather ridge of mountains, as it forms into several, is by far the highest land on this part of the coast; much loftier than Mount Edgecombe; and I think nearly the height of Mount St. Elias. At six o'clock the appearance of an opening presented itself, bearing North 10° East; and having then a light breeze from North West

Monday 6.

by West, we stood in for it. Next morning at four o'clock

o'clock Mount Fairweather bore North West by West, twelve leagues distant. What was taken for a wide opening in the land on the preceding evening now appeared to be joined by low land, as we could from the mast-head see the low land extending from side to side, and no good appearance of an harbour. Indeed, our distance from the land was so great, that we could not determine this point with certainty; but as the wind was now rather scant for proceeding in towards the place where we had supposed the opening to be, and a fine wind for running towards Cape Edgecombe, I desisted from standing any further in the North North East direction, and edged away to the East North East, with an intention of getting pretty well in shore, in order to look for a harbour, as we stood towards the Cape. At ten o'clock we saw an opening in the land bearing North East, which promised well for a good harbour. On running in for it, another good appearance of an harbour presented itself, bearing North by East, and seems to be situated about eight leagues to the South East of Cross Cape.

All the land next the sea, beginning about eight leagues to the South East of Cross Cape, and trending to within ten leagues of Cape Edgecombe, seems to be composed of low woody islands, among which there appear several places of good shelter. The inland country forms into a number of peaked hills, some well wooded, and others quite bare. On drawing near the opening, and about two miles from the shore to the North West of it, we had twenty and twenty-five fathoms water over a muddy bottom, and just in the entrance were some high barren rocks. A large Indian boat came out, probably to view the ship: there were twelve people in her, and only three of them men, the reft women and children. On getting into the entrance of the paffage, which is about a mile acrofs, we deepened the water to thirty fathoms over a fandy bottom, the barren rocks juft mentioned forming the South fide; the Northern fide is low land, forming itfelf into feveral fmall bays, from whofe points are breakers at no great diftance. About half a mile within the barren rocks we had thirty fathoms water over a rocky bottom, which depth and bottom we carried at leaft a mile farther, fteering North Eaft by Eaft, which is nearly the courfe into the harbour. The paffage fo far is nearly a mile acrofs, with bold rocky fhores on each fide. Prefently afterwards we fhoaled the water to ten fathoms, being then in the narroweft part of the channel, which in that fituation is not more than half a mile acrofs, formed on the Northern fide by fome bold rocks, and to the Southward by a bluff point of land; to the Eaftward of which, a fmall diftance from the fhore, are fome rocks that juft fhew themfelves above water. Immediately on paffing thefe rocks we deepened the water very quick, having from thirty to forty fathoms; and a moft fpacious and excellent harbour opened itfelf to our view, trending to the North Weft and South Eaft, and running deep into the Northward, with a number of fmall iflands fcattered about. We run up towards the North Weft part of the harbour, and after paffing a fmall ifland near the North fhore covered with trees, we anchored about noon with the fmall bower in thirty-one fathoms water over a muddy bottom, and moored with the beft bower to the Eaftward, entirely land-locked; the rocks lying in the inner part of the paffage, juft fhut in with the fmall ifland already mentioned, and bearing South three or four miles diftant.

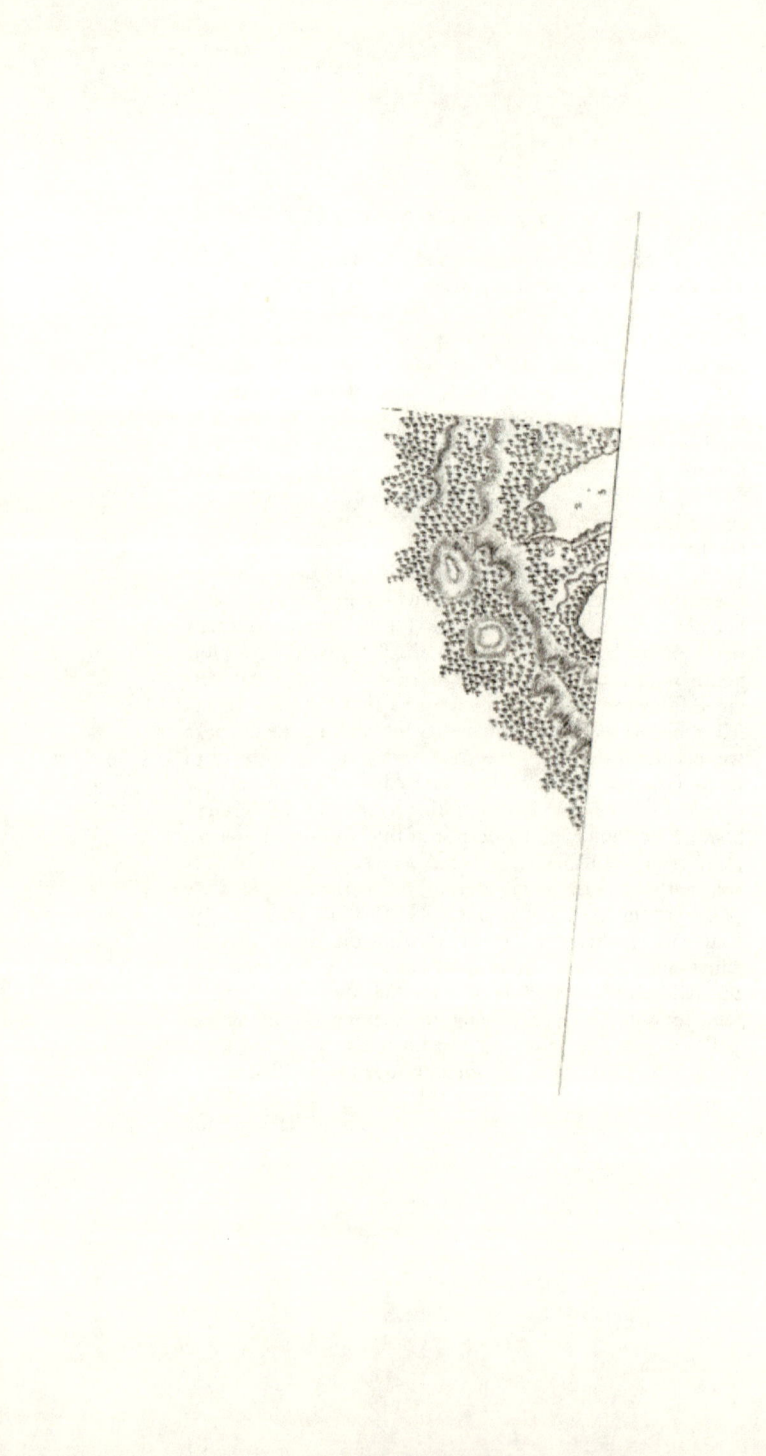

Soon after we were moored, the Indian boat, which had followed us in, came along-side, and the people gave us a song in the usual Indian manner. I found their language totally different from that spoken by the natives in Prince William's Sound; but they extended their arms as a token of peace, nearly the same as those people. Their boat was the body of a large pine tree, neatly excavated, and tapered away towards the ends, until they came to a point, and the fore-part somewhat higher than the after-part; indeed, the whole was finished in a neat and very exact manner. I made my new visiters a few trifling presents, and inquired for the sea-otter skin, by the name it bears at Prince William's Sound; but they not understanding me, I shewed them a sea-otter skin, and made signs for them to bring me some, which they seemed inclined to do. They were ornamented with beads of various sorts, and had some other articles, which induced me to think that the Queen Charlotte had touched near this neighbourhood on her way to King George's Sound, particularly a tin kettle and some towes, exactly the same sort as ours. They made me understand by signs, that the vessel from which they procured those articles had been in a port to the Eastward of Cape Edgecombe, and described her as having two masts. This little information led me to think that possibly the Queen Charlotte might still be somewhere about the Cape; and as I before had formed an intention of sending the long-boat on a trading expedition, I determined to fit her out with all possible dispatch, and accordingly I ordered a proper assortment of trade to be got ready, and six weeks provisions of all kinds that the ship afforded. The Indians, after receiving a few presents,

sents, left the ship and went on shore, where they remained a short time, and then returned with a few good dry sea-otter skins. I took notice that these Indians were not so particular in dressing or stretching their skins as the inhabitants of Prince William's Sound and Cook's River; neither were any of them marked with paint, as if intended for a market, which is the general practice in the Sound and River. I shewed a man in the boat, who appeared to be the chief, a marked skin, and he immediately knew (probably by the mark) what country it came from, and described the inhabitants as having their under lips slit, and wearing ornaments in them. He also described their canoes, with their method of paddling; and on being shewn a model of the Prince William's Sound canoes, he gave me to understand that it was the same sort with those he had been describing. I learned that they had an intercourse with the natives of Prince William's Sound; in the course of which, quarrels often arose, and battles frequently ensued; and one of the men shewed me a deep wound near his lip, which he received in an engagement with them. That these people have communication with each other, is pretty certain; and I am apt to think that this part of the coast, and farther on to the North West, is the country which the inhabitants of the Sound call Wallamute; as I saw two daggers in the possession of two men belonging to old Sheenawaa's tribe, which were made exactly in the same manner as those worn by the natives at this place, and they gave me to understand that they had bought them at Wallamute. The daggers which the people hereabouts use in battle are made to stab with either end, having three,

four,

NORTH WEST COAST OF AMERICA.

four, or five inches above the hand tapered to a sharp point; but the upper part of those used in the Sound and River is excurvated.

CHAP. XII.
1787.
August.
Monday 6.

TOWARDS evening our visiters prepared to go on shore; but, by way of securing my friendship, were desirous to leave one of their party on board for the night, and take one of our people with them on shore. As they seemed to betray neither a mischievous nor thieving disposition, I had no objection to the proposal, particularly as I thought the person who went might have an opportunity of observing what number of sea-otter skins they possessed, and might also form some idea of their manner of living. Accordingly, I permitted one of my people to go on shore, and that I might be under no apprehension about his safety, two of the Indians (instead of one, as was first proposed) remained on board, and behaved remarkably well: they were both young, very well made, good-looking men, and appeared to be brothers. The other man, who appeared to be the chief of this small tribe, went away with my man and the rest of his tribe at seven o'clock. I observed they went to the Northward, and turned round a point of land, beyond which most probably their habitation was situated.

ABOUT eight o'clock next morning, the Indians returned with our man, but they brought very little trade. The person who went on shore with the Indians informed me, that their residence was at the foot of a hill near a run of fresh water, which issued out of an adjacent valley. Their house (for they had only one) appeared to be only a temporary habitation, and he could observe very few articles of trade among

Tuesday 7.

among them. The way to this Indian hut was to the North East through a little sound, full of small islands covered with wood.

AT daylight the long-boat was hoisted out, and some hands were employed in fitting her for an expedition to the Eastward. The seine was hauled in several parts of the harbour; but we did not meet with any success.

THE long-boat being properly equipped, at five o'clock she set out on a trading expedition towards Cape Edgecombe, and among the islands to the South East of that Cape, with the same officers and men that went in her to Cook's River. I gave them particular orders to return in seventeen days; and in case they fell in with the Queen Charlotte, to desire captain Dixon to sail with them towards our present harbour, and remain in the offing until I should join him; as I proposed leaving the coast towards the latter end of the month, and proceeding for China, unless our success in trade warranted my staying on the coast to a later period.

THE adjacent country abounding with white cedar, I sent the carpenter on shore with a party on the 8th, to cut some for sawing into sheathing-boards: the remainder of the ship's company were busied in various necessary employments. In the course of the day we had a small canoe along-side, with one man and a woman; but they brought nothing to dispose of; and probably were out on a hunting party, as they had all the implements for that purpose: however, after staying a short time with us, they returned towards the Eastern point of the Sound,

from

from whence they came, in order to give their tribe intelligence of our being in the harbour. Towards evening our first visiters came along-side, and the two young men again requested to sleep on board, which I permitted, and Joseph Woodcock, one of my apprentices, slept on shore with their party. When the Indians left us, they did not go to their habitations round the North point, as on the preceding evening, but took up their abode in a small bay near the ship, where they erected a miserable hut, insufficient to keep out either wet or cold.

Not having any success in hauling the seine near the ship, I sent the whale-boat with the seine round a point to the North East; round that point they proceeded up an arm of the Sound, which took a direction about North and North by East, for four or five miles: this arm has two or three small woody islands lying at the entrance, and is navigable for a ship of any size, almost the whole way up; at the head of it they found a small fresh-water rivulet, where they caught a few good salmon and a great number of very indifferent ones, most of which were suffered to escape. The indifferent salmon appear to be a different kind from the others, and I am inclined to think were out of season. They had a most disagreeable colour, to appearance as if in a state of putrefaction; and the upper jaw had a number of large teeth projecting almost right out of it. Since our arrival I had frequently seen in the fresh-water creeks (in which places these kind of salmon get a considerable height) many of them dying, and great numbers on the banks quite dead; indeed there is reason to suppose that few of them survive the approach of winter, but the other sort keep in deep water, and about the

mouths

mouths of the creeks. Those caught by our people were fine large fish, of a very good colour, and without the teeth, or rather tusks, in the upper jaw, which so particularly distinguish the inferior sort.

The small canoe which visited us in the morning from the Eastward returned again at eight o'clock, in company with two large boats, containing about twenty-five men, women, and children. They entertained us near an hour with singing, and afterwards took their leave and went on shore to the little bay just mentioned, where some of them erected temporary huts to lodge in, but others contented themselves with such kind of shelter as some rocks which hung over the beach afforded. On leaving the ship they gave me to understand that they had some excellent skins to dispose of, and would bring them in the morning: accordingly, soon after daylight the Indians again came along-side, bringing five very good sea-otter skins (which were all they had of the kind) and a number of beautiful black skins, such as I had never seen before; but am apt to think they were a species of seal.

This tribe (as well as our former visiters) traded very fairly; and as they did not seem to be of a thieving disposition, I admitted a number of them on board. When dinner was brought into the cabin, my guests required very little invitation to partake, but began to eat very heartily; and so well did they relish our victuals, that the table was presently cleared, and there was occasion for another course, which was brought in, and they fell to with as keen an appetite as at first, till at length, being fairly satiated, they gave over, though with some reluctance.

tance. After looking at various parts of the ship, and receiving some little presents, they returned to the shore well satisfied with their entertainment.

IN the forenoon we got several fine logs of cedar on board, and two of the people were set to work in sawing them into sheathing-boards. The cooper was sent on shore to brew spruce-beer and essence of spruce for sea-store; there being an abundant quantity of excellent pine for that purpose not far from the ship: others of the ship's company were employed in wooding and watering, and I sent two of the boys with the canoe into the passage to try for fish; but they returned without meeting with any success.

ABOUT one o'clock an Indian boat came into the Sound with two men, a boy about twelve years old, and a young child in her; one of the men was a remarkably fine looking fellow, and appeared to be a person of great consequence. This small party came from the North Westward, and I am inclined to think their usual place of residence is near the spot where I have before mentioned there is a probability of finding a good harbour between this Sound and Cross Cape: they came through a passage that leads into another Sound to the North West of that we lay in, and which passage makes the land to the Westward of us an island.

I BOUGHT from our new visiters a few very good sea-otter skins, and a number of wild geese. The method they make use of in catching those birds is to chase and knock them down immediately after they have shed their large

large wing-feathers; at which time they are not able to fly.

These Indians had a number of beads about them of quite a different fort to any I ever faw; they had alfo a carpenter's adze made in a different manner to ours, with the letter B and three fleurs-de-lis on it. The chief informed me that he received thefe articles from two veffels which had been with them to the North Weft, and defcribed them as having three mafts: he gave me to underftand that they had a drum on board, and a number of great guns. Thefe circumftances inclined me to think that the veffels defcribed by this chief were the French men of war that were fitting out for difcovery at the time we left England.

Besides thefe fhips juft mentioned, I was informed by fome of the Indians, that another veffel had vifited the coaft a little way to the North Weft of our fituation, and from their defcription, I fhould rather fuppofe her to have been the Queen Charlotte than any other veffel; as they defcribed her having only two mafts, and her boat like our whale-boat. They alfo made me underftand very clearly, that an unfortunate accident happened to one of her boats, which was fifhing at an anchor in the mouth of the port where fhe lay: whilft fifhing, the wind came in frefh from the fea, which caufed a good deal of fea to fet in, and when endeavouring to weigh their anchor, the cable flipped on the broad-fide of the boat, which overfet her; and before any affiftance could be given them from the fhip five men were drowned. The boat to which this misfortune happened they gave me to underftand was

exactly

exactly the model of our whale-boat; and I was afraid that an accident of the kind might possibly have happened to the Queen Charlotte's boat.

AFTER this small party had finished trading, the chief requested leave to stay all night on board with the elder boy, which I granted, and sent Joseph Woodcock on shore with the other man and child.

THE chief from the North West, with his little party, took leave of me the next morning, and proceeded towards home; telling me at the same time that he would return in ten days with more sea-otter skins.

CHAP. XIII.

A new Party of Traders from the East.—Under a Necessity of exchanging Hostages.—Part of the Ship's Company go on Shore.—Meet with Indian Tea.—Visit the Natives at their own Residence.—Their Habitations and Manner of Living described.—An Account of the Spaniards having been on the Coast, and left the Small-pox.—The Long-boat returns from an Expedition to the Eastward.—Examine the Sound.—Another Visit from our North West Friends.—Ceremonies to be observed before commencing Trade.—Joseph Woodcock sent as an Hostage—Three Days in the Country.—An Account of the Natives—Their thieving Disposition—Nastiness, Ornaments, Dress, and Language.—Observations on the Advantages likely to accrue from a Settlement on the Coast.—Some Thoughts of an Expedition by Land.—Leave Portlock's Harbour.

CHAP. XIII.
1787.
August.
Saturday 11.

IN the morning of the 11th two large boats came into the Sound from the Eastward. This tribe were entire strangers to us, and consisted of twenty-five men, women, and children, from whom I bought a few very good seaotter skins, a cloak made of the small black skins I have before taken notice of, and several skins of the same sort. This new party of traders did not associate with the other Indians; but after their business was over, and their curiosity gratified by looking at the ship, they went on shore

shore in a bay not far from the ship, where the cooper was employed in brewing spruce-beer, and took up their lodging in a good convenient house, which he and his assistants had built to shelter themselves from the rain, and which was well covered with cedar bark. The seine was hauled in the afternoon, and we caught a good supply of excellent salmon.

Some of our old acquaintance came on board in the evening to sleep with us, and I sent a person on shore by way of hostage as usual. Indeed I found it absolutely necessary to conform to their custom in this particular; for more than once, when I had refused to exchange hostages with them, in consequence of the appearance of bad weather, they were immediately alarmed, and would not come near the ship on any account whatever; but on my permitting a person to go along with them on shore, they would receive him on entering their boat with a general shout of exultation, and seemed perfectly convinced that no harm was intended them. On these occasions, instead of one Indian staying on board in exchange for the person I sent on shore, more than half a dozen would offer themselves as volunteers, and I sometimes permitted three or four of them to sleep with us. The two young men who first visited us were generally of the party; and indeed one of them was almost constantly on board.

On the 12th I gave part of the ship's company leave to recreate themselves on shore; as a walk I knew would be highly serviceable to them; and the adjacent country was pleasant and agreeable, and afforded great quantities of blackberries and wild raspberries, quite ripe, and exceedingly

CHAP.
XIII.

1787.
August.
Sunday 12.

ceedingly good. This party, in the course of their ramble, fell in with a large spot of low swampy ground, situated at a small distance behind the brewery beach, on which grew a large quantity of the Indian tea. This discovery was a timely one; for by this time the greatest part of our other tea was expended, and our newly-discovered tea was a most excellent substitute. It grows on a low small shrub, not more than twelve inches from the ground; the leaf about half an inch long, and tapers gradually to a point; the under-part covered with a light downy substance.

In the forenoon I went in the whale-boat, accompanied by Mr. Wilbye and one of the young Indians, to visit their residence; he undertaking to direct the way. We rowed to the North West for about two miles, and then came to what had the appearance of a point of land from the ship, but we found it to be an island, situated at the entrance of an arm of the Sound, which trends away between North and North East. The Indian informed me that their place of abode was up that arm, therefore we proceeded on, and found it to run in a zigzag direction between North and North East, about five miles to the head of it from the island in the entrance, and near seven miles from the ship. This arm appears to be navigable for at least four miles up, for vessels of any size, and there are a number of small islands covered with trees scattered in various parts of it. We arrived at the Indian's habitation about noon, and found one small temporary house, and the ruins of two others which had been much larger, and appeared to have been made use of as winter habitations; the uprights or supporters were still remaining, and some boards that were intended for a floor. On the beach

was

A View in Guadalupe, Northern West coast of America.

was a large boat, and three of a smaller size; the large boat capable of holding thirty persons, and the others about ten people each. From this circumstance I expected to have seen a numerous tribe, and was quite surprised when I found that it consisted only of three men, three women, the same number of girls, two boys about twelve years old, and two infants. One of the women was very old, I should think not less than eighty. I observed the oldest of the men to be very much marked with the small-pox, as was a girl who appeared to be about fourteen years old. The old man endeavoured to describe the excessive torments he endured whilst he was afflicted with the disorder that had marked his face, and gave me to understand that it happened some years ago. This convinced me that they had had the small-pox among them at some distant period. He told me that the distemper carried off great numbers of the inhabitants, and that he himself had lost ten children by it; he had ten strokes tatooed on one of his arms, which I understood were marks for the number of children he had lost. I did not observe any of the children under ten or twelve years of age that were marked; therefore I have great reason to suppose that the disorder raged a little more than that number of years ago; and as the Spaniards were on this part of the coast in 1775, it is very probable that from them these poor wretches caught this fatal infection. They, it should seem, are a nation designed by Providence to be a scourge to every tribe of Indians they come near, by one means or other.

The Spaniards were among them in the height of summer, and probably they caught the infection about the month

CHAP.
XIII.
1787.
August.
Sunday 12.

month of August. To see their manner of living at that season of the year, one would think it a miracle that any of them escaped with their lives. I found men, women, and children, all huddled together in a close house near a large fire, and entirely surrounded with stinking fish. Round the house, for at least one hundred yards, and all along the banks of a little creek that ran down by this miserable dwelling, were strewed stinking fish; and in several places were beds of maggots a foot deep, and ten or twelve feet in circumference: nay, the place had really such a dreadfully offensive smell, that the young Indian himself, though habituated to such wretched scenes from his earliest infancy, having remained on board with us a few days, could not bear it, but intreated me very earnestly to leave the place, which I did, and returned to the boat, accompanied by him and the rest of our party. Possibly the small-pox only raged during the warm weather, and the infection was destroyed by the setting in of a severe winter; but the sufferings of the poor Indians, when the disorder was at its height, must have been inconceivable, and no doubt the country was nearly depopulated; for to this day it remains very thinly inhabited.

A NUMBER of the Indians who visited us from the Eastward were marked with the small-pox, and one man who had lost an eye gave me to understand that he lost it by that disorder; but none of the natives from the Westward had the least traces of it. I cannot account for this circumstance any other way than by supposing that the vessel from which these unfortunate people caught the infection, was in a harbour somewhere about Cape Edgecombe; and
perhaps

perhaps none of the natives further to the Westward than this Sound had an opportunity of having any intercourse with her, and by that means happily escaped the disorder. After I left this miserable habitation, the seine was hauled, and we caught a good supply of fine salmon. In the evening, our late visiter from the Northward returned and slept on board, together with the rest of his party, and we hauled his boat up along-side. He informed me that the weather was so bad that he could not possibly get home; however, he set off again at day-light the next morning to make another trial. In the forenoon part of the ship's company had leave given them to go on shore, and though rainy weather came on, yet they were so intent on picking Indian tea, and berries of various kinds, that few of them returned on board before the approach of evening. In the course of the day, our neighbours in the Sound brought us a few sea-otter skins, and some others of various kinds; and a few of the natives that had been out on a hunting party returned with three very fine sea-otter skins just taken from the animal.

On the 14th part of the ship's company were employed in wooding and watering, others hauled the seine, and caught a supply of good salmon, and the sawyers were busied in sawing cedar into sheathing-boards.

At nine o'clock in the morning of the 15th the long-boat returned from her expedition to the Eastward; she had been just to the Eastward of Cape Edgecombe, where they met with some inhabitants, and purchased about twenty pretty good sea-otter skins. Between the harbour we lay in and the Cape, they fell in with a strait about a league

league wide at the entrance, and running in about East, or East South East, with bold shores and good anchorage. Soon after getting in (the Southern and Eastern point of the strait in 57° 30′ latitude, and the Northern and Western point in 57° 36′ latitude), they stood up between South and South by East, near four leagues, the strait for that distance appearing near three leagues across, with several small islands scattered about it. From the Southern point there were several appearances of fine openings branching out in various directions; however, they did not examine any of them, but kept along under the Southern shore, as the most likely place for leading out near Cape Edgecombe. After getting up this passage about four leagues, they found it not more than half a league across, with good anchorage all the way up; and after carrying that width two leagues higher, it became very narrow and shoal, one part in particular so shoal, that it became dry at low-water for near two miles. In this narrow part they struck a rock, which shivered one of the planks in the loof of the bow, and caused the boat to make a good deal of water. This accident might have been attended with serious consequences; however, they hauled the boat on shore, and nailed a piece of sheet-lead over the damaged part, which effectually stopped the leak. After passing the narrow part, which they did by taking a proper time of tide, they found the passage to grow wider (still trending away to the North East); the depth of water increased gradually, and nearly as salt as sea-water. This circumstance gave them great hopes that the passage they were in had a communication with the sea to the South East, and consequently that they should get to the South Eastward of the Cape, by a very safe and easy navigation. In this opinion

opinion they were soon confirmed by coming into a large Sound, where they saw a great number of whales. They also had a sight of Mount Edgecombe, and some islands lying to the South East of Cape Edgecombe. In the course of their cruise thus far they had landed several times in a fine level pleasant country, where they could perceive the traces of inhabitants having been there recently, but what is rather extraordinary, they saw neither huts nor Indians.

ON getting round the North point of this passage, through which they had come thus far, they saw an opening that appeared to run about a league up in a North direction, and then branched out various ways. In the entrance of the main opening were several small islands (I think it very probable that the North West arm of this opening runs into the first large sound that we entered). They still saw no inhabitants, therefore continued to steer on to the South East for a passage about a mile and a half across, made by the Northern part of an island just under Mount Edgecombe (which was distinguished by the name of Pitt's Island), and the opposite point of land which we suppose to be the main. Through this passage they had a view of the sea, and the islands lying to the South East of Cape Edgecombe.

AFTER getting through the passage, they steered among a cluster of islands lying near the shore to the Northward of Cape Edgecombe, and anchored to the Northward of the largest. This island bore North from the Cape about three leagues distant, and several other islands lay to the South East of this cluster, six leagues distant.

CHAP.
XIII.

1787.
August.
Wednes. 15.

They remained here some time without seeing any inhabitants; and as the wind had set in from the South East, which prevented them from proceeding any further in that direction, they were preparing to return back again, when a canoe made its appearance with six people in her, from whom they procured some sea-otter skins, and soon afterwards they were visited by a few other canoes; but the people were not by any means so numerous as might naturally have been expected in so fine a situation. Their visiters gave them to understand, that a vessel with two masts had lately anchored near the place where the boat then lay; and from the articles of trade which the natives possessed, I had scarcely a doubt but this vessel was the Queen Charlotte. The different articles our people saw were hawks bells, tin kettles, buckles, and rings, all of them the same pattern with our own; they had also a Sandwich Island calabash, and a number of towes. The boat lay in this situation two days, during which time the people were on shore, but they did not see any appearance of wood having been recently cut down, or any other sign of a ship's crew having lately been on shore; so that I should suppose if the Queen Charlotte had anchored near this situation, it was in her passage to King George's Sound; and having wooded and watered before she left Prince William's Sound, they would have no occasion to carry on any operations of that sort at this place. Messrs. Hill and Hayward observed many of those people to be marked with the small-pox, and made the same observations there respecting that disorder that I had done in this harbour, which was, that none under ten or twelve years of age bore any marks of the disorder.

A SHORT

A SHORT time before they intended sailing to return to the ship, and while the people were busy in putting the boat to rights on deck, the Indians went in two boats, and took an opportunity of cutting their cable. The anchor lay in twenty-eight fathoms water without a buoy, so that there was no chance of recovering it. After doing this piece of mischief, the Indians made for the shore with all the haste imaginable, and landed at a little distance from the long-boat. Our people pursued them, and being a good deal exasperated at their daring and insolent behaviour, they landed with the boat, and entirely destroyed both the Indian boats. The natives fled with precipitation into the woods, which put a stop to our people's pursuit; and I believe they did them no further injury. I was sorry that the boat's crew should have been under the necessity of taking this step; but undoubtedly this crime committed by the Indians was of so very mischievous a nature, that it became necessary to punish them in some measure for it; and it is very probable that destroying their boats (which it must cost them much time and trouble to rebuild) would make a greater impression than even taking away numbers of their lives. After filling their water, and getting a little wood on board, the long-boat returned to the ship by the same passage that they went through, and during the whole passage did not see a single canoe.

THE night before they got on board, James Blake, one of the boat's crew, fell overboard: the boat was going very fast through the water when this accident happened, and had got a considerable way to leeward before they brought her to. Blake could swim but very indifferently, but fortunately was saved by John M'Coy (another of the boat's boat's crew) swimming to him with an oar, which supported him until he was pulled into the boat, and it was near an hour before they got him on board, owing to a fresh breeze, and his being directly to windward.

Thursday 16.   ON the 16th the ship's company were employed in wooding and watering, and getting the ship ready for sea. In the forenoon two Indian boats came along-side, from whom I bought a few tolerably good sea-otter skins. In the afternoon we completed our water, and the long-boat's crew had leave given them to go on shore.

Friday 17.   THE weather during the whole of the 17th was squally and unsettled, the wind blowing very fresh from the Eastward, which prevented any business from going forward. In the course of the day we were visited by one canoe, which brought a few indifferent sea-otter skins.

Saturday 18.   AT eight o'clock in the morning of the 18th I went in the whale-boat to the South point of the entrance into the Sound to see how the wind prevailed out at sea. I landed on a part of the point that was sheltered from the surf by some rocks, from which situation I had a good view of the sea and the shores to the North West and South East of this entrance. I found the wind in the entrance and at sea to be about South West by South, blowing strong and in squalls, which sent in on the rocks and shores a tremendous surf. After taking some bearings from this point, I embarked with an intention of examining the Eastern part of the Sound. About noon we rowed under the lee of a small island, and took shelter under some trees that hung over the water, where we refreshed ourselves

with

with some smoked salmon. From this we proceeded on to the Eastward, under the Southern shore of the Sound, and after rowing about two leagues, came to another passage leading out to sea in the direction of South West. This passage is about three quarters of a mile across, with bold rocky shores, against which the surf broke with great fury; and the wind being directly in, a heavy sea set up the passage. I found in the mid channel between twenty and thirty fathoms water over a bottom of hard sand, and the passage from the inner to the outer points appeared to be about two miles long. The wind blowing fresh, and there being a very heavy sea, I was prevented from going through it as I at first intended, and got only two thirds of the way: from which situation I could see the sea break on some rocks that run out a little way from the outer point; but between them the passage appeared good and clear. This passage I guess to be about two leagues to the South East of the one we came in at with the ship. Finding it impossible to proceed further out, we bore up, set our sails, and run in again to the Sound. I proceeded on, and found the South shore to run nearly East for one mile and a half, when a small river emptied itself into the Sound. The shore then took a North North East direction for about two miles more, in which situation the land took a quick turn round, and there appeared a passage near half a mile across, navigable, and trending away directly to the Eastward. I did not follow this passage, as the boat's crew were quite wet, and a good deal fatigued with pulling; but landed in a small bay to the Northward of it, where we took some refreshment.

IN

CHAP.
XIII.

1787.
August.
Saturday 18.

In this bay, and not more than ten yards from the beach, there was a kind of monument erected probably to the memory of some distinguished chief. This edifice was composed of four posts, each about twenty feet long, stuck in the ground six feet distant from each other, and in a quadrangular form. About twelve or fifteen feet from the ground there was a rough boarded floor, and two of the sides were boarded four feet higher up, the other sides were left open. In the middle of this floor an Indian chest was deposited, which most likely contained the remains of some person of consequence; and on that side of the edifice to the Westward, and which pointed up the Sound, there was painted the resemblance of a human face. This wooden edifice, from its tottering condition, had certainly been erected a considerable length of time; and as it began to decay, I could perceive that the Indians had fixed supporters to the original uprights, and the painting appeared to have been frequently touched over. As none of the inhabitants were near us, I was desirous to know what the chest contained; but on one of the boat's crew attempting to get up in order to examine it, the whole fabric had like to have given way, on which I ordered him to desist, as I was not willing to destroy a building that probably was looked upon by the Indians as sacred, and which they apparently took very great pains to preserve.

Some of the inhabitants had lately visited this bay, as we saw a place where a fire had lately been made, and which appeared not to have been long put out. From this place Joseph Woodcock took a view of the land as
given

given in the annexed plate. We now steered nearly West for the ship, and as we rowed along, I found the North shore of the Sound to run in a North West direction for about a mile and a half; it then took a quick turn in to the Northward, and formed a fine harbour, with a few small islands well covered with trees scattered about the entrance, and the harbour seemed to run in for three or four miles. About six o'clock in the afternoon I got on board, and understood from Mr. Hill (to whose direction I left the trading business), that some of the natives had been on board, from whom he purchased a few pieces of sea-otter and some good ermine skins.

On the 19th we had a fresh gale from the South South West, with violent squalls and heavy rains. Towards evening the wind shifted to the Eastward, and grew moderate; but the weather still continuing rainy, none of the natives came near us. Neither the wind nor weather appearing settled enough to get out to sea with, I kept the cooper on shore brewing spruce essence for sea store; the rest of the people were employed in other necessary works.

In the forenoon of the 20th our late visiter from the North West made his appearance in a large boat; his party consisted of twenty men and women, besides ten or twelve boys and girls, and a few infants.

As this chief, when he last took leave of me, had promised to return with a good cargo of sea-otter skins, I expected a brisk trade to commence every moment, and prepared myself accordingly; but I presently found that at this time my old acquaintance was not for transacting his business in a hurry; and perhaps he thought that on his last visit we were not impressed with a sufficient idea of his importance; for now he came along-side with his party in great pomp and solemnity, all of them singing; and in addition to the vocal concert, they entertained us with instrumental music, which consisted of a large old chest, beaten with the hands, by way of a drum, and two rattles. The rattles were two feet long, and about two inches round, made of hollow pieces of wood neatly joined together, and a number of small stones being put in, they were closed at both ends. The chief held one of these rattles in his hand, which he frequently shook with an air of meaning intelligence, and the rest of his tribe seemed to follow his directions, in singing in the most exact manner.

His dress was an old coat, made of cloth which formerly had been scarlet, with some old gold or silver fringe about the shoulders; but that ornament being esteemed of little value, the cloak was decorated down each side with buttons, and small lead pipes, each about an inch long. His hair, after being well rubbed with oil, was entirely filled with down taken from gulls, and which is always worn by the Indian chiefs when in full dress. In this grotesque figure he displayed as much importance as any Spanish don could possibly have done. Besides the curious dress which the chief himself wore, he had another in the boat not less remarkable than his own, and ornamented nearly in the same manner, which was worn during the time of their singing by a woman whom I took for his wife.

AFTER

AFTER this long ceremony was over, the chief made me a present of half a sea-otter skin, but did not produce any thing for sale; giving me to understand at the same time that he must go on shore before any traffic could be carried on. After staying there some time (which I apprehend was taken up in assorting their furs) he returned with his party; and now I expected our trade to begin in good earnest; but in this I was again disappointed; for the singing again commenced, and by way of varying our amusement, the chief appeared in different characters during the time his people were singing; and always changed his dress when he varied his character; in doing of which some of his companions held up a large mat, by way of scene, to prevent us from seeing what was going on behind the curtain. At one time he appeared in the character of a warrior, and seemed to have all the savage ferocity of the Indian conqueror about him. He shewed us the manner in which they attacked their enemies, their method of fighting, and their behaviour to the vanquished enemy. He next assumed the character of a woman, and to make his imitation more complete, he wore a mask, which represented a woman's face with their usual ornaments; and indeed it so exactly resembled a woman's face, that I am pretty certain it was beyond the reach of Indian art, and must certainly have been left by the Spaniards in their last visit to this part of the coast.

AFTER this entertainment was over (with which it was necessary for us to appear pleased), the chief and some of his people came on board, and trade at last commenced between us. In the course of the day I bought twenty-five pieces of tolerably good sea-otter, equal to about ten whole

whole skins; but it should seem as if the chief wanted me to pay for the entertainment he had given us, as well as his furs; for I could not purchase a good skin for less than a light-horseman's cap, two yards of inferior broad-cloth, a pair of buckles, two handfuls of small beads, and two fish-hooks. The articles we bartered with were light-horsemen's caps, striped woollen blankets, towes, eighteen or twenty inches long, buckles, buttons, and beads of all sorts, but particularly small transparent ones, either green, blue, or yellow. However, I could not procure even a piece of a skin with any of the latter articles; they only were given by way of concluding a bargain, as were tin kettles, brass pans, and pewter basons; but hatchets, adzes, and howels, they would scarcely take for any thing whatever.

My visiter was equally tedious in trading as he had been in his entertainment; so that I could not get every thing he had to dispose of during the whole day, and about eight o'clock in the evening, our traffic for the day being over, he sent his boat on shore, and remained on board with one of his people for the night; and as he required an hostage, I sent Joseph Woodcock on shore with his party.

Woodcock having frequently been on shore as an hostage, was well known to the natives, and they seemed very fond of his company. On one of these occasions he remained among the Indians for three days; during which time he had a good opportunity of seeing their customs and mode of living; and his account perfectly agreed with my own observations when on shore. Their filth and nastiness

nastiness were beyond conception; their food, which consisted chiefly of fish, was mixed up with stinking oil, and other ingredients equally disagreeable, and the remains of every meal were thrown into a corner of their hut, upon a heap of the same kind that was in a state of putrefaction, which, together with large quantities of fat and stinking oil, caused a very loathsome and offensive smell; and what rendered it still worse, the same apartment served them both to eat and sleep in.

This uncomfortable situation frequently induced Woodcock to take a ramble into the woods; but he was always very narrowly watched by some of his new companions, who seemed to apprehend that he was endeavouring to make his escape from them. Once in particular, having wandered a considerable distance from the Indians place of residence, he began to amuse himself with whistling part of an old song, not expecting, if the natives heard him, that it could possibly be a matter of offence; but in this he was mistaken, for several of them immediately ran up to him, and insisted on his giving over: at first he did not comprehend their meaning, and went on with his tune; however, one of them soon put a stop to it by laying his hand on Woodcock's mouth; being apprehensive that he meant the whistling as a signal for some of his companions to come for him. Except their watching him so closely, they treated him with great kindness; and at their meals always gave him what they considered as choice dainties, mixing his fish with plenty of stinking oil, which in their opinion gave it an additional and most agreeable relish; and he found it no easy matter to persuade them to let him eat his fish without sauce.

These

THESE poor wretches, by living in so filthy a manner, were intirely covered with vermin; but this they seemed to consider as no kind of inconvenience; for at any time when the lice grew troublesome they picked and ate them with the greatest relish and composure: sometimes indeed, when they were greatly pestered, and had not an opportunity of ridding themselves of their guests in that manner, they would turn their jackets, and wear the inside outwards, by way of giving them a few hours respite.

POOR Woodcock soon became as much incumbered with vermin as his companions, but use had not as yet reconciled him to such troublesome guests, and he felt his situation extremely disagreeable. The Indians endeavoured to persuade him to dispose of them in the manner they did; but this was so totally repugnant to his feelings, that they soon perceived his dislike to their proposal. At length he persuaded one of the women to rid him of the vermin, and she (probably considering them as a peculiar dainty) accepted the office with pleasure, and entirely cleared him from every thing of the kind.

AT daylight in the morning of the 21st, I sent Mr. Hayward in the yaul out to the entrance of the Sound, to see what wind prevailed there and in the offing: he returned about eight o'clock, and informed me that the wind was at South West by West in the offing, which threw a heavy sea into the passage. As there was no prospect of our getting to sea with the wind in that quarter, I kept the people to work in brewing, sawing plank, and other necessary employments.

ABOUT seven in the morning the Indian chief with his party returned on board, and our trade again commenced; but I found him equally tedious in the disposal of his furs as on the preceding day. Towards noon I sent Mr. Hayward to the South point of the entrance into the Sound, to get a meridian altitude. He landed on the South point, and got one which gave the latitude of that point 57° 44′ North; the latitude of the ship's place in the harbour was 57° 46′.

DURING the day I bought of my visiters about the same quantity of furs as I had done the day before, and nearly at the same prices. About seven o'clock, our trading was finished; and as I knew the neighbourhood was cleared of all the furs, I determined to quit the Sound the first opportunity; and this evening the ship was put in a state fit for sea.

I FOUND this party from the North West much more addicted to thieving than any of our former visiters in the Sound were; and it is really astonishing to see with what patience a thief will wait when once he has fixed his eye on the thing he means to steal, and with what secrecy and dexterity they will convey their booty away. One fellow in particular took a liking to my drinking-mug, which was a black-jack; and he had got it under his frock, which are made in the same manner as at Prince William's Sound; but very unfortunately for the poor fellow, it happened to be about half full of beer, a part of which splashing over, discovered the thief and his intentions. Notwithstanding I kept two people constantly in my cabin to watch the by-standers, whilst I traded with

any

any of them, one fellow found an opportunity to get a cutlafs under his frock, and was not difcovered till he was going down the fide of the fhip: I immediately took it from him, and gave him a very fevere chaftifement with the flat fide of it, and afterwards drove him out of the fhip; yet notwithftanding all our vigilance and attention, another of them found means to fteal out of a box in my cabin four pair of worfted ftockings and fome other things, with which he found means to get out of the fhip undifcovered. Our vifiters from the Eaft were much eafier to deal with, and much honefter. It appears to me that the inhabitants of this Sound, and thofe farther to the Eaftward, ftand much in awe of them; for they frequently importuned me very earneftly to drive them away; being extremely uneafy all the time they were on board. The Weftern people appear to me to be much more warlike and favage than any of their neighbours; their language varies a little from the others; but their fongs and mufic are entirely different; their boats, weapons for war, and hunting implements, are much the fame. They appear to be very indolent and dirty, which naturally expofes them to all manner of vermin, and which is difpofed of in the manner already mentioned. They have not the ufe of bladderfkin frocks for their drefs, but make dreffes of the fkins of land and fea animals, made up in the fame manner as the inhabitants of Cook's River and Prince William's Sound. The men do not ufe the method of flitting their under-lips; but wear their ornaments of beads, fhells, &c. at their ears, through which they have fmall holes bored: they likewife bore a fmall hole through the griftle of the nofe, through which they will fometimes put a needle or nail that they purchafe in trade, or may have given them as a present; but the women disfigure themselves in a most extraordinary manner, by making an incision in the under-lip; in which part they wear a piece of wood made in an oval form a little hollow on each side, and about the thickness of a quarter of an inch; the outer part of the rim is hollowed all round: this curious piece of wood is thrust into the hole, and is secured there by the rim of the lip going round it, fixed in the hollow which is made round the wood. They appear to be worn large or small in proportion to the age of the women, or perhaps to the number of the children they have bore; those that I took to be between thirty and forty years of age wore them about the size of a small saucer, and the older larger in proportion; one old woman, I remarked particularly, having one as large as a large saucer. The weight of this trencher or ornament weighs the lip down so as to cover the whole of the chin, leaving all the lower teeth and gum quite naked and exposed, which gives them a very disagreeable appearance. When they eat, it is customary for them to take more in the mouth at a time than they can possibly swallow; when they have chewed it, the lip-piece serves them as a trencher to put it out of their mouths on, and then they take it occasionally. It seems a general practice among the females to wear the wooden ornament in their under-lip; the children have them bored at about two years of age, when a piece of copper-wire is put through the hole; this they wear till the age of about thirteen or fourteen years, when it is taken out, and the wooden ornament introduced; its first size is about the width of a button. They likewise have their ears bored, where they wear their ornaments of beads and other things. Their apparel is the same kind as wore by the men; both men and

and women being very fond of long hair, which is considered as a great ornament. At the death of a friend the hair is cut off pretty short, which seems to be the general mourning of all Indian tribes. The women wear the hair either clubbed behind or tied up in a bunch on the crown of the head; the men wear theirs either loose or tied at the crown. The method of dressing the hair with birds-down is only practised by the men. The women in general are hair-dressers for their husbands, which office they seem to perform with a great deal of dexterity and good-nature.

POLYGAMY I think is not practised here, as I never observed any one of them to have more than one woman whom he seemed to consider as his wife, to whom they pay very strict attention and treat with a great deal of affection and tenderness: you cannot affront them more than by attempting to make advances to their wives. They likewise are very fond of, and remarkably affectionate to, their children. The women are the keepers of their treasures or riches, which they generally have in a box or basket, and always take the lead in fashions, which they shew by the placing of their ornaments, or fixing such a curiosity to be the favourite of the day. It is not the custom with those people, as with the South Sea islanders, for the men and women to eat separately, nor are the women confined to eat meats of a particular description; but for men, women, and children, to sit down indiscriminately at their meals, which chiefly consist of fish of different kinds; such as salmon, which they have in the greatest abundance, mussels, and various other shell-fish, sea-otters, seals, and porpoises; the blubber of the porpoise

they

they are remarkably fond of, and indeed the flesh of any animal that comes in their way. I could never observe that they had any quantity of dried salmon provided for a winter's stock; so what they live on at that severe part of the season I am at a loss to find out, unless they catch land-animals in the neighbourhood of their winter quarters. I am greatly inclined to believe the principal part of their provision at that season is confined to the inner fine bark of the pine-tree. Any tin kettles they get from us they make use of to drink out of. They boil their victuals in wooden vessels, by constantly putting red-hot stones into the water.

Their persons are in general much about the size of Europeans. The men have a very fierce and savage aspect, which, with their dress, gives them much the appearance of warriors; their weapons of war are daggers and long pointed spears; they are very easily irritated, and would make very little scruple to kill you when they think themselves injured. More than once I had nearly experienced that fate, from some trifling disagreements in trade; but being pretty well acquainted with their tempers, I guarded as much against them as possible; and on all occasions took care to be well provided for them in case of an attempt, by keeping my pistols ready-charged before me.

Their women, were it not for the filth and nastiness which continually cover them, would be by no means disagreeable; their features in general are pleasing, and their carriage modest. They frequently gave us opportunities to observe their wish to please, particularly when the wooding

wooding party were on shore; at these times they would place themselves in a line, and begin singing and making motions all the time the men were at work; and if their drollery happened to please the people, and make them laugh, they all immediately joined in a loud burst of laughter; and when the Indians were not there, they would assist the people in getting wood and taking it to the boats. They were particularly useful in taking the wood from the beach through the surf to the boat, as they were not encumbered with shoes and stockings; and it saved the men from wetting themselves. But if at any time the Indians came to them at the time when they were thus making themselves useful, they would instantly drive them all away with very little ceremony. Upon such occasions as these, I used to give the people small bright buttons to make them presents, with which their pride and ambition were highly gratified. One time, not having an opportunity of sending the boat on shore at the usual hour, to fetch the wooding-party on board, the women gave them an invitation to their habitations, which was about three hundred yards from the place where they were at work; and upon this occasion treated them (or offered to do it) with every thing their wretched habitations afforded, and behaved very kindly to them. Their huts are made of a few boards, which they take away with them when they go to their winter quarters. It is very surprising to see how well they will shape their boards with the shocking tools they employ; some of them being full ten feet long, two feet and a half broad, and not more than an inch thick.

THE

NORTH WEST COAST OF AMERICA.

The country is very mountainous, and covered with the pine-tree, a great number of which grow to an amazing fize.

Their language is harfh and unpleafant to the ear: a fpecimen of which I have here given, fpelled as near the manner of their pronunciation as I could give it:

Hat-feene	give or hand me.
Youtes	fea-otter.
Hatata	bring.
Caw-wout	beads.
Hoetaa	iron.
Caa-congo	blanket.
Een	water.
Youtes-Gaatea	young fea otter.
A-gua-goone	bed.
Cow-a-ka-na	beftoge or friendfhip.
Onowfka	a box.
La-la	the tongue.
Claake	berries like a wild rafpberry.
Sulk	marmot or ermine fkin.
Clacke	one.
Taike	two.
Nufk	three.
Ta-koon	four.
Kacheene	five.
Clay-too-fhoe	fix.
Tack-a-too-fhoe	feven.
Nufk-a-too-fhoe	eight.
Coo-fhuck	nine.
Cheene-caught	ten.
Cheene-caught ca-ka-cheene	fifteen.

They have a great number of curiofities amongft them, many of which fhew them to be a people of great ingenuity and contrivance. They make a curious bafket of twigs, in which they frequently boil their victuals, by putting

CHAP.
XIII.

1787.
August.
Tuesday 21.

ting red-hot stones into them. They have tolerable ideas of carving, and indeed almost every utensil they make use of has some kind of rude carving, representing one animal or other. Whilst Woodcock was with them, one of the women gave him a comb, which is made in such a manner as to represent an eagle; an engraving of both sides of which I have given in the annexed plate. But as curiosities were not the articles we were in pursuit of, I gave strict charge to my people not to purchase any thing, being apprehensive that if I allowed a traffic of that nature, the natives would not have been induced to have brought us any skins for sale, as they are very useful, and necessary for their clothing, whilst the others are only the amusements of their leisure hours, and many of them made by their women.

I shall now take leave of my Indian traders, and for the last time of the American coast. The inestimable value of their furs will ever make it a desirable trade, and whenever it is established upon a proper foundation, and a settlement made, will become a very valuable and lucrative branch of commerce. It would be an easy matter for either Government or our East India Company to make a settlement of this kind; and the thinness of the inhabitants will make it a matter of easy practicability; and as the Company are under the necessity of paying the Chinese in cash for their teas, I look upon it a settlement on this coast might be affected at a very inconsiderable expence, which would more than pay them for every article that is brought from China. Another convenience likely to accrue, is from a well-known enterprising character having, if he meets with proper encouragement from the country, intentions

Knife from Sandwich Islands.
N.º 1

Comb from the Coast of America.

Back
N.º 2

A Lance from Sandwich Islands
N.º 3

Front
N.º 2

Another Knife from Sandwich Islands.
N.º 4

tentions of going over land to thefe parts; by this means will be finally determined the long fought North Weft paffage, with fome account of the interior parts of the country, to which we are yet entire ftrangers. That fuch an event may take place, muft be the wifh of every lover of his country; and though the enterprife is fraught with every danger that idea can fuggeft, yet what is it that Britifh valour dares not attempt?

CHAP. XIII.
1787.
Auguft.
Tuefday 21.

ON the 22d at daylight I fent Mr. Hayward out to fee what wind prevailed in the paffage; in the meantime unmoored. About five o'clock Mr. Hayward returned; he found the wind light and variable, with fome fwell in the paffage. At feven o'clock a breeze fprung up about Weft North Weft, with which we weighed, and came to fail, and proceeded towards the entering of the Sound, which as we approached, we found the wind very light and variable, from Weft to Weft South Weft, with a confiderable fwell. Heaving into the paffage about ten, the wind very faint, and almoft directly in, got the whale-boat and yaul a-head to tow the fhip. At eleven very near calm, making very little progrefs; but foon after a fteady moderate breeze fprung up from the Weft, and juft about this time the tide of ebb making, and the two boats a-head, we got out apace, the Indians in their boats following us at fome diftance, and on our getting out of the paffage, they returned and went into the Sound.

Wednef. 22.

ON the 23d about one o'clock we cleared the rocks which lie off the South point of the harbour, and ftood away South, the wind at Weft South Weft. On the 24th a breeze at South Eaft by South, with thick rainy weather, with which we ftood to the South Weft by South,

Thurfday 23.
Friday 24.

the

the land in sight; no observation. The 25th light winds and variable, with thick drizzling rain, steering South West half South. On the 26th a fresh breeze and foggy, steering South South East, the wind at South West. The 27th a fresh gale from West North West, and cloudy, steering South South East. On the 28th a fresh gale from North West, with fog at times. Passed some drift wood, a seal, and several pieces of sea-leek: our latitude 50° 6′ North.

CHAP. XIV.

Passage from the Coast to the Sandwich Islands.—Transactions there.—Letters received from Captain Dixon and Mr. Ross.—Some Particulars received from Taa-boo-a-raane respecting the Death of Captain Cook.—Description of the White Tern.—Cruelty of the Chiefs to their Inferiors.—Observations on a Trade to Botany Bay from these Islands.—Our final Departure from them.—Passage to China.—Arrival there.

WEDNESDAY 29th August 1787, to Sunday 16th September: nothing in the course of this time occurred which claims particular notice; but being now in longitude 136° 24′, there is a small island said to have been discovered by some Spanish navigator, and laid down, the North part of it, in latitude 26° 50′ North, and longitude of the West part of it 135° 0′ West; and at two judging myself about five leagues to the Northward of that latitude, and in the longitude of 136° 20′ West, I thought it not prudent to run nearer its latitude until daylight; therefore at two in the morning tacked and stood to the West North West until half past three, when I stood again to the Southward. At four, a moderate breeze and cloudy weather, the wind at South West, standing to the South South East, and at daylight there was no appearance of land.

CHAP.
XIV.

1787.
September.
Monday 17.

On the 17th, at two in the morning, standing to the South by East, saw a large flight of flying fish, the first during the passage. At 2ʰ 30ᵐ I got two sets of distances of the sun and moon, which gave the longitude at that time 136° 8′ 15″ West. I judge these sights to be the most accurate I had taken, and therefore shall suppose the longitude deduced from them to be the true longitude of the ship. At

Tuesday 18.
Thursday 27.

five in the morning saw a few tropic birds, and some bottle-nosed porpoises. From this time to the 27th nothing happened to engage attention; and then, at half past eight we saw the high land of Owhyhee, bearing West South West half West, distant fifteen or twenty leagues; and

Friday 28.

on the 28th at five in the morning, at which time it was daylight, we found ourselves about two leagues and a half from the land: at which time we bore up, and made sail towards the shore. At half past five we were about six miles from the shore, when a multitude of canoes came off with the different productions of the island; such as hogs, fowls, bread-fruit, taro, plantains, and a few cocoa-nuts. Of the other articles they brought us an abundant supply; and although there was a heavy swell, and the day unsettled, some of them made three or four trips to shore before the evening came on for other cargoes, as they disposed of their first. We remained within four or five miles of the shore, from seven in the morning until about seven in the evening, during which time I suppose we bought of hogs and pigs near two hundred; fowls about six dozen; about three tons of bread-kind; some bass rope and fishing-lines, enough, when laid up, to make about 150 fathom of two-inch rope, the best lines that can be made; and we found very little trouble in trading with them, and bought provisions very cheap. They brought

very

very little salt; and I think very little of that article can be procured about the island, except on the West side, where it may be bought in great abundance. The whole day about fourteen hands were employed in killing and salting for sea store, and by the evening we had salted about two tierces. A number of the large hogs we skinned, finding their skins of great use, for the purpose of leathering the foot of our sails. To preserve the skins we let them lie twenty-four hours in pickle, and then hung them up to dry. After they had been two or three days hanging out, we made them up in bundles, and, by airing them now and then, found they would keep any length of time. At noon, squally unsettled weather, with some rain, the wind about East North East; the Northernmost parts of the island in sight West by North; the East part of the island covered with squalls; our distance from the nearest part of the island about five miles. I could not learn from these people of any ship having been lately at this island.

SATURDAY, September 29th, 1787, light variable winds, with frequent showers of rain, a very heavy swell from the North East rolling in on shore, which made the surf very furious on the rocks. At four in the morning, although only four or five miles from the shore, the weather was so thick, that we could not see it: at half past five in the morning it cleared up a little, when the Northernmost part of the land in sight bore West by North half North, eight or ten leagues distant, and the East point bore South by East. At six in the evening a light breeze at East, with open cloudy weather. Two canoes remained with us until this time, when they went for the shore. At eight

CHAP. XIV.
1787.
September.
Saturday 29.

in the evening, judging myself about three leagues from the land, at which distance I wished to keep during the night, we hauled up our courses, and under our top-sails stood to the North by East about a knot and a half per hour, until midnight; then wore ship, and stood to the South East by South a knot and a half per hour, until two in the morning; then wore again, and stood to the North North East, until four in the morning, at which time we wore and stood to the South East until daylight, which was about half an hour past four. We then found ourselves about three leagues from the land, bore up, and run in about South West, until about half past seven. We were then about five miles from the shore, the canoes coming off in numbers, and at eight a brisk trade began for provisions and other necessaries; hauled off to the North by East, with a light breeze from the East by North. A heavy swell rolling in, made it necessary to keep the ship under sail; and with all the sail we could make, we could scarce hold our own against it.

At noon a moderate breeze from the Eastward, with clear weather, the East point of Owhyhee bore South East by South about twelve leagues, and the Northermost part of the island in sight West by North about nine or ten leagues, our distance from the nearest shore about four or five miles: no observation to be depended on. During the day caught several very large sharks. It is really astonishing to see how little these people appear to dread those fish. I have seen five or six large sharks swimming about the ship, when there have been, I dare say, upwards of an hundred Indians in the water, men and women; they seemed quite indifferent about them, and the sharks never

offered

offered to make an attack on any of them, and yet at the same time would seize our bait greedily; whence it is manifest, that they derive their confidence of safety, from their experience that they are able to repel the attacks of those devouring monsters.

On Sunday, September 30th, a moderate breeze from the Eastward, with pleasant weather. A vast number of canoes about the ship, which remained with us till between three and four in the evening, when having sold all their cargoes, and gratified their curiosity, they returned to the shore. By this time I suppose we had bought about three hundred hogs and pigs, and an abundant supply of bread-kind. About four in the evening, with a fine little breeze from the North East by East, we made sail from the island, and stood to the North West by North, meaning to run down on the North side of the islands to Atoui, where, if the Queen Charlotte had been before us, I should expect to receive some intelligence; if not, I should have an opportunity of leaving a letter with our old friend Abbenooe for captain Dixon, in case he should call at that island. At four in the evening the Northernmost part of Owhyhee in sight, West three quarters North, and the East point South South East half East, from the nearest shore about four leagues. At six the North point of Owhyhee bore West about nine or ten leagues, and the East point South by East three quarters East, twelve or fourteen leagues distant, and the high land of Mowee from West North West half West to North West by West half West. At eight, moderate and cloudy weather; at midnight, light winds, with open cloudy weather; steering North West by North, about two knots and a half per hour, the wind

CHAP.
XIV.

1787.
September.
Sunday 30.

at East North East. At four in the morning a light breeze from the East South East, with cloudy weather. At eight the East point of Owhyhee bore South East by South, and the North point bore South West, distant from the nearest shore seven or eight leagues; the island of Mowee extending from West half South to West by North. During the day a number of hands were employed in killing and salting pork for sea store.

October.
Monday 1.

MONDAY, 1st October, soon after dark, I was surprised to hear some Indians calling out to us, and immediately saw a canoe paddling towards the ship. She came alongside, and remained a few minutes; when she returned towards the shore: she was from Mowee, and had nothing for sale except a few bits of cloth. It is surprising how these people do venture off in their ticklish canoes. This one was so small that she would hardly contain the two men that paddled her.

Tuesday 2.

TUESDAY the 2d, at noon a moderate breeze at East by North, with fair pleasant weather: the extremes of Woahoo South 38° East, and South 73° East, distant from the nearest part about seven or eight leagues: the island of Atoui extending from South 80° West to North 80° West, distant about twelve leagues. Latitude observed 21° 58′ North.

Wednes. 3.

AT four in the morning a moderate breeze at North by East, and fair weather. Soon after four hauled in for the land, and at daylight (which was soon after five) we found ourselves about two leagues from the South point of Atoui, at which time we edged away for Wymoa Bay. In running

ning along-shore a number of canoes, both large and small, came off to us, but brought hardly any articles of provision. I learnt from them, that the king and most of the principal men of the island were at Oneehow, and that, previous to their setting off for that island, they had tabooed the hogs, which effectually put a stop to our getting any. I also learnt from these people, that the Nootka and Queen Charlotte had been at the island. The Nootka, they gave me to understand, did not anchor, but proceeded to Oneehow, where she lay some time. The Queen Charlotte, they told me, anchored in Wymoa Bay, and remained two days, when she left the island and stood to the Southward. I found from their information, that captain Dixon had left a letter for me with Abbenooe, and that it lay at his house at Wymao; I therefore stretched in for the bay, and when about a mile and a half from the shore, brought-to, with the main-topsail to the mast.

Between eight and nine a young man, named Tahiree, a son of Abbenooe's, came on board, and informed me that the letter was tabooed in the house, and that I could not get it until Abbenooe either came himself, or sent directions for its being delivered. I thought the best step I could take was, immediately to push for Oneehow, and anchor, where I might have an opportunity of procuring some yams, whilst a messenger was going to Atoui for the letter. I accordingly bore up about ten in the morning, and made sail for Oneehow, with a fair breeze at East South East, and fair weather. At noon a moderate breeze with fair weather, Atoui extending from East by North to North North East, Wymoa Bay North East by East about

CHAP. XIV.
1787.
October.
Wednef. 3.

about four leagues; the South point of Oneehow South West by West, three quarters West, seven or eight leagues; and the island of Orehaw North West by West, eight leagues: latitude observed, 21° 51′ North.

TAHIREE, Abbenooe's son, and one or two others, took their passage with us from Atoui to Oneehow; and from them I learnt, that there had been some disturbance between the Nootka and them, and that Tyaana, a principal chief of Atoui, had gone off with the Nootka.

Thursday 4.

A MODERATE breeze from South East, with fair weather, steering to the South West half West, at the rate of three knots an hour. At four, the Northernmost part of Oneehow in sight North North East, distant about three leagues, and the South head West by South, distant about two miles. At six in the evening came to an anchor on the South West side of Oneehow in sixty-two fathoms water, a fine white sandy bottom, and veered to a cable and a half, the South head bearing over a point of land East South East half East, distant about four or five miles, the West point North 10° East, distant about two leagues; and the Peaked Mountain bearing over the low land, North 40° East, our distance from the shore about two miles. It was by no means necessary to anchor in such deep water as we then lay in, as, by going about half a mile nearer the shore, you may anchor in forty fathoms, a tolerable good bottom, and at a sufficient distance from the shore; and I would advise no person to anchor in less water about this island, as, if they do, they stand a hazardous chance of being in foul ground. No canoes came off. At midnight light and variable winds, with clear pleasant weather. At

nine

nine in the morning two canoes came along-side, of which we purchased a present supply of yams. The people of those canoes told me that Abbenooe would be on board in a little time, accompanied by the king and his principal men. Towards noon no appearance of any canoes; I came to the determination of sending our whale-boat and yaul on shore, to try if any yams could be purchased from the natives; meaning, if Abbenooe did not make his appearance towards the evening, to sail from the island. At noon light variable winds, with some smart showers of rain. Sent the boats on shore under the direction of Messrs. Hayward and Bryant.

The most of these twenty-four hours a fresh breeze and variable from East South East, around by the East to North East, with some showers of rain. About two in the afternoon the king, accompanied by Abbenooe and most of the other principal men of Oneehow and Atoui, came on board, and brought with them a good quantity of yams and potatoes. I learned from Abbenooe, that captain Dixon's letter was at Wymoa, to which place he assured me he would send for it immediately; pressing me very hard to remain until the return of the messenger, which he told me would be in about thirty-six hours. Judging that I could procure yams sufficient to last us to China, I promised him I would stay; and he accordingly dispatched a canoe immediately for it, under the care of a trusty messenger; and in the mean time we carried on a very brisk trade for yams and water, which the natives brought off to the ship in their canoes; the water in large calabashes. Towards the evening the boats returned on board, not having purchased many yams. Abbenooe observing

serving one of the people who was just returned from shore to have only one shoe on, enquired what was become of the other; and the man telling him he had lost it in the surf just as he got into the boat; my old friend desired him to point out the place and he would go and look for it; observing at the same time, that one shoe only was of little use. I attempted to dissuade him from going, as the evening now came on and the wind blew very fresh, but all to no purpose. Abbenooe, bent on going to search for the shoe, took a canoe that we kept for his use, and paddled away for the beach; and in less than an hour he returned on board, bringing the shoe and buckle, and was pleased to the last degree that he had been successful in his undertaking.

My old friend acquainted me of the Nootka having sailed from this place about a month ago, and captain Dixon having sailed from Atoui about eighteen or twenty days ago. He gave me to understand that the Nootka and them parted on bad terms, but that captain Dixon and they parted on terms perfectly friendly. He told me that they had been fired on by the Nootka, but that no person had been hurt; he also confirmed the account of Ty-e-a-naa's having gone off with the Nootka. Towards the evening the king and most of the principal people went on shore; Abbenooe and a few others remained on board with us all night. In the morning began again a brisk trade for yams and water. At noon a fresh breeze from the North East, with open cloudy weather.

Fresh breezes from North East, with open cloudy weather. The whole of these twenty-four hours employed purchasing

purchasing yams and water. In the morning I received a letter, by the hands of one of the chiefs, from Mr. David Rofs, chief mate of the fnow Nootka; in which he mentioned their having failed from this island on the 5th day of the laft month: he likewife informed me that they left an anchor in Yam Bay, and fuppofed that their cable was cut by the Indians; but I should rather fuppofe by the rocks. Some other letters were received by different people on board from the Nootka, which gave an account of their having loft an anchor at Mowee, and a large grapnel at fome other place.

A FRESH breeze from the Eaftward, with open cloudy weather, moft of thefe twenty-four hours. In the evening bufily employed in purchafing yams and water; and by fix o'clock had completed that bufinefs; having procured about twelve tons of yams, a quantity of potatoes, and filled feven butts and two puncheons of water; at eight in the morning the meffenger returned from Atoui with captain Dixon's letter, which I found dated the 18th of September; and that he had left the coaft on the 9th of Auguft, all well, and with fifteen hundred fkins. He likewife informed me, that off King George's Sound he fell in with a ship and floop under Company's colours; I should fuppofe our Company's, the ship called the Prince of Wales, commanded by a captain Colnett; the floop's name he did not mention; fhe was commanded by a captain Duncan; and Mr. John Etches was fupercargo. Captain Colnett informed him that he had juft come out of King George's Sound; at which place he had found lying a ship under Imperial colours, commanded by captain Barclay, and manned

manned by Englishmen. He said nothing of their succeſs or intentions.

Immediately on the receipt of this letter I began to heave ſhort. About half paſt nine we were under way. We lay-to until near noon; when, having finiſhed a letter for captain Colnett, or Duncan, or any other commander belonging to the King George's Sound company, and delivered it to the care of my old friend Abbenooe, we made ſail from the iſland at noon, and ſteered to the Weſt by South, intending, after getting clear of Taahoora, and the ſhoal (called by the Indians Modoo-papapa, which I never ſaw, but judge from the information I have received from different Indians, to lie about Weſt South Weſt from Tahoora at a little diſtance), to haul to the Southward as far as 14° or 13° 30′ North, as the ſafeſt track, until we got the length of the Ladrones.

On quitting our friends thereabouts, I muſt do them the juſtice to ſay we have ever found them friendly and uſeful. A man of ſome note, named Ta-boo-a-raa-nee, belonging to Owhyhee, took his paſſage with us to this place, and was received by the king and principal men with much ſatisfaction. I ſaw a very ſtriking likeneſs between him and Ka-nee-na, who was killed at the time captain Cook fell, and who was always a moſt friendly chief. I inquired if he knew Ka-nee-na; at which he ſeemed ſurpriſed, and heſitated for ſome time, ſeemingly conſidering what anſwer he ſhould make me; at laſt he informed me that he was his own brother; of which I had little doubt, from the great reſemblance of their features.

tures. Ta-boo-a-raa-nee is a well-made, tall, handsome fellow; and from what I could judge of him, had a disposition equally good with his unfortunate brother. He could scarcely refrain from tears while speaking of him, and assured me that to the last moment of his life he was our sincere and faithful friend. I asked him if captain Cook was killed with a pa-ho-a? He told me no; that he was killed with another weapon; the point entering in between the shoulders, and coming out at his breast. And I am certain he was right in his explanation of the instrument; for on my shewing him a pa-ho-a, he said that was not it, and hunted about the cabin till he found a bayonet, and assured me that the Orono was killed with an instrument of that kind. And it is very probable it might be so, as the natives had got some from the ships, either by stealth or by trading with the people; and I am inclined to believe the man knew, as he informed me, that he was present when captain Cook was killed. He said a great number of their people were wounded from the fire at different times, the greatest part of whom died, particularly those that were wounded in the body; such as recovered were only wounded in the fleshy parts. He told me that the present king Co-ma-aa-ma-a and other chiefs were very much afraid of coming on board; dreading our resenting the fate of our countrymen. He informed me that Pa-reea is the principal chief around Karakakooa Bay, and is at present in great esteem. He confirmed the account of old Te-ree-o-boo's dying a natural death, and being succeeded by his relation Co-ma-aa-ma-aa, and that he was much lamented by his subjects. Ta-boo-a-raa-nee likewise gave gave me an account of two vessels having anchored in Karakakooa Bay, where they

they remained five days. He said they were ships from Britania, and in the two had fifteen women and eight children on board, and described them as European women. This I looked on as a strange account; and well knowing that these people are very apt to invent stories, I gave no credit to that part of the account respecting the women and children being on board: the rest might possibly be true, though one improbable circumstance rendered the whole doubtful and suspicious; for though there seems to be a kind of propensity generally prevailing among these people to invent and contrive reports, with a view to please and oblige, yet there is another quality which seems the most predominant in them of all others, and which is always visible in those who are vested with any degree of authority or power, or are anyways elevated or exalted to a station superior to their neighbours; for arrogance, insolence, and voracity, are the distinguishing properties by which their inferiors are taught to dread them, and be awed into the most submissive obedience to their commands, however opposite to their ease, interest, or safety; insomuch that I have seen a considerable chief at Woahoo sit in his canoe alongside, without an article for sale himself, and watch a poor fellow that had perhaps paddled from the opposite side of the island with all his family, and perhaps all their worldly property and substance; such as two or three pigs, a few plantains, pieces of cloth, and some bread-fruit; and after selling their little cargo, and getting for it a few bits of iron and some little trinkets, things (the iron in particular) that are inestimable to them, that greedy and tyrannical chief hath jumped out of his canoe into the water, swam to the poor man, and demanded of him every article which he had seen him receive, which was instantly

instantly given up. On these occasions I spoke to the king, who made me understand that it was warranted by their established custom. And after receiving such an answer, I was apprehensive that any further attempts to intercede on the poor man's behalf might aggravate the injury to the sufferers, and be productive of worse and more serious consequences to him, as well as create some disgust to me, for presuming to call in question, or suggesting the impropriety of the rules by which they were governed; and therefore I waved the subject, and desisted from my purpose, though urged to it by all the feelings of pity and compassion.

Among the variety of occurrences that happened during our last visit to Atoui, the reader may recollect the circumstance of Pooareare (a messenger belonging to the king) obliging an old chief by force to discover where his treasures were deposited, and afterwards seizing on them as his own. As we left the island soon after that transaction, I had no opportunity of learning how it terminated; but when Abbenooe came on board at Oneehow, he informed me, that when Taaao heard of the affair, he was so much displeased with the messenger, that he ordered Pooareare (although a favourite) to be put to death for the robbery, and his cruelty to the poor old man. This order was executed by a chief named Namaateerae, whose courage and activity have already been spoken of.

Namaateerae found the culprit in a village situated a little to the Eastward of Wymoa, where he attacked, and, after some resistance, killed him with a pahoa.
The

CHAP.
XIV.
1787.
October.
Sunday 7.

The messenger also happened to have a pahoa, but was so unequal a match for the warrior, that it was of no use to him.

These instances serve to shew, that though the common people are plundered at the pleasure of their superiors, yet the chiefs are not suffered to assault and rob each other with impunity.

Most of the birds met with at the Sandwich Islands are already well known. However, I brought a specimen of the white tern home with me; and as I do not find that it has yet been figured in any English work, I have procured a correct drawing of it, from whence the annexed engraving is taken; and with *Mr. Latham*'s permission, have taken the following description from the sixth volume of his *Synopsis of Birds*, p. 363, where an account of it is given.

White Tern.—Length thirteen inches, breadth thirty; bill slender, black; eyelids the same; the general colour of the plumage white as snow; but the shafts of the scapular quills, and tail, except the three outer feathers, are black; the tail is forked in shape, and shorter than the wings when closed by an inch; legs brown; webs orange; claws black. In some there is a slight mixture of brown on the head. This bird inhabits various places of the Southern hemisphere; having been met with off the island of *Saint Helena*, the *Cape of Good Hope*, *India*, and many of the islands of the *South Sea*.

WITH

White Tern from Sandwich Islands.

Published May 1784 by J. Stockdale & G. Goulding

WITH respect to the description of the natives of these islands, I mean their persons, their houses, canoes, customs, civil, military, and religious, I refer the reader to the more full account of captains Cook and King. But one piece of advice I will venture to give to those whose business may lead them to these islands, for the purpose of watering and refreshing, is this, that they make the island of Owhyhee, a little to the Southward of the East point, and run down the South side of the island. There is no danger but what shews itself, nor indeed did I perceive any that lay half a mile from the shore, until you come the length of the South point. There is off that point a reef that runs off about a mile, which is easily discovered by breakers and coloured water. In this run you may get small hogs and vegetables enough for present supply; and after hauling round the South point, you will begin to get a supply of salt, which article cannot be procured at the Eastern part of the island; I mean not after you get to the Eastward and Northward of Karakakooa Bay; and as you draw towards Karakakooa, you will get a plentiful supply of fine hogs, bread-fruit, and sweet potatoes, taro, sugar-cane, and cocoa-nuts.

THIS island is not famous for the sweet root; and between Karakakooa and the South point you may procure all the refreshments the island affords, and you may also get the natives to bring off fresh water enough for present use. Take care they do not cheat you, by filling their callabashes with salt water, which they will do, and sell it, if you are not careful in tasting: several of my people were cheated this way. And hereabouts is the situation I would recommend for salting pork; you will have the open and unconfined

confined air, and at the same time moderate breezes and smooth water, which enables the canoes to come off with greater care and safety with their hogs and salt.

From this part I would advise the navigator to run for the West end of Ranai (the bearings and distances of these islands from each other will be found, by consulting the chart of them in captain Cook's last voyage), and from that point sail directly for the West point of Morotoi. Should night come on, there is anchorage to the Northward of the West point of Morotoi, sheltered from the prevailing winds. After leaving this island, sail directly for the South East point of Woahoo, and on rounding that point anchor in King George's Bay. If found necessary to stay there any time, it would be advisable to buoy the cables. At this island I would advise the watering and wooding business to be done, not by sending on shore for either article, but by encouraging the natives to bring them to the vessel.

To give any further directions respecting the navigation amongst these islands would be superfluous, as every particular on that head may be collected from the detail of occurrences during our second visit to them. I cannot help observing, that I think their situation and produce may be productive of material benefit to our new settlement at Botany Bay, and at the same time be a considerable saving to government in the articles of provisions, which may be purchased here at a trifling expence.

Monday 8. A fresh breeze, with hazy weather, the wind at East; the West end of Tahoora bore South 15° East, distant seven

NORTH WEST COAST OF AMERICA.

seven or eight leagues, the South head of Oneehow East about eleven or twelve leagues distant, and the Northernmost part of the island in sight North 65° East.

CHAP. XIV.
1787.
October.
Monday 8.

At noon a fine gale, with pleasant weather, latitude observed, 21° 26′ North, longitude about 161° 56′ West. Taking our departure from the island of Tahoora, it lying in the latitude of 21° 43′ North, and longitude 160° 24′ West of Greenwich, variation about 9° East. From this time to the 4th of November nothing particular occurred.

A FRESH gale from the North East, with hazy weather, steering West North West half West, five knots per hour. At five in the evening I got a set of azimuths, which gave the variation 7° 54′ East; at eight hauled in the lower steering-sails. At this time, according to the situation given Tinian by captain Cook, East point latitude nearest 14° 55′ North, and longitude 213° 45′ West of Greenwich, I judged it to bear North 84° West, and distant eighty-four miles; and as we had a fine brisk gale from the North East, with clear weather, I determined to run on all night, hoping to get a sight of the island about daylight, which is between five and six. At midnight a fine steady six and a half knot gale from the North East. At two in the morning a seven knot gale, hauled in the topmast steering-sails. Just at daylight, which was about half past five, saw the islands of Saypan and Tinian, the North point of Saypan bearing West North West, distant about seven or eight leagues, and the East point of Tinian bearing South West half West, distant eleven or twelve leagues, the North point of Tinian shut in with the

November.
Sunday 4.

CHAP. XIV.
1787.
November.
Sunday 4.

South point of Saypan. At this time our latitude, by account, was 15° 16′ North, and longitude, from obfervations brought forward, 213° 16′ 30″ Weft. The Eaft end of Tinian, according to captain Cook's chart, fhould then have bore 55° 00′ Weft thirty-feven miles, and the bearing we then had of it was 58° 00′ Weft, and as near as I could guefs diftant about thirty-three miles; therefore I fhall conclude, that the fituation given thofe iflands by captain Cook is very nearly the truth. We continued to ftand on to the Weft North Weft half Weft, with a frefh gale from the North Eaft by North until fix, when we altered the courfe to Weft, and fet fteering-fails. We ftood in Weft until feven o'clock, then fteered South Weft by Weft and South Weft by South, ranging along the Eaft fide of Saypan, at the diftance of about two leagues and a half. At half paft eight, the paffage between Saypan and Tinian open, fteered for it, and about nine paffed clofe to the South end of Saypan; immediately to the Weftward of which point is a good bay, with perfect fmooth water and a fine fandy beach, on which there was fcarce any furf. I did not ftand into the bay, therefore cannot fpeak as to the foundings; but I dare fay the anchorage may be very good. A little to the Weftward of this bay is another, which looks well for anchorage. In paffing through this paffage, which trends about Weft by North and Eaft by South, diftance from one ifland to the other between two and three leagues, we obferved no foul grounds lying off from either ifland, until we got nearly through; then difcerned a reef lying from the South Weft point of Saypan, North Weft, diftant about half a mile. Indeed, all the Weft fide of Sayphan appears to be bounded by a reef running nearly the fame diftance from the fhore; and from the faid

South

View of part of the South Side of the Island SAPAN, one of the Ladrone Isles.

South West point is a small island, bearing North half West, distant three or four leagues; from which island there is a reef running off in the direction of about South West, to the distance of a league and a half; and there is also a reef running off from this small island that seems to join to Sayphan.

We observed a number of white animals grazing on the plains of Tinian, which we suppose to be the white cattle that Lord Anson says the island of Tinian so much abounds with. We could not, although within half a mile of Saypan, observe an animal of any kind. Both islands appear beyond description beautiful, abounding in immense quantities of cocoa-nut and other trees. We could not pass so near these beautiful islands without wishing very much to partake of the refreshments they could so amply furnish us with, particularly the fresh beef and acid fruits, articles to which we have been strangers for upwards of two years: but as through the blessing of God we were all in perfect health, and not being in need of any refreshments, and having a fine steady brisk gale, I thought it most advisable to push on for China; therefore, after getting through the passage, stood away to the West North West, with a brisk gale at North East by North. And to the honour of the King George's ship's company be it ever remembered, that on this so tempting an occasion (as indeed on all others), not a murmur was heard, nor a discontented face seen. From this time to the 15th November nothing occurred in particular to excite the reader's attention.

A FRESH

CHAP. XIV.

1787.
November.
Thursday 15.

A FRESH breeze from the North East, with hazy weather and a heavy sea from the North East, with which we are steering about West South West, down towards the South point of the small Botel Tobago Xima. About two in the afternoon we passed the reef, which runs off its South East point at the distance of about half a mile, and then hauled to the West by North, with a six knot gale at North East. Those islands I found to lie in the latitude of 21° 52′ North, and longitude of 238° 35′ West, lying nearly North and South of each other, with an apparently good passage of about two or three miles broad between them. On the South West part of the large island the land appeared to bend in and form a good bay, well sheltered from the North East winds. We observed a little wood, but it appeared to be low and small. The Western side of the large island appeared very green and pleasant, and in many places was laid out in cultivated plots, and in several places along the shore were towns of considerable extent. We did not attempt to haul in for anchorage, but continued to steer over West by North to make the island of Formosa, and at half past three I saw it, the South point bearing West by North, distant about ten or eleven leagues. At four a fine gale at North East, with which we steered West by North six knots per hour; the large Botel Tobago Xima bearing North by West half West, and East by North, distant from the nearest part of it about four leagues, and the small Botel Tobago Xima bearing East 74° North, distant about five leagues. At five hauled to the North West by West, the wind at North North East, the extremes of Botel Tobago Xima bearing North East by East half East, distant about five leagues, and

and East by North six leagues, the South point of Formosa West half South, distant about eight leagues. At six a fresh gale at North North East, with dark cloudy weather. We then close-reefed the topsails, wore ship, and stood to the Eastward. At half past four saw a large light on the isles of Botel Tobago Xima, bearing East South East: wore ship, and stood to the North West, the wind at North East. At midnight a fresh gale, with cloudy weather. At four in the morning wore ship, and stood to the East by North; and at half past five day-light, when we bore away to the South South West, and made sail, set steering-sails. In the course of the night we had a current, which set us about six leagues to the Northward along the coast of Formosa; the South point of which island bore South West half South, distant about five leagues, and the Northernmost part of the said island in sight North by West, distant about twelve leagues. Up main-topgallant yard, and set the sail: we were steering along shore South South West towards the South point, at the rate of six and a half and seven knots per hour, our distance from the shore abreast about two leagues, and in running down saw a good appearance of an harbour about four or five leagues to the Northward of the South point, which seemed to run in in about a South West direction, and between that and the South point several small hammock rocks, lying at a little distance from the shore. The coast that we run down along might be approached within three or four miles without any danger. At half past ten passed around the South point within about a mile of the shore. From off this point there is a reef runs off about half a mile. In about a South South East direction we saw nothing of the Ville Rete rocks, it being very thick in their direction, and after passing the South point,

CHAP.
XIV.

1787.
November.
Thursday 15.

point, we hauled to the West North West, at the rate of six and seven knots an hour. Immediately on getting round the South point, I observed the land to bend short in to the Northward, and form a very good bay for shelter against the North East winds, the water in the bay quite smooth, and scarce any surf on the beach. I had an intention of anchoring upon this coast, and would have done it, had I seen any inhabitants or habitations to have entered into a traffic with them; but as I saw no appearance of this part of the land being peopled, I gave up the idea, and proceeded on towards the coast of China, with a fresh gale at North East by North, with frequent gusts from the land, and dark cloudy weather. At noon moderate with unsettled looking weather, the South point of Formosa bearing East by South, distant about five leagues, and the Northernmost part in sight on the Western side North West one quarter West, distant four leagues. No observation. Latitude account 22° 06' North, longitude by account 229° 37', longitude by departure 239° 2'.

Sunday 18.

This morning at daylight we were surrounded by a multitude of Chinese fishing-vessels or junks; at seven saw the land through the haze, bearing from North to West North West, and at eight saw Pedro Branca, bearing West by North, distant four or five leagues. A moderate breeze at North, with very hazy weather, with which we steered West by North, about four and a half knots per hour. In this run from the South point of Formosa, the ship a-head of the reckoning nearly eighty miles of longitude. At half past nine, seeing a Chinese vessel steering down towards us, we shortened sail, and brought-to, in hopes of getting a pilot out of her. Sent the whale-boat on board her,
which

which returned soon after, accompanied by a boat from the Chinese vessel, in which came a pilot, with whom I agreed for his carrying the ship to Macao for fifty dollars. At half past ten filled, and stood to the West North West, the wind at North, a three knot breeze. At two, hazy weather; sounded in twenty-four fathoms black muddy sandy bottom, Pedro Blanco bearing North East by North, distant about four miles, and the coast in sight to the North North West, distant eight or nine leagues. No observation; latitude by account 22° 38′ North; longitude by departure 242° 16′ West.

LIGHT winds from the Northward, with hazy weather, with which we steered to the West North West, one knot six fathoms per hour, sounding from twenty-two to nineteen fathoms over a bottom of black muddy sand. At four in the evening the land in sight extended from North by East to West by North, distant from the nearest part five or six leagues, and Pedro Blanco, North 88° East, distant about seven leagues. A strong tide or current setting us to the Westward, at five sounded in seventeen fathoms, black muddy sand. At half past five the land extended from North North East to West North West, distant from the nearest part about five leagues, a small island lying off the coast, bearing North West, distant about four leagues. Moderate breeze from the North, with hazy weather, with which we steered to the West North West, about two knots per hour, regular soundings, from nineteen to seventeen fathoms and a half, over a bottom of fine black muddy sand; at nine anchored with the best bower in seventeen fathoms and a half over a bottom of black muddy sand, the small island before mentioned bearing North East half North,

CHAP.
XIV.

1787.
Monday 19.

North, about four leagues, the coast in sight from North East by North to West South West, distant from the nearest point four or five leagues. During the night moderate and variable winds; at six in the morning a moderate breeze at North East by North, with which we weighed, and came to sail; up topgallant yards, and set the sails, and steered to the South West by West about three knots per hour. At eight a light breeze at North East, with hazy weather, the Westernmost part of the Grand Lema bearing South West by West, distant six or seven leagues, the Easternmost part of the coast or islands North East half North, about the same distance. And the small island before mentioned, North East half East, nine or ten leagues distant, and our distance from the nearest shore four or five leagues. During the forenoon a brisk breeze at North East, with which we steered in West South West, at the rate of four or five knots per hour, for the passage to the Northward of the Grand Lema, regular sounding from fifteen and a half to nineteen and a half fathom over a bottom of muddy sand; and at eleven squally, hauled in the steering-sails. At noon a fresh breeze at North North East, with squalls, and with which we steered West South West, in the passage to the Northward of the Grand Lema six knots per hour, the East part of the Grand Lema bearing South East by South thirteen or fourteen miles, and the Northernmost land in sight North East by East, our distance from an island to the North North West about one mile. No observation.

Tuesday 20.

A FRESH breeze at North North East, with hazy weather, with which we steered West North West four knots per hour, sounded frequently as we run in, and found depth of water from thirteen to fifteen fathoms over a

muddy

muddy bottom. At four in the evening a moderate breeze at North, with which we stood to the West North West half West, three knots per hour, almost surrounded by islands. At five anchored with the best bower in eight fathoms and a quarter water, over a bottom of mud; the extremes of Lanton bearing South East by East a quarter East, and South East half East; islands all round; our distance from the nearest shore about two miles; down topgallant yards. During the night light and variable winds, with cloudy weather. At six in the morning, with a light breeze from the Northward, we weighed, sounded frequently as we approached the passage leading to Macao, and found from eight to six fathoms over a muddy bottom. About nine, by borrowing too near the Southern and Eastern shore, we suddenly shoaled our water to three fathoms and a half; but by keeping a little to the North, we deepened it again to six fathoms, and then stood through the passage: a fresh breeze at about North East by North, with clear weather. At half past ten, the tide of ebb having made, we came to an anchor with the best bower in nine fathoms, muddy bottom; the city of Macao bearing North West half North, distant about five or six leagues. At noon a moderate breeze, with fair weather; latitude observed 22° 10′ North.

A MODERATE breeze at North, with hazy weather. At one in the afternoon, the ebb-tide having slacked, we weighed and stood towards Macao; and at half past four anchored with the best bower in four fathoms and a half, muddy bottom, in Macao Road, the town bearing West by South, distance two or three leagues; and Lanton Peak East. At five sent the whale-boat on shore to Macao. At six in the morning a fresh breeze at North by West; with

with fine weather. Saw lying in the Typa two large ships under French colours: one of which I found to be a thirty-two gun frigate, and the other an armed store-ship: their destination, after leaving this, is generally supposed to be to the island of Formosa, where it is believed the French mean to get a footing.

ABOUT seven in the morning the boat returned, having finished her business. The officer in her brought me a letter from captain Dixon, informing me of his safe arrival in China; and that in consequence of cargoes being procured for our two ships, he had proceeded up to Wampoa, where the Nootka was also arrived from Prince William's Sound, and a ship called the Imperial Eagle, commanded by a captain Berkley, from King George's Sound; English property; under Imperial colours. We heard of two vessels from India to the North West coast being missing; the one commanded by a captain Peters, and the other by a captain Tipping; most likely cut off by the natives of that coast. After receiving on board for the use of the ship's company 257 pounds of fresh beef and some vegetables, sent the boat on shore again to get a pilot for the ship to Wampoa.

LIGHT winds at North by West, with pleasant weather; in the afternoon moored ship with the kedge anchor; arrived on board nine seamen, late belonging to the ship Imperial Eagle, and two late of the Nootka, to take a passage to Wampoa.

MODERATE breezes from the North North East, with fair pleasant weather. At seven in the evening the pilot came

came on board. At four in the morning weighed, and came to sail from Macao towards Wampoa; and at noon was turning to windward between Macao and Lanton. Before we left Macao, received on board eleven Lascars and four seamen more as passengers for Wampoa.

A MODERATE breeze from the Eastward, with fair pleasant weather. At one in the afternoon, the flood being spent, came-to with the best bower in ten fathoms water, loose sandy bottom: the island of Lanton, the Peak, bearing East by South, and the South west point of Macoa West South West. At half past four weighed and came to sail; set steering-sails. The tide of flood being expended, at ten came-to with the best bower in nine fathoms and a half water, muddy bottom. At seven in the morning weighed and came to sail. At eight passed the Bocco Tigris; and at noon were plying to windward up Canton river.

LIGHT breeze from the Eastward, with pleasant weather. At two in the afternoon came-to with the best bower in seven fathoms and a quarter water, muddy bottom. At the same time came on board captain Dixon of the Queen Charlotte: the first pagoda bearing North West half West, four or five leagues. At seven in the afternoon weighed and came to sail. At eleven came-to with the best bower in six fathoms, two miles below Wampoa; and at ten in the morning weighed again, and dropped up to Wampoa, and moored ship with both anchors in five fathoms water.

WHILST we lay at Wampoa, our principal business was to refit the ship, and take a cargo of tea on board on account

CHAP.
XIV.

1787.
November.
Sunday 25.

count of the East India Company. An account of the disposal of our furs, and other material incidents, being given in captain Dixon's voyage, I refer the reader to that publication.

DURING this interval, a dangerous mutiny happened on board the Belvidere, captain Greer, then lying at Wampoa. A thing of this nature being of the most dangerous consequence to a commercial country, I have captain Greer's permission to publish the examination of the mutineers before a court of inquiry; which, together with some anecdotes of Tyaana, whom I met with at Canton, will be the subject of the next chapter.

CHAP. XV.

An Account of a Court of Inquiry held at the Request of Captain Greer, of the Belvidere, on his People who mutinied in his Absence.—The Court's Determination thereon, and Punishment inflicted upon the Mutineers.—Account of meeting with Tyaana at China.—His Behaviour there.—Attention paid him.—Return to his own Country.—A short Description of his Person.

Wampoa, 9th December 1787.

At a Court of Enquiry held on board the Earl Fitzwilliam in consequence of the following Letter from the Council of Supercargoes:

To Captain James Dundas, Commander of the Earl Fitzwilliam, and senior Commander.

SIR,

HAVING taken into serious consideration the circumstances of the late riot and mutiny on board the Belvidere, and the dreadful consequences that might be apprehended to the honourable Company's property, and the general interest of the nation, in the trade of this place, were such an instance of licentiousness passed over without due punishment; and being of opinion with the commanders whom we have consulted on the occasion, that the

the inflicting immediate and severe corporal chastisement on the principal offenders will more effectually contribute to the end proposed, of deterring others from following so dangerous an example, than consigning them over to the more dreadful punishment which they have incurred from the laws of their country, on account of the distance of time which must necessarily intervene, and the probable absence of those on whom we wish it to operate as an example:

We request you will, at such time as shall be most convenient to you, assemble the commanders of the several ships, to consult and determine on such punishment to be inflicted on the offenders as shall appear to you proportioned to their several offences, and report to us your opinion of the same.

We are,

SIR,

Your most obedient humble Servants,

(Signed) HENRY BROWNE.
JOHN HARRISON, junior.
G. CUMMING, junior.
ALEX. BRUCE.
CHA^s EDW^d PIGOU.
HENRY LANE.

CANTON,
8th December 1787.

On receiving the foregoing order, made the signal for all commanders; read the said letter; sent for the prisoners and principal evidences on board the Earl Fitzwilliam; and desired them to prepare themselves for a court to be held here at eight o'clock next morning.

Wampoa, 10th December 1787.

PRESENT:

Captains, JAMES DUNDAS, President.
ALEX^R MONTGOMERY.
JOSEPH HUDDART.
J. H. DEMPSTER.
JAMES MONRO.
HENRY CHURCHILL.
GEORGE BLACHFORD.
W^M HARDCASTLE.
DAVID TOLME.
GEORGE MILLETT.
RICHARD PENNELL.
WILLIAM STOREY.
PHILIP DUNDAS.
JOHN DENNIS.
JOHN PAIBA.
CHARLES LINDEGREN.

THE court being met, read the above order from the council of supercargoes.

CALLED the prisoners, and read the following charge:

You John Berry, Abraham Lilly, Henry Ladson, James Keiff, Anthony Garland, Robert Skinner, Thomas Langford, William Conner, Timothy Kelly, and John Haftings, not having the fear of God before your eyes, are

are charged with the high crime of mutiny; in firſt meditating aforethought a deſign to inſult the officers of the ſhip Belvidere, to which you belonged; and carrying the ſame into execution, by refuſing to obey the commanding officer, by ſeizing him, beating him, and otherwiſe ill-uſing him, on Saturday night the firſt of December in this preſent year, and continuing your mutinous behaviour till Sunday noon, when you attempted to carry the command of the ſhip Belvidere againſt your officers; which you in ſome meaſure effected, by turning the guns aft upon them, and threatening to murder them; by breaking open locks, and threatening to fire the powder and blow up the ſhip. And further, even when aſſiſtance was called from the reſt of the Company's ſhips, for the purpoſe of enabling the officers to reſume their command, and procure peace to ſuch of his Majeſty's ſubjects as were willing to return to their duty on board the Belvidere, you wantonly armed yourſelves with ſhot and other dangerous weapons, and attempted the life of ſuch of his Majeſty's ſubjects as endeavoured to ſuppreſs your mutinous behaviour; intreating and perſuading the reſt of the ſhip's company to aſſiſt you, and threatening to murder them if they did not join you in this mutiny: but, thank God, the murders that might have been the conſequence were happily prevented by the immediate aſſiſtance from the commodore.

We are therefore called upon by our honourable maſters to make inquiry into this matter.

Mr. David Dunlop, chief officer of the ſhip Belvidere, called in and examined. Deſired him to inform the court of what he knew of the prisoners and the mutiny they are accused of; which he did as followeth:

On Saturday night the first of December, between ten and eleven o'clock, I was going to bed, and heard Ladson, Keiff, and Conner singing and making a noise on the gun-deck; I desired them to leave off and not make such a noise to disturb the people on board the ship; to which Ladson replied, that he thought it was hard he had not the liberty of singing a song. I told him he might go on the forecastle and sing till he was tired, but he must not sing on the gun-deck. They left off making a noise, and I went to bed; in half an hour afterwards was surprised to hear them make more noise than before. I turned out, and desired my servant to bring me a light; I went forward to them, and desired them to leave off; when James Keiff laid hold of the candle that was in my hand. I seized him by the collar, and endeavoured to get the candle again, when he put the candle out. I was very ill used in the dark by Keiff and others: I received several blows: there were several billets of wood hove. I then called for lights. The mates who were on board were soon with me. I held Keiff fast by the hair of the head; being determined to put him in irons. The people turned out, and said he should not be put in irons. The men who made the people turn out were Abraham Lilly, John Berry, Henry Ladson, James Keiff, Anthony Garland, Robert Skinner, Thomas Langford, and William Conner. James Keiff was handed upon the quarter-deck, and while the carpenters were getting the irons, the prisoners behaved in a mutinous manner; and William Conner threatened the fifth mate, Mr. Law, and said he would

would be his butcher. Berry, Lilly, and Ladson, appeared at their head near the quarter-deck, and declared they were on board of a merchantman, and no man should be put in irons or punished for any offences whatsoever. The man James Keiff was put in irons. I desired the people to go to their hammocks; but they would not quit the deck, where they remained till between two and three o'clock on Sunday morning, when they began to drop off; and I believe by three the deck was clear of them. I then ordered one of the officers, with two midshipmen and a quartermaster, to keep watch; and in case of any disturbance to call me. I then went to bed.

On Sunday morning, when the hands were called, the boatswain informed me the people refused to turn out; on which I went forward among them; telling them the bad consequence that would attend refusing to do their duty, and behaving in such a mutinous manner, for which I was convinced they had no cause. Upon which they went and washed the decks, and remained very quiet till one o'clock of the same day, when they rushed suddenly up from the gun-deck, armed with gunners handspikes, billets of wood, marlinspikes, and double-headed shot, and rushed aft on the quarter-deck, with John Berry and Abraham Lilly at their head, threatening they would murder any man who should attempt to oppose their releasing the prisoner. The sixth mate, Mr. James M'Culloch, was knocked down by John Berry with a marlinspike which he held in his hand with a lanyard to it. I attempted to stop them, but was very near being thrown over-board; I saved myself by getting hold of the lanyard of the foremast main-shroud. They took the prisoner on the main-deck,

deck, knocked off his irons and threw them over-board. Berry then said the day was their own, and ordered to give three cheers, which they did. I ordered the gunner to hand the arms out of the gun-room, that I might secure the ringleaders and take them into custody. The people then went down on the gun-deck, secured the ports, knocked away all the ladders, and pointed the two bow-guns aft; they also broke open the fore-scuttle, and cleared away a quantity of cordage that was on the magazine scuttle; they clapped bolts and the poker into the fire, to serve as matches. Being afraid I would come down upon them, they raised a report that they had broke open the magazine and loaded the two bow-guns. Seeing that all the officers were of opinion that it would be dangerous to attack them in that situation, lest they might accidentally or wilfully blow up the ship, I went forward to the fore-hatchway on the upper-deck, and desired them to keep from the magazine. Berry, Lilly, Ladson, Skinner, and Garland were the men that spoke to me from the gun-deck; they said if any of the officers attempted to come down on the gun-deck they would certainly murder them, and sooner than they should be taken would blow the ship up. In a few minutes after this, the second mate, Mr. Craig, came on board. Finding that there was no probability of getting them from the magazine while I remained on board, I left the ship; leaving orders to the second mate not to let any boats come along-side, nor let our people out of the ship, or suffer them to have any liquor. I then went on board the Earl Fitzwilliam, and returned with Mr. Raitt, on board our ship, and sent for the third mate, and ordered him, as soon as all hands were called, to take possession of the lazaretta, with six quarter-masters

masters armed, and if any attempted the magazine, to run him through. I ordered the gunner, with his two mates, to defend the gun-room, and if any attempt was made, to shoot those that did. All hands were then called, and appeared upon the upper-deck, with John Berry and Abraham Lilly at their head; and Mr. Raitt and myself endeavoured by fair means for them to deliver up the ringleaders, which Berry and Lilly absolutely refused to do. Berry said he would fight all the ships at Wampoa so long as the Belvidere's sides stuck together, and would die to a man before any of them should be punished. I found that the boats were advancing; and the people, armed with shot, threatened to sink the boats if they attempted to come along-side. I immediately ordered the officers to arm, and clear the deck of them, and to kill any man who should attempt to throw shot at the boats. The upper-deck was immediately cleared; they jumped down the fore-hatchway and rushed to the fore-scuttle. There was immediately a cry on the gun-deck that they had got possession of the magazine. While Mr. Raitt and myself attempted to clear the main-deck, John Berry and John Hastings were armed with shot, and threatened to throw them at us; I went down then on the main-deck by the main-scuttle; the first man I met with was Keiff, whom I secured and handed upon the quarter-deck. I believe in the space of five minutes all the prisoners were secured.

Questions to the Witness.

Abraham Lilly. Was I the head man present with Berry when Keiff was taken out of irons?

Answer. You was.

Lilly.

Lilly. Was I one of the men that answered you from the gun-deck?

Answer. You was.

Lilly. Was I one of the six that threatened to cut the people down to turn out?

Answer. To the best of my knowledge you was.

Anthony Garland. Was I seen at the fore-hatchway?

Answer. Yes.

Garland. Was I on the quarter-deck when Keiff was rescued?

Answer. To the best of my knowledge you was.

Henry Ladson. Was I at the fore-hatchway when the people spoke to you from below?

Answer. To the best of my knowledge you was.

Garland. Was I one of the six that threatened to cut the people down to turn out?

Answer. To the best of my knowledge you was.

Robert Skinner. Was I one of the six that threatened to cut the people down to turn out?

Answer. To the best of my knowledge you was.

Skinner. Was I one of those that spoke to you from the fore-hatch?

Answer. To the best of my knowledge you was.

John

John Berry. Was I one of the six that threatened to cut the people down to turn out?
Answer. To the best of my knowledge you was.

Court. Did you see or know who those men were that took off the irons and threw them over-board?
Answer. I cannot say.

Court. At what hour was it when those people spoke to you from the fore-hatchway?
Answer. About a quarter past one o'clock, when the ports were lashed in.

Court. Was any officer present at the above conversation at the fore-hatchway?
Answer. Yes, the third and sixth mates.

Court. This witness further says, there are two of the prisoners, Hastings and Conner, always behaved well till this affair, and he believes they were led into it by the rest.

Court requested to know of the prisoners if they wanted to ask Mr. Dunlop any more questions?
Prisoners. No.

Mr. Milliken Craig, second officer of the ship Belvidere, called in and desired to inform the court of what he knew respecting the prisoners and the mutiny.

It was near one o'clock on Sunday when I met captain Clarkson between the Earl Fitzwilliam and Hilsborough,

Hillsborough. He inquired if captain Greer was in the boat; he said not; when he immediately told him there was a mutiny in the Belvidere.

WHEN I came on board at one o'clock I found the ship in a mutinous state. The people would not permit boats to come along-side; they threatened to sink them with shot if they did. I went into the cuddy with Mr. Dunlop and the rest of the officers of the ship, to dinner. When I came out again Mr. Dunlop left the ship. The orders that Mr. Dunlop left were, I was to endeavour to keep the ship in quietness if possible, and to prevent liquor coming into the ship; I was to do nothing else till I received further orders; the men at that time in a state of madness with liquor. When Mr. Dunlop was out of the ship, all the mutineers came aft, among whom were the prisoners now before me; they said they intended to be obedient to my command, till such time as they saw captain Greer; I told them I immediately expected they would. I desired they would point the guns forward they had pointed aft; to give up the possession of the magazine, to haul up the ports, and in every other case to put the ship in order; which they did. They asked, if Keiff was a free man? I told them I should wait for orders how to act with him. I then sent for the gunner, and desired him to see the magazine and the guns secured; he reported it was done; the officers at the same time were allowed to walk the deck or any part of the ship they pleased. The ship was perfectly quiet till the note came from the commodore, and also afterwards till Mr. Raitt and Mr. Dunlop came on board: they then objected to their coming on board, and came aft in a mutinous manner; upon which I prevented their obstruct-

obstructing the passage of the above gentlemen. Mr. Dunlop desired all hands to be called: Mr. Raitt and Mr. Dunlop delivered these orders sent by the commodore, which was to deliver up the ringleaders; they all objected to it, and swore they would die to a man before they would permit it. Mr. Raitt then pointed out the folly of standing out against so many ships here; they said they did not care, they would give it red-hot on both sides, particularly Berry. The attack was then made on the mutineers by the officers on board and in the boats; they were drove below and taken prisoners.

Questions from the Court.

What boats were those that were prevented from coming along-side?

Answer. Mr. Temple was in the boat; do not know what ship the boat belonged to.

Court. When the people came aft to prevent Mr. Dunlop coming into the ship, who were the men that came forward?

Answer. Berry and Lilly.

Court. What did Mr. Dunlop say to you when you went in to dinner? Did he mention the circumstance of the man being taken out of irons, and what steps he had taken previous to your coming on board?

Answer. Yes.

Court. When the ship's company refused to give up the ringleaders, were there any of the men that you particularly observed to take the lead?

Answer.

Answer. Yes; Garland, Ladson, Berry, and Lilly.

Court. When you was going along-side, did they endeavour to prevent you?
Answer. No.

Court. When the attack was made on the mutineers, where was you, and did you observe any man take a more active part than another in the mutiny?
Answer. I was on the quarter-deck loading my pistols; the most active men were Berry and Lilly.

Court. Was you present at the securing the whole, or any part of the prisoners?
Answer. I recollect sending Skinner up the fore hatchway.

Court. What was his behaviour at the time? did he resist much?
Answer. No, he did not.

Captain Greer. When Mr. Dunlop quitted the ship, did they demand any terms of you? if so, what were they?
Answer. None.

Court. Did you give orders to prevent boats coming along-side after Mr. Dunlop left the ship?
Answer. I did, not to let boats come along-side without my knowledge.

THE prisoners were then asked by the court if they had any questions to put to the witness? They all answered, No, they had none.

MR. Adam Cumine, third officer of the ship Belvidere, called in, and desired to inform the court of what he knew of the prisoners and mutiny.

AT about half past ten o'clock of Saturday night, the 1st of December, I heard the chief mate get up and call for a light, as the people were then singing and making a riotous noise; I suspected he meant to go forward and quiet them. The fifth mate followed them immediately, and myself very soon after. I had at that time no idea the chief mate would meet with any ill treatment; but by the time I got forward, was much surprised to find that James Keiff had seized the light out of his hand; and the chief mate, who had then got Keiff down upon a chest, was attempting to retrieve the light, the fifth mate giving him every assistance in his power. We dragged Keiff aft into the steerage; I then perceived the people meant to make a general mutiny, there being a cry from all quarters, Turn out, turn out; at the same time a stool and some other things were hove aft amongst us in the steerage. The petty officers then interposing in our favour, we got Keiff upon the quarter-deck, and put him in irons. The people were by this time all upon the quarter-deck, and were insisting upon having the prisoner delivered up to them; but being opposed by the officers at the break of the quarter-deck, they did not attempt to force their way aft. Ladson, Conner, and Kelly, being the principal ringleaders,

gave

gave the chief mate a great deal of abuse, and even threatened to take the fifth mate's life. The chief mate begged they would go to their beds, assured them if they offered to relieve the prisoner, he would instantly arm and proceed against them, represented how dreadful the consequences might be, and he would at any time get assistance from the other ships, with which he could with the greatest ease secure every one of them. They still continued their abuse, and even resolved not to quit the deck without the prisoner; however, about two o'clock, many of them began to slip off the deck, and by three there were very few remaining, and every thing was once more quiet, and remained so till the next day at noon. Some time after we had piped to dinner, the chief mate sent for me, told me he believed the people intended forcibly to relieve the prisoner after dinner, and desired I would order all the quarter-masters to be ready. Before we could get armed, they all rushed aft in a body; Berry at the head, who threatened to knock the first man down, who came in their way, with a marlin spike which he carried in his hand. We the officers and petty officers threw ourselves in before them, and Berry struck the sixth mate on the shoulder with the marlin spike, which brought him to the deck. We found it impossible to detain the prisoner, whom the mutineers carried forward, knocked off his irons, and threw them overboard: then Berry called out, We have got the day, let us give three cheers; which they accordingly did. They then went down below, pointed the two bow guns aft, lowered down the ports, and unshipped all the ladders. Berry and Lilly came aft into the steerage, and gave the officers every abuse they could think of; they were even heard to say from below they would break open the magazine. The boatswain

swain then went down below, to see if they intended to take such a dangerous step; they told him they were all ready for doing it, and would certainly do it the moment they were attacked by the officers, which prevented the chief mate from attacking, as he intended to have done. Having ordered every body to arms, the chief mate ordered me to take the yaul and go on board the Fitzwilliam, and request captain Dundas to give his advice. In the dangerous situation the ship was, captain Dundas desired I would return, and if the chief mate wanted assistance from the other ships, to let him know immediately and he would send a boat from every ship in the fleet. By the time I returned the second mate came along-side, and the people seemed inclinable to return to their duty; but in a most daring manner came aft, and insisted upon terms which were not granted them, as they had possession of the gun-deck and magazine, and we had every reason to think from their behaviour when the second mate came along-side, that they would be perfectly quiet when he was left commanding officer. The chief mate quitted the ship in a sampan, it being his opinion, the second mate's, and my own, that the ringleaders could be secured when the people were in a state of sobriety. It happened as we expected: the moment the chief mate quitted the ship, they returned to their duty, got the guns in their places when ordered by the second mate, and every thing appeared perfectly quiet. About three o'clock the Locko's boat came along-side, to know if we wanted any assistance. The people let the officer come on board without any disturbance. He soon after left the ship. About four o'clock the chief mate, and Mr. Raitt the chief mate of the Fitzwilliam, came on board. The mutineers let the officers come on board

board after some altercation, but ordered the boat to shove off, threatening to stave her if they refused. The chief mate then called me, and ordered me to take six quartermasters down to the lazaretta armed, and defend the magazine, and to run any man through that should attempt to enter it. I can give no account of what passed after this upon the upper-deck and gun-deck, as I did not come up till most of the mutineers were seized.

(Signed) A^M CUMINE,
December 4, 1787.   3d Mate, Belvidere.

HAVING read this to the court, and affirming it as true, he then proceeds as follows: After I had been some time in the lazaretta, they lifted the scuttle leading to the magazine, and were going to jump down; being opposed, they afterwards laid the scuttle over again. A little time after they lifted it off again, and then they said they were determined to jump down. I assured them if they did, I would run the first man through. Notwithstanding which, a man (Paterson) jumped down, and I wounded him. After him numbers immediately jumped down, first throwing billets of wood and shot, and drove me from the lazaretta. I cannot recollect if any of the prisoners were there.

Court. Do you know who took Keiff off the quarter-deck, and who knocked his irons off?
Answer. Berry and Patterson.

Court. What were the terms that the people demanded of the chief mate, and what officers were present when they did so?
Answer.

Answer. They demanded that they should have an allowance of grog, and likewise that Keiff should be at liberty. The officers present were the chief, the second, fifth and sixth mates, and the witness.

Court. Who were the men that asked those terms?
Answer. Lilly and Garland.

Captain Greer. Did they not demand a midshipman (Mr. Clayton) to be turned before the mast?
Answer. I heard it called out, but do not know from whom.

Court. Did it appear to you during the mutiny that the people were in a state of intoxication?
Answer. Very few of them I think.

Court. Do you recollect any of that few that were in that state?
Answer. Kelly; none else among the prisoners but him.

Court. Do you know the man that threatened the fifth mate's life?
Answer. Yes; Conner.

Questions asked by the Prisoners.

John Berry. Whether he saw me knock the irons off Keiff?
Answer. The witness saw him carry Keiff forward, and very active about him; but cannot say who immediately knocked them off.

MR. Law, fifth officer of the Belvidere, called in, and desired to inform the court of what he knew of the prisoners and the mutiny.

At half past ten o'clock on Saturday night, the 1st December, I heard Mr. Dunlop call for a light. I was then in the great cabin; I followed him, and saw Mr. Dunlop collar Keiff, and Keiff take the light from Mr. Dunlop. A scuffle then ensued. Keiff tore Mr. Dunlop's shirt. I assisted Mr. Dunlop in getting him aft; during the time a billet of wood was thrown from forward, which struck me on the leg. Conner came aft; I did not know his intentions, and pushed him forward. Keiff was put in irons with difficulty. I was last in coming upon deck, and turning round, I saw the people assembling a-breast the main-mast; Ladson, Berry, and Conner, laying down terms to Mr. Dunlop, and insisting on having Keiff out of irons. Berry said, Don't let us stand about it, let us take him out. A long altercation ensued till one in the morning; they then began to disperse. An officer was then ordered to keep the watch through the night; during which in my watch they were quiet. At twelve o'clock the next day, Sunday the 2d December, the people came up armed, Berry in particular. With a marline-spike they rushed aft, with Berry at their head, and took the prisoner forcibly out of irons. They then began to make a great disturbance, threatening Mr. Dunlop, and calling him a number of abusive names, saying, that the ship was now their own, and that no man should be punished without they thought he deserved it. They barricaded the ship, and swore that no boats should come along-side: all the prisoners and most of the people making use of these or like expressions.

They handed up shot upon deck, and got every thing necessary to keep the boats off in case they were boarded. Berry and Lilly said they would die upon deck rather than give the ship up.

Court. Did Berry strike the sixth mate to the deck, and at what time?
Answer. I cannot say.

Court. Did you see any body attempt to push Mr. Dunlop overboard, or did you see him nearly in that situation?
Answer. I saw him nearly in that situation, but saw no man do it.

Court. In what state was the ship's company as to sobriety during the Saturday night and Sunday?
Answer. Kelly was the only drunken man I saw amongst them.

William Conner. Did you hear me threaten your life?
Answer. Only my ears.

Court to the prisoners. Have you any more questions to put to the witness?
Prisoners Answer. No.

Mr. James M'Culloch, sixth officer of the ship Belvidere, called in, and desired to inform the court of what he knew of the prisoners and the mutiny.

Upon the 1st of December at night, I as usual put the lights out at nine o'clock, and immediately went to bed; but before I was long asleep, I was awakened by a noise I heard upon deck. I then got up, and without putting any other clothes on but my breeches, went upon deck, and there saw all the foremast-men together in the waist: but the man who was then spokesman was William Conner, who then said they were all determined to have James Keiff out of irons that night; and Henry Ladson, who declared there should nothing prevent them having him to sleep on the gun-deck that night, and in his own hammock; and John Berry said, What signifies talking, let us one and all go and take him, and see who dares hinder us. Robert Skinner and Samuel Walker likewise were resolved upon relieving the prisoner; as for the rest of the people, they stood behind their backs, declaring and signifying their approbation of every thing the ringleaders proposed; however, seeing the officers and petty officers were determined to guard the prisoner all night sooner than suffer him to be relieved by them, they wisely went to bed. However, Mr. Dunlop thought proper to make one officer keep watch with two midshipmen and two quarter-masters; the rest turned in, but were ready upon a moment's warning to be upon deck; but we had the satisfaction to remain quiet for the rest of the night. Next morning the people got up and washed the main-deck without making any noise; and for my own part I thought the men had reflected deliberately on their behaviour: but at twelve o'clock, when the boatswain and his mates had piped to dinner, they all of course went below, and the ship's steward as usual served out their grog. But I do not think they had time to eat their dinner, when they came upon deck

deck with their champion ringleaders at their head, armed with fids, marlinspikes, pump-bolts, handspikes, crows, and belaying pins, with John Berry first encouraging them, by saying, We will murder the first bugger that offers to oppose us. Mr. Dunlop just then came out of the cuddy, and I myself not having time to get either pistols or any defensive arms, run in between the mutineers and the prisoners. What with the force of them all running upon me, and the blow I received from John Berry's marlinspike, I fell down amongst their feet, and was hustled forward to the waist before I could recover myself; but upon my getting up, I saw the mutineers breaking the lock. They then, by order of John Berry, gave three cheers, he saying they had got the day. They then went below, unshipped the ladders, let down all the ports, pointed the two foremost guns aft, and handed up the shot, and declared, if any violent measures were proposed, they would break open the magazine. At that time Mr. Craig came on board, when Mr. Dunlop and the rest of the officers agreed to let them alone until such time as we had it in our power to get between them and the magazine, as they seemed to be then quiet. Mr. Dunlop then called a passage-boat, and took leave of us, as I imagined, to go to Canton. At this time the people were quiet, and said they would go to their duty. At half past three o'clock the commodore's boat came along-side; but before this, the ringleaders came aft, in a daring manner insisting upon terms; and John Berry, Abraham Lilly, and Anthony Garland, insisted upon having Mr. Clayton, a midshipman, turned before the mast, that they might have him to murder; but upon Abraham Lilly's saying so, John Berry said, I will not take his life; I will break one leg and

and one arm; and as for Mr. Law, I will cut one of his ears off. When the commodore's boat came, Mr. Raitt, his chief officer, read a letter, the contents infisting upon the ringleaders being given up; upon which the mutineers put themselves in a posture of defence, and swore no boats should come along-side. They immediately some of them went to break open the magazine, and began throwing at the boats along-side and upon the quarterdeck; but the officers and petty officers being armed, we made a sally from the quarter-deck, and cut several down with cutlasses, when they went to the magazine, and found a warm reception from the third mate, who was then guarding it with five quarter-masters. The pinnaces all got along-side, we then took all that were on the maindeck prisoners, went down upon the gun-deck, hauled up the ports; but before we had that done, several were hurt by shot hove by the mutineers. However, by five o'clock, we had all our foremast-men prisoners in the cuddy, when John Berry, Abraham Lilly, Anthony Garland, William Conner, Robert Skinner, John Hastings, Thomas Langford, Henry Ladson, Timothy Kelly, and James Keiff, were sent prisoners on board the commodore. Samuel Walker, Thomas Paterson, Oliver Butler, and James Brown, were the only men not concerned.

Questions asked Mr. M'Culloch.

Court. What terms were demanded by the prisoners?

Answer. Anthony Garland insisted upon grog that day and liberty; he likewise demanded Mr. Clayton midshipman to be turned before the mast, because he had on that day nearly got him a flogging. Abraham Lilly threatened

to

to murder the said midshipman; John Berry said he would break one leg and one arm.

Court. Do you know who knocked the irons off Keiff?

Answer. I do not know who knocked the lock off the irons, but I saw Berry and Paterson throw them overboard.

Court. Did you hear any of the people threaten to blow the ship up?

Answer. Yes, but cannot say who.

Court. Were there any locks broke open to enter the lazaretta?

Answer. The lock of the fore-scuttle, but cannot tell who did it.

Abraham Lilly. Question. Did you hear me threaten Mr. Clayton's life?

Answer. Yes, I did; you and Garland.

Court to the Prisoners.

Court. Have you any more questions to put to the Witness?

Prisoners Answer. No.

Mr. Christopher Spencer, gunner of the ship Belvidere, called in, and desired to inform the court of what he knew of the prisoners and the mutiny.

Questions

Questions by the Court.

Court. Where was you when you heard of the chief mate's light being taken from him?
Answer. In the gun-room.

Court. Was you upon deck when Keiff was put in irons?
Answer. Yes.

Court. Was there any resistance made, or any abusive language made use of, and from whom?
Answer. Ladson and Conner said that the man should not be put in irons without their going with him.

Court. Was you sent by Mr. Dunlop to secure the gun-room, and did any body attempt to break in, and who?
Answer. None.

Court. Were the ship's company drunk or sober, or what sort of state were they in on Saturday and Sunday?
Answer. A little drunken on Saturday; all sober on Sunday except Kelly.

Court. Did you receive any orders from Mr. Craig when Mr. Dunlop left the ship, and what were they?
Answer. To go down and see the magazine secured.

Court. What situation were the guns in?
Answer. They were in their places.

Court.

Court. When Mr. Dunlop left the ship were the ports down?
Answer. No, they were up.

Court to the Prisoners.

Court. Have you any questions to put to the witness?
Prisoners. None.

Mr. William Frost, Boatswain of the Belvidere, called in and ordered to inform the court of what he knew of the prisoners and the mutiny.

Questions by the Court.

Question. Did you see the guns pointed aft on Sunday?
Answer. Yes the two foremost.

Question. Were the ports ever lashed in?
Answer. I do not know; but they were lowered down and hauled up several times.

Question. What state were the ship's company in on Saturday and Sunday?
Answer. On Saturday only Keiff and Payne drunk; on Sunday between twelve and two only Kelly that appeared to be drunk to me.

Question. Did you hear any of the people say they would blow the ship up?
Answer. I heard it, but cannot tell who.

Question. Who appeared to you to be the leading men, and who was most active in the mutiny on Saturday and Sunday?

Answer. On Saturday night Conner and Ladson, on Sunday Berry and Lilly.

Court to the Prisoners. Have you any questions to put to the witness?

Prisoners Answer. No.

Court to Mr. Dunlop, chief mate.

Question. Did the ship's company any time on Sunday ask any terms of you?

Answer. They asked if I had released Keiff. I answered, No; that they had done it themselves. They also demanded Mr. Clayton, midshipman, to be turned before the mast.

MR. Charles Raitt, chief officer of the Earl Fitzwilliam, called in, and desired to inform the Court of what he knew of the prisoners and the mutiny.

Questions by the Court to Mr. Raitt.

Question. What state did you find the Belvidere in when you went on board with Mr. Dunlop?

Answer. In a very mutinous state; and the first thing that made me believe they were, was their ordering my boat to put off instantly from along-side.

Question. Did you see them armed to keep any boats off?

Answer. Yes; but not at first.

Question. Did they refuse to give the ringleaders up when you told them you came with the commodore's orders?

Answer. They refused to a man, and said they would sooner die. Berry in particular said he would fight the ship as long as her sides stuck together; took off his cap, and gave three cheers. When I was telling him the consequence, Ladson replied, he could only be hanged; as to flogging, he did not mind it.

Question. Did the people seem drunk or sober?
Answer. Perfectly sober and very deliberate. I did not see one drunk.

Question by Henry Ladson to the Witness.

Question. I wish to know where I was when I made that answer?
Answer. On the upper-deck on the chock starboard side of the deck. When they found the boats coming, they armed themselves with round shot and double-headed shot; called, Stand by and divide yourselves, the boats are coming on both sides.

The Prisoners upon their defence.

John Berry, Have you any person to call on your defence, or to speak to your character?
Answer. No.

Abraham Lilly, Have you any person to call on your defence, or to speak to your character?
Answer. No.

Henry Ladſon, Have you any perſon to call on your defence, or to ſpeak to your character?

Anſwer. I was not on the fore-hatchway when Mr. Dunlop ſpoke from the upper-deck.

James Keiff, Have you any perſon to call on your defence, or to ſpeak to your character?

Anſwer. I deny taking the candle from Mr. Dunlop but to hold it.

Anthony Garland, Have you any perſon to call on your defence, or to ſpeak to your character?

Anſwer. I am not guilty of going on the fore-hatches, nor with the ſhot, nor with taking the man out of irons. Mr. Donaldſon, Mr. Young, and Mr. Perry, will ſpeak to my character. Thoſe gentlemen not preſent.

Robert Skinner, Have you any perſon to call on your defence, or to ſpeak to your character?

Anſwer. No.

Thomas Langford, Have you any perſon to call on your defence, or to ſpeak to your character?

Anſwer. Can get a character in the fleet.

William Conner, Have you any perſon to call in your defence, or to ſpeak to your character?

Anſwer. Says he was in liquor, as an excuſe for his conduct.

Timothy Kelly, Have you any perſon to call in your defence, or to ſpeak to your character?

Anſwer. Pleads drunkenneſs.

John Haftings, Have you any perfon to call in your defence, or to fpeak to your character?

Anfwer. They were running forward with cutlaffes; I took up a fhot to defend myfelf. Captain Greer gives him a good character till this mutiny.

Adjourned to Saturday the 15th inftant at eleven o'clock in the forenoon.

Saturday, 15th December 1787.

The Court being refumed,

PRESENT:

Captains, JAMES DUNDAS, Prefident.

ALEX^R MONTGOMERY.
JOSEPH HUDDART.
J. H. DEMPSTER.
JAMES MONRO.
HENRY CHURCHILL.
GEORGE BLACHFORD.
W^M HARDCASTLE.
DAVID TOLME.
GEORGE MILLETT.
RICHARD PENNELL.
WILLIAM STOREY.
PHILIP DUNDAS.
JOHN DENNIS.
JOHN PAIBA.
CHARLES LINDEGREN.

The Court having gone through the evidence, and asked the prisoners what they had to say for themselves; it has not appeared that there has been the least cause for murmur amongst the ship's company, either for ill usage from any one officer or petty officer in the ship; that this daring mutiny has arose from a spirit that prevailed, that they were on board of a merchantman, where, according to their own expressions, they would not meet with due punishment; that it also appears, that on Sunday, the second day of the mutiny, the prisoners were all sober and deliberate but one man, Kelly, and who pleaded drunkenness; the others never attempting any defence of that sort, or saying any thing in their own vindication. We therefore are of opinion that this daring mutiny, had it not been immediately suppressed by about eighteen boats manned and armed from the Company's ships, the consequence might have been dreadful, not only to that ship; but this spirit spreading to the fleet in general, where there are above three thousand of his Majesty's subjects, the greater number of which might have, by joining the mutineers, committed depredations against the inhabitants, and put a stop to the Company's trade, with the loss of many lives: We therefore are of opinion, that severe and immediate corporal punishment be inflicted upon the ringleaders; and that Berry and Lilly at different ships of the fleet receive, *Berry* one hundred, and *Lilly* seventy lashes; that the rest be punished on board the Belvidere, and that *Ladson* and *Keiff* receive sixty lashes; *Garland*, *Skinner*, and *Conner* forty-eight lashes; *Hastings* and *Langford* twenty-four lashes; that *Kelly*, as least culpable, receive twelve

twelve lashes. The latter recommended to mercy by the Court.

(Signed) J. Dundas.
A. Montgomery.
J. Huddart.
J. H. Dempster.
James Monro.
H^y Churchill.
George Blachford.
Wm Hardcastle.
D^o Tolme.
Geo. Millett.
Richd Pennell.
Wm Storey.
Ph. Dundas.
John Dennis.
John Paiba.
Charles Lindegren.

John Berry and Abraham Lilly, after having the last of their punishment along-side of the Belvidere, were liberated, and taken on board, when they went down on the gun-deck, and were spiriting up the seamen to mutiny again; on which, and being insolent to captain Greer on the quarter-deck, he ordered them on shore at Dones Island, with their clothes, &c. which is the island the English are permitted to walk on, and within a cable's length of the ships.

TYÅANA

On the Belvidere's arrival in England, they brought an action against their captain in the court of Common Pleas, which was tried on the 15th December 1788, before Lord Loughborough and a special jury, when a verdict was given in favour of captain Greer.

Berry had been an old offender in the navy and on board the Granby East Indiaman, captain Johnson, 1777.

SOON after my arrival at Canton I took an opportunity of paying a visit to Mr. Cox, an English gentleman resident there; and I was much surprised to see my old friend Tyaana, whom the reader may recollect I met with at Atoui, on my second visit to the Sandwich Islands. Tyaana immediately recollected me; and so sensibly was he affected with the interview, that he clasped his arms about me in the most affecting manner, reclined his head on my shoulder, tears ran unheeded down his cheeks, and it was some time before he became calm and composed enough to utter the name of his old acquaintance Popote; but when the first transports of joy, which so unexpected a meeting excited, had a little subsided, he seemed happy in making every enquiry that could please or afford satisfaction respecting his friends at the Sandwich Islands; and on my enquiring how he came to China, I found that captain Mears had touched at Atoui in his passage from the coast of America to China, and Tyaana expressing a wish to accompany the captain to Pretane, he had taken him on board

board and brought him to Macao; at which place he left him in the care of Mr. Rofs, his chief mate, of whom Tyaana was remarkably fond. They remained some time at Macao; and Tyaana was generally indulged in walking about wherever his inclination led him; and on thefe occasions he conftantly wore a beautiful feathered cap and cloak, and carried a fpear in his hand to denote himfelf to be a perfon of grandeur and diftinction; nor did he like to wear any other drefs, except the maro, which is always worn by the Sandwich iflanders about the waift: such an appearance however being scarcely modeft in a civilized country, Mr. Rofs got a light fattin waiftcoat and a pair of trowfers made for him, and which he was prevailed with to wear, but not without great feeming reluctance at firft, but with which he was better pleafed after they became familiar and habitual to him.

TYAANA, though *no profeffed papift*, would frequently go to the places of divine worfhip at Macao, and always obferved the manner, motions, and attitudes of the congregation, ftanding or kneeling, and as they did, fo did he, appearing very ftudious to imitate them, by an exact conformity to all their actions, geftures, and behaviour.

His noble and generous fpirit vifibly difcovered itfelf on various occafions. One time he went up to an orange ftall, and picking out half a dozen oranges, gave the woman who fold them a couple of nails for them, which in his eftimation was a very ample, and indeed a fuperabundant compenfation for her oranges; nails in his country being things of very great and precious value; obferving at the fame time that he had paid her for the oranges and made

her

NORTH WEST COAST OF AMERICA.

her a present beside; but the good woman was by no means satisfied with such payment, and was about to raise a disturbance, by a loud, rude, offensive clamour of her not being paid; when some gentlemen luckily happening to be with Tyaana at the time, they readily pacified her complaint, by paying her to her satisfaction.

WHEN the Queen Charlotte arrived in Macao Roads, Mr. Ross and Tyaana often went with captain Dixon to Wampoa. During this short passage Tyaana often expressed his dislike of the Chinese, particularly that custom of shutting up and excluding the women from the sight of all strangers. And he seemed likewise to have contracted a prejudice, as well against the form, shape, and manner of their persons, as against their practices and customs; and carried it even to hatred and antipathy, insomuch that he was once going to throw the pilot over-board for some trivial matter of offence.

WHEN he arrived at Canton he was particularly noticed by the gentlemen of the English factory, from whom he received invitations, and every mark of civility which could testify their respect and regard to his rank and dignity; nor was he less caressed and admired by all classes of people at Canton.

A CAPTAIN Tasker, of the Milford, from Bombay, gave a sumptuous entertainment to a number of English gentlemen, and of course Tyaana was among the rest. After dinner, being upon deck, a number of poor Tartars, in small sampans, were about the ship asking alms, as is customary there on such occasions of entertainment and festivity.

festivity. Tyaana immediately enquired what they wanted, and being told that they were beggars who came to supplicate the refuse of the table, he expressed great concern, saying that he was very sorry to see any persons in want of food, and that it was quite a new scene to him; for that they had no people of that description at Atoui; he seemed to be under great impatience to procure them relief, and became a very importunate soliciter on their behalf. The captain's generous disposition readily co-operated with his importunities, and he ordered all the broken victuals, being a large quantity, to be brought upon deck, and Tyaana had the distribution of it among the poor Tartars, which he did, observing the most equal, impartial division he was able to make of it; and his pleasure and satisfaction in the performance of that task were not less visible in his countenance than his actions.

I asked him if he was willing to go to Pretane; but he told me that he expected to have been there in twelve moons, but that now he should be glad to return to Atoui. It seems captain Mears had engaged in a Portuguese expedition to the coast of America, and promised to leave Tyaana at Atoui in his passage thither. The gentlemen at Canton, desirous to give him lasting proofs of their friendship and esteem, furnished him with whatever could be useful or acceptable; such as bulls, cows, sheep, goats, rabbits, turkies, &c. with oranges, mangoes, and various kinds of plants; so that his safe arrival with his cargo would prove of the utmost value to his country, and an honourable testimony to his countrymen of the distinguished esteem and regard with which he had been treated,

and

and his very name revered by all ranks and conditions of the people of Canton.

TYAANA is tall; being six feet two inches in height, and so exceedingly well made, that a more perfect symmetry and just proportion of shape is rarely to be met with; but he is rather inclined to corpulency; has a pleasing animated countenance, a fine piercing eye; but the annexed engraving, which is taken from a painting for which he sat at Canton, and which was deemed a striking likeness, will give a more perfect idea of him than can possibly be conveyed by verbal description.

CHAP. XVI.

Leave Macao.—Proceed through the Straits of Banca and Sunda.—Anchor at North Island.—The Vessels part Company.—Arrival at Saint Helena.—Departure from thence.—Five of the People nearly poisoned by eating Fish.—Arrival in England.

ON the morning of the 6th of February a fresh breeze, with open cloudy weather; latter part moderate breezes and hazy. At seven in the morning weighed and came to sail, with an intention of taking a birth below the shipping, to be in readiness for going down the river immediately on the pilot's coming on board. At eight, a rope getting into the tiller rope block in stays, occasioned the ship's touching the ground. It was very near the pitch of low water, and by the time we had run out a kedge, and hove taught on the hauser, she floated off. At nine the pilot came on board; employed sailing and warping down the river with a light breeze from the North East. About noon had got down nearly to the lower parts of the shipping, where we anchored for a few minutes, and gave the ship's company an opportunity of getting some dinner; and I have to remark, that Robert Spencer, John Harrison, and Thomas Potts, stole a boat from along-side the ship at about eight or nine in the evening, and absented themselves for some time; and on my sending Mr. Hayward with another boat to look for them, he picked them up near the Bankshalls. They had been purchasing a quantity of liquor, sufficient to have kept the ship's company in a state of drunkenness for some days. Those three persons, since our arrival at Wampoa, either from drunkenness, or sickness occasioned by it, scarcely did a week's duty.

ON Thursday the 7th very light winds from the East North East, with close hazy weather; employed sailing and towing down the river; and at six in the evening the tide of ebb being done, and not enough wind to stem the flood with, we anchored with the small bower anchor in five fathoms, muddy bottom, about three or four miles below the shipping at Wampoa; Queen Charlotte in company. At midnight the wind light and variable between the North and West. At five in the morning weighed, and came to sail with the ebb, with a light breeze from the North North West, and fine weather; Queen Charlotte in company. Soon after getting under way, the wind chopped round to the East South East: employed turning down the river until ten in the morning, at which time we anchored in about five fathoms, muddy bottom, with the small bower.

ALL this morning we had light winds from the South East, with fine weather. At three in the afternoon the ebb-tide having made strong, we weighed and came to sail, Queen Charlotte in company. At eight in the evening came-to with the small bower in five fathoms water, muddy bottom. At six a breeze at North North East, weighed and came to sail. At eight passed through the Boca Tigris with a fine breeze at North West,

CHAP. XVI.

1788.
February.
Friday 8.

West, with which we were standing towards Macao. At noon a breeze at West North West, with fine pleasant weather, a number of Chinese boats along-side, with vast quantities of oysters, which we bought very cheap. At nine in the morning sent the whale-boat on board a ship at anchor. She proved to be the Diana, country ship, from India for Wampoa, who had been missing some time.

Saturday 9.

MODERATE breeze from the West, with fine clear weather. At two in the afternoon the wind hauled round to the southward. At seven in the evening, the ebb being down, we anchored with the small bower in eight fathoms water, muddy bottom. At midnight a moderate breeze at East South East. At two in the morning a breeze at North East, and the ebb having made, we weighed and came to sail. At eight very light airs, and variable. At half past eight came-to with the small bower in five fathoms water. At ten a moderate breeze at South. At half past eleven weighed and came to sail.

Sunday 10.

CALM, with fair weather. At two in the afternoon a light breeze from the West by South, standing down towards Macao. At five Macao bore North West by West, distant about four leagues, and the Westernmost part of the Grand Ladrone South by East one quarter East, distant about eight leagues; the island of Patoe, which is a small island, lying just to the Westward of the Grand Ladrone, bearing South three quarters East, distant about seven leagues. A moderate breeze from the South East by East, with which we were standing through between the Patoe and the islands lying to the Westward. At half past five, hoisted in the whale-boat and secured her, and placed

placed the Sandwich Island canoes on the quarter in room of the whale-boat. At this time the pilot left us; I sent by him a letter for Henry Browne Esq. president of the council at Canton, signifying the situation and good condition of the King George and Queen Charlotte; also a letter of advice for Mr. John Etches, or the commander of the Prince of Wales or Princess Royal, to be delivered on either of their arrivals. At half past seven the breeze having failed, and the tide setting to the Westward, we came-to with a small bower in six fathoms water, Queen Charlotte in company, the Grand Ladrone bearing from South East half East to South East half South, distant about five leagues, the island of Patoe South East by East three leagues. At midnight calm and very hazy. At three in the morning a light breeze sprung up at North North East, weighed and made sail, Queen Charlotte in company. At half an hour after nine in the forenoon the South East point of the Grand Ladrone bore North East half North, distant about twenty-five miles, from whence I took my departure: Grand Ladrone latitude 22° 2′ North, longitude 246° 4′.

The 11th, 12th, and 13th February, for the most part fair weather. A number of the ship's company ill with fluxes, and others with fevers, owing (in the opinion of the surgeon) chiefly to their hard drinking whilst at Wampoa. On the 12th saw many dark-coloured gulls and some boobies, all white except the tips of their wings, which were black. At half past seven in the morning of the 13th saw a sail in the North East quarter standing to the Southward. At nine the strange sail being near enough

CHAP.
XVI.

1788.
From Sunday
10, to Thurs-
day 14.

enough to see our colours, we hoisted them; the stranger
answered us by shewing her's, which we took to be Prussian;
latitude observed 18° 01' North, latitude account 18° 09'
North, course South, 3° 0ʹ West, distance from the Grand
Ladrone fifty-four miles; longitude account 246° 04' West,
longitude observation 246° 35' 15" West, variation 0° 0'.
On the 14th instant spoke with the ship which we had
been within sight of all day, which proved to be a vessel
formerly called the Lowden, British built, and about fifteen months ago fitted out in the river Thames, from
whence she sailed under Imperial colours to King George's
Sound on the North West coast of America, and from
thence to Macao in China. She is now called the Imperial Eagle, commanded by captain Berkley, and manned
by British subjects. She at this time sailed under Portuguese colours, and was bound for the Mauritius. Our
people were now all upon the recovery; the Queen Charlotte in company.

Friday 15.
Saturday 16.

ON Friday the 15th light winds from East by South.
On the 16th a moderate breeze, with the wind at North
East; at eleven, judging myself pretty near the Macclesfield
shoal, hove to, and sounded with sixty fathoms line; no
ground. At midnight sounded again with sixty fathoms
line; no ground. At one in the morning a vast number
of porpoises about. Between midnight and seven sounded every hour without getting ground, sometimes with a
hundred fathoms of line. At seven o'clock, judging myself far enough to the Southward, I altered my course
to South West by South, with a view of making Pulo
Sapata, the wind at North East, a two knot breeze. I
supposed,

NORTH WEST COAST OF AMERICA.

supposed, from our not striking soundings on the Macclesfield, that it does not extend so far to the Westward as laid down in the charts, and that we passed just to the Westward of the bank. I supposed this, from our being pretty certain of our longitude; having at 2ʰ 30ᵐ past midday got some very good observations of the sun and moon, the sun West of the moon, which gave the longitude at that time 245° 54′ West of Greenwich. Saw many birds of the booby kind. At eight in the morning hailed the Queen Charlotte. Captain Dixon informed me that his vessel made some water when she lay along, three inches per hour; his surgeon and cooper's mate very ill; our people all on the recovery. On the 17th I took my surgeon on board to give his advice or assistance, and took with me about ten or twelve gallons of Port wine for the use of the Queen Charlotte's sick; saw a few birds of the tern kind, a number of flying-fish, and some dolphins. About the 18th I found, by comparing our compasses with the Queen Charlotte's azimuth compass, half a point difference, ours shewing half a point more to the Southward than her's did. I believe the azimuth compass to be the most exact, and allowed accordingly. At half past three in the afternoon I returned on board, hoisted the whale-boat in, and made sail. Our surgeon was of opinion, that the people on board the Queen Charlotte were in a fair way of recovery, and that there was no necessity of removing them into this ship, as I intended, for the purpose of having the surgeon's assistance. Captain Dixon informed me that the Queen Charlotte made about three inches of water an hour. She soon after leaving the Ladrone made one and two inches, and as her leak increased, I thought it right to stay by her until

3 B

CHAP. XVI.

1788.
February.
Wednes. 20.

until we saw how it turned out. Pulo Sapata at noon bore South 51° West, distant 285 miles. On the 20th we had fresh gales with cloudy weather, and the wind being North by East, I steered South West half West, to avoid the Vigia rock. At a quarter past ten saw the island of Sapata, bearing South West one quarter South, distant about eleven miles Hauled to the South South West to go to the Eastward of the island. A small hummock rock in one with Sapata, bearing from Sapata North West by West, three quarters West, and distant from Sapata about three or four miles. This island is perfectly bold on the North and East sides, the South and West not so safe, owing to the small hummock rock, and a few breakers. It is well named, for it is exactly shaped like a shoe, and no person can be deceived in it, for it seems to bear the same likeness on all sides, not a tree or bush to be seen on it; but there were boobies in great abundance, the island being made white by their dung.

Thursday 21.

On the 21st we shaped our course about South West by West, thinking to make Pulo Condore at about five or six leagues to the Eastward of the island; from thence we steered for Pulo Timoan and Pulo Cloz. About two in the afternoon saw another small island bearing about North West by North, and distant about four or five leagues. I imagined this to be one of the small islands laid down by Dalrymple, lying to the Westward of Pulo Sapata. He also lays several down to the Eastward of Sapata; none of which I found to be there. At three in the afternoon Pulo Sapata bore North East, distant eleven miles. With a fine steady gale at North East, we steered South West half West, four knots per

NORTH WEST COAST OF AMERICA.

per hour; this South West half West by our compass being nearly South West by West true. On the 22d our people continued very ill; several of them in fluxes. On 25th saw the islands of Aramba bearing from North East by East to East by North, our distance from the North end about eight leagues. At six Pulo Domer bore South East.

CHAP.
XVI.
1788.
February.
Friday 22.
Monday 25.

On the 26th, a light breeze from North North East, with close hazy weather, steering to the South half West, two knots and a half per hour, soundings from thirty-three to twenty-eight fathoms, over a bottom of dark muddy sand and some small shells. At captain Dixon's request, I sent my surgeon on board to give his assistance to Mr. Lowther, surgeon of the Queen Charlotte, who continued very ill. The Queen Charlotte's Peruvian bark being very indifferent, I sent them a supply of ours, which was much better. Captain Dixon returned with the boat, and was also much indisposed with the flux, which was very prevalent among us. We saw the land making in separate small islands, extending from South South West to South West by West half West, the Southernmost land the island of Pulo Panfang, and distant about eight leagues; Queen Charlotte in company. Latitude observed 1° 11' North; light breezes from North East, with exceeding hot sultry weather. On the 27th the peak of Linging made its appearance through the haze, bearing West North West half West, I suppose twelve or fourteen leagues distant. This peak, or rather two peaks, are very remarkable, making very much like two glass-house-chimnies, quite high and close together; the North Easternmost of the two appearing rather rounder at the top than the other, and of nearly an equal height: at the

Tuesday 26.

Wednes. 27.

same

CHAP.
XVI.

1788.
February.
Wednesf. 27.

same time the largest, and I think the most Easterly of them bore North West by West half West, distant about eight or nine leagues; the island of Taya South West three quarters West, distant eight or nine leagues, depth of water eighteen to fifteen fathoms dark grey sand; saw the cluster of islands, called the Three Islands, bearing South, distant about five leagues. Instead of three islands, we found islands and rocks, upwards of a dozen, the largest of the cluster of islands and rocks, and which is nearly the Northern and Western extreme of them, bore from South South East half East to South by East half East, distant three leagues; some small rocks above water lying a little to the Northward and Westward of this island South by West, Pulo Taya North West three quarters West, seven or eight leagues distant. We run along the West side of the cluster Three Islands, at the distance of three or four miles from them in fifteen or sixteen fathoms water, over a dark grey sandy bottom. These islands are a moderate height, very woody, and appear to be safe and bold too; there are some sandy beaches, which I dare say afford plenty of turtle, and no appearance of any breakers any where about the isles, except at a little distance from the points of the small rocky isles. At half past eleven the Queen Charlotte hoisted her colours half mast high; on this we shortened sail, spoke her, and found her surgeon dead. At noon cluster Three Islands bore from North East by East half East to South East by East half East, distant from the nearest island about three leagues; the small islands lying off the North end of Banca, bearing South South West, distant ten or twelve leagues, and Pulo Taya about North North West, distant ten or twelve leagues. I make the Northern and Western extreme of the cluster Three Islands to lie in

the

NORTH WEST COAST OF AMERICA.

the latitude 1° 4′ South, and longitude from lunar observation 254° 34′ West, and latitude of the South extreme of said cluster 1° 17′ South, and longitude 254° 28′ West. Those islands seem to stretch in a South by East and North by West direction of the same small rocky islands, but may lie a little out of that direction to the Eastward and Westward.

THE 29th we had a fine steady breeze at North North East, and steered to South by West, four knots and a half per hour, the depth of water varying as we increased our distance from the cluster Three Islands, from twelve to twenty-one fathoms. At four the Southernmost of the cluster Three Islands bore North North East three quarters East, distant about eight leagues; this bearing and distance, and Mount Monopin South half East, distant about twelve leagues. This bearing and distance by me, places the Mount almost exactly in the same situation that captain King places it in. We now altered the course to South South West and South West by South, thinking before dark to get the Mount to bear about South East by East, or East South East, distant six or seven leagues, as, according to captain King's account, with that bearing and distance, we should have been clear to the Westward of the shoal called Frederic Hendric, and then we could have hauled up for Banca Straits; but we could not accomplish this point before dark, therefore I thought it most prudent to stand off and on during the night, and to enter the Straits in the morning. At six in the evening Monopin bore South South East, distant about eight or nine leagues, and the point of Banca that forms the Eastern entrance into the Straits South three quarters East, ten or eleven leagues; the

islands

CHAP. XVI.

1788.
February
Friday 29.

islands lying off the North end of Banca East half North, six or seven leagues. We had soundings in twenty-one fathoms, dark grey sand. Saw a strange sail to the Northward standing to the Southward; suddenly shoaled our water to thirteen fathoms, standing to the North West, and at half past nine suddenly shoaled the water to seven and a half, soft muddy bottom. This shoal water I supposed to be the Frederic Hendric shoal, or a shoal laid down in Hamilton Moore's account, lying near the Sumatra shore.

Saturday,
March 1.

A FINE breeze from the North West, with rather squally weather and some showers of rain, steering from East by South to East by North, four knots per hour along the Banca coast, at the distance of about four miles from the shore. At half past twelve, we shoaled our water to seven fathoms, and there being an appearance of a bank lying to the Southward of us, hauled up East by North, and just run along its edge in six and a half and seven fathoms water, this appearance of a bank on our starboard hand, and the shore of Banca on our larboard, the Banca shore distant about four miles, and the bank distant a quarter of a mile. Soon after hauling nearer the Banca shore, we deepened our water to fifteen fathoms, and then edged away again to the South by East. About one I got sight of some rocks and a dry white sand-bank, bearing about East by South half South; we hauled to the East by North, and passed between Banca and this shoal, in never less than seven fathoms water over a sandy bottom. At half past one Mount Monopin bore North West by North, and near about the middle of the shoal South East by South, our distance from the Mount about five leagues I judged, and from the sea-shore under the Mount about nine

NORTH WEST COAST OF AMERICA.   375

nine or ten miles, the shoal distant about a mile or a mile and a half, our depth of water at this time fifteen fathoms sandy bottom. The dry part of the shoal appears to be about a quarter of a mile long, trending East and West; it seems narrow; but the coloured water appeared two or three miles to run from the East and West ends in an East and West direction. The shoal I suppose to be entirely covered at high water, I think a perfectly safe passage may be made into those straits, by keeping the Banca shore on board, and passing between it and this shoal. Indeed I would prefer it rather than run down on the Sumatra shore, where should the winds hang Easterly, it may prevent a ship for some time in entering the Straits. When we had Monopin Hill bearing North North East half North, saw a large town on Banca in the same direction close down to the sea-side; at the same time saw four large proas coming towards this town from towards the Straits of Malacca, and one going towards the Straits. At two in the afternoon the tide began to run to the South East through the Straits at South, a light breeze from the North East with small rain, and Mount Monopin bore North West half West, seven or eight leagues distance, and the Northernmost part of Banca in sight North West by West half North, five leagues, and the Northernmost part of Sumatra in sight South West half West. The third point on the Sumatra shore bore South South East half East, three or four leagues distant; our distance from the nearest part of Banca three leagues; the Queen Charlotte in company. Saw a strange sail to the North West standing to the Southward. At noon we had light winds from West by North, with constant rain, steering South by East, two miles per hour; at the same time the second point on the Sumatra shore

CHAP. XVI.

1788. Sunday. March 2.

West

CHAP. XVI.
1788.
March.
Sunday 2.

West three quarters North, distance about five miles; and Mount Permisang, on the island of Banca, North East half East, distance about four or five leagues.

On the 2d March we passed by a Dutch ship lying at anchor. She appeared to be a man of war of twenty guns. At four in the afternoon the first point on the Sumatra shore South East half South, five or six miles, and the Southernmost point of Banca East half South, four or five leagues; Mount Permisang, on the island of Banca, North West six or seven leagues. Hove-to for the ship that was standing after us, and at a quarter past four we spoke her, and found her to be the ship Lansdown, captain Storey commander, from China, bound to London.

Monday 3.

On 3d March light winds and very variable, with close sultry weather. At half past one weighed and stood over to the Sumatra shore; the wind very faint, and a strong tide setting to the South East, which drove us very near the other shoal, that lies between the island of Luspura and the first point of Sumatra; at the same time anchored in five fathoms, a little to the South East; the Lansdown anchored in three fathoms and a quarter. Soon after a breeze springing up from the North East, we weighed and stood to the North North West, as did the Queen Charlotte and Lansdown, to clear the North point of the above-mentioned shoal, and at five we passed over it in three fathoms water; as did the Queen Charlotte; the Lansdown in going over struck and stuck fast, and made a signal of distress. We immediately anchored in five fathoms water, muddy bottom; as did the Charlotte, and sent our boats with kedge anchors and hawsers

to

NORTH WEST COAST OF AMERICA.

to their affiftance. When at anchor, the firft point on the Sumatra fhore bore North North Weft about two or three leagues; the Southernmoft point on the ifland of Sumatra in fight. At half paft nine the Lanfdown made the fignal for more affiftance; hoifted out our yaul, and fent four hands and an officer to their affiftance. At half paft ten the yaul returned, having got her off without receiving any damage. From this time to the 8th nothing particular occurred; when the Lanfdown almoft out of fight. Latitude obferved 4° 50′ South; latitude per bearing, and diftance of the Sifters, 4° 54′ South; longitude per ditto 253° 44′ from Greenwich.

CHAP XVI.
1788.
March.
Monday 7.

ON the 9th, ftrong gales and fqually weather, with thunder and fharp lightning: down topgallant-yards and ftruck the topgallant-mafts. At midnight frefh gales at Weft North Weft; loft fight of the Queen Charlotte; fuppofe fhe was driven off. At daylight faw the Queen Charlotte to the Eaftward; fhe had drove during the gale about two leagues; got under way to join us. The 10th a light breeze from the Northward, with cloudy weather. The Queen Charlotte in company; the Lanfdown barely in fight. Several of our people ill with fluxes.

Sunday 9.

Monday 10.

ON this day at one o'clock in the morning Thomas Pafford, armourer's mate, departed this life, and at fix o'clock in the evening was buried, after having read the ufual funeral fervice over the body. Hoifted out the whale-boat, and fent her with an officer and fix hands on fhore, to look about the reef, by which thefe iflands are furrounded, for turtle. Latitude obferved 5° 7′ South;

Tuefday 11.

3 C

latitude

CHAP. XVI.

1788.
March.

Wednes. 12.

latitude per bearing, and distance of the Sisters, 5° 1' South; longitude per ditto 253° 50' West.

ON the 12th light winds and clear. At three o'clock in the morning the whale-boat returned without any success; having seen no signs of any turtle, nor any kind of fruit on shore; but saw great flocks of wild pigeons.

Thursday 13.

ON the 13th light winds and cloudy. Saw lying in the road two Dutch ships and three Dutch ketches. Came to anchor. Soon after an English cutter came along-side, in which was Mr. Wood, late commander of the Charlotte sloop packet from the Presidency of Bombay, with intelligence for any English Company's ships from China. This gentleman had unfortunately lost his packet on a small island near Cracatoo; and after getting on shore, was attacked and beat off by a country pirate, who, after plundering her, burnt the vessel down to the water's edge. Notwithstanding this gentleman's misfortunes, he has been lucky enough in executing his commission so far, with a boat spared him from the Lascelles, captain Balintine; as no one ship has passed without being spoke with and receiving the intelligence. Before he met with, and got this cutter from the Lascelles, he did his business with a small canoe that he found on the island on which his vessel was lost.

Friday 14.

AT noon standing on towards the roads with a gentle breeze from the Northward; came to anchor, Queen Charlotte in company. On the 14th the island of Java extending from South East by East to South, distant from the nearest part of it five or six leagues. On the 15th the Lansdown anchored in these roads for the purpose of filling water. Sent a boat with a party of men to the North Isle to cut wood; also sent our sick people on shore to take a walk. Served turtle to the ship's company. On the 16th completed our wooding and watering; having filled thirty-seven puncheons, five butts, and one hogshead, and got on board one boat-load of wood. This evening hoisted in the boats, lashed all our water-casks, and in every respect got the ship ready for sea. At eight weighed and came to sail; the Queen Charlotte in company. From this time to the 26th nothing particular. This day died John Coppertwaith, landsman, after experiencing near two months illness of the flux.

From this to the 30th we had fresh Northerly breezes. This day I brought-to for the Queen Charlotte to come up. About nine I sent the whale-boat on board the Queen Charlotte for captain Dixon, and sent our surgeon to look at their sick, and to make up any medicine he thought necessary, and leave directions with them in case of illness. On captain Dixon's coming on board, we agreed to part, and each of us to make the best of our way for Saint Helena. At four, the wind at North East, altered our course to South West. Captain Dixon took leave of me, and returned to the Queen Charlotte; and our surgeon returned on board. Hoisted in the boat, and made sail. From this time to the 12th of June we had a great deal of bad weather, frequently attended with heavy rains and thunder and lightning. This day saw the island of Saint Helena bearing West by North, distant six or seven leagues.

CHAP. XVI.

1788.
June.
Friday 13.

On the 13th a brisk breeze at South East, with heavy weather. At half past noon shortened sail and brought-to. Hoisted out the whale-boat and sent her on shore with an officer, to acquaint the governor of our arrival off the island. At three o'clock the boat returned, with directions from the governor to come in. Bore away and made sail for the bay, and at five anchored with the small bower in thirteen fathoms: hand away and moored with the best bower to the North West in nineteen fathoms, over a bottom of fine black muddy sand; the points of the bay bearing North East by East half East, and South West by West half West, the town South East by East, our distance from the shore about half a mile. From this time to the eighteenth, the carpenter with his party employed in repairing the sheathing, cleaning the bottom, and other necessary repairs; others employed in receiving fresh provisions on board, likewise pitch and tar. The people had leave given them to go on shore. Abundance of fine mackrel and bonettas to be always caught along-side the ship. Completed our water, having got on board thirteen tons and a half.

Wednes. 18.

Thursday 19.

On the 18th arrived here the Queen Charlotte, all well; received the governor's dispatches, and at eleven unmoored and hove short on the best bower, waiting for a breeze. On the 19th a light breeze from the South East, with fine weather; weighed and came to sail; saluted the garrison with nine guns, which was returned with an equal number. Hoisted in the whale-boat and made sail. At four o'clock in the afternoon St. Helena bore East South East, and South South East half East, and the Valley Town South East; our distance from the shore about twelve or thirteen miles. From this time to the 25th moderate

NORTH WEST COAST OF AMERICA.

derate breezes from the South East. This day five of my people, after eating a hearty dinner of bonettas, which had been caught while at Saint Helena, and salted and hung up for sea-store, were in about an hour afterwards taken very ill of a violent pain in the head, an eruption on the skin, and every part considerably swelled and inflamed; these alarming appearances in a great measure subsided after their drinking a little sweet oil, and towards the evening they were all nearly recovered. In consequence of those fish having such a poisonous effect, I ordered all that remained to be thrown over-board.

CHAP. XVI.
1788.
June.
Wednes. 25.

FROM this time to the 22d August afforded little variety, when we made the Isle of Wight; and on the 24th came to anchor in Margate Roads; the people all in high spirits, and rejoiced to see their native shore again. I cannot take leave of my readers without doing justice to the tradesmen that fitted us out with provisions; particularly Mr. Stevens, who supplied us with the very best of every kind; and Messrs. Seale and Waters, a puncheon of whose bread I opened in the river, and found it equally good as when first put on board.

August.
Friday 22.
Sunday 24.

THE grand object of the Voyage, of which an account is given in the preceding sheets, being to trade for furs, with an expectation, no doubt, of gaining more than common profits, by an undertaking which at once was new, hazardous, and uncertain; the world will naturally enquire whether such expectation has been answered; and more particularly as reports have been industriously propagated to the contrary.

THAT

CHAP.
XVI.

THAT the King George's Sound Company have not accumulated immense fortunes may perhaps be true; but it is no less certain that they are *gainers* to the amount of some thousands of pounds; and that the voyage did not answer the utmost extent of their wishes, undoubtedly was owing to their own inexperience; for when the King George and Queen Charlotte arrived at Canton, and even a month after that period, prime sea-otter skins sold from eighty to ninety dollars each. Of this quantity these ships had at least *two thousand* on board, besides a large quantity of furs of inferior value: but though we could have sold our cargo with ease, we were not at liberty to dispose of one material article; the sole management of it being vested in the hands of the East India Company's supercargoes; and at length the skins just mentioned were sold for less than *twenty dollars* each.

FROM this plain statement of *facts*, the public may at once perceive that this branch of commerce, so far from being a losing one, is perhaps the most profitable and lucrative employ that the enterprising merchant can possibly engage in.

A LIST of PLANTS, BIRDS, and FOSSILS, seen in *Cook's River*, and which are nearly the same all along the Coast of America.

PLANTS.

Vaccinium vitis idæa
Red whortle-berries
Erica
Adoxa moschatellina
Tuberous moschatel
Rubus idæus, raspberry bush
Fragaria vesca, wood strawberry
Leantoden taraxicum, common dandelion
Artemisia vulgaris, mugwort
Ribus Alpinum
Vaccinium myrtillus, bilberries
Gnaphalium dioicum, cat's foot
Erigeron acre, blue fleabane
Archillea millefolium, yarrow
Empetrum nigrum, crow-berries
Lilium Kamtschatchense, or Savanne
Plantago major, great plantane
Heracleum penaces, or sweet grass
Veronica
Iris
Angelica sylvestris
Rume acetosa
Alisma plantago aquatica
Ledum palustre
Arbutus uva ursæ
Myrica gale
Rubus chaineemorus
Aconitum napellus
Ranunculus
Astragalus alope euroides
Polygonum bistorta, snake-weed
Orchis latifolia
Betula mana
Lupinus luteus
Allium vineale
Imperatoria
Sedum vesticillatum
After
Pinus Canadensis
Birch alder
Populus alba
Wild rose bushes
Senapis juncea
Astragalus uralensis
Aquilegia
Saxifraga nivalis
——— granulata
Sisymbrium Monensis
Draba verna
Polypodium vulgare
Convallaria stellata
Rumex acutus
Rumex aquatic

BIRDS.

BIRDS.

White-headed eagle
──────bellied──────lath
Crows, ravens, common swallows
The jay of Steller, black grouse
Black sea pies, with red bills
Kingsfisher of a bluish colour, speckled with white
Snipes, grey sand piper
Wild geese and swans
Shags, gulls, the razor bill
The little lusk, the common shearwater
Numberless brown petrels, terns.

FOSSILS.

The composition of the mountains of a grey granite, mixed with glimmer and quartz; the first usually black, and the last purplish
This is covered with a stratum of clay, and above that with a bed of rich vegetable earth
Sulphur, pelluadum, black lead
Copper stone of a blue colour
Iron stone of a black colour
Red oker, cannel coal.

APPENDIX.

TABLES of the ROUTE of the KING GEORGE and QUEEN CHARLOTTE, the Variation of the Compass, and Meteorological Observations, during the Voyage.

N. B. In these Tables, the Situation of the Ships at Noon is set down, and the Variation as observed some Time the same Day.

TABLE I.
From Falkland's Islands to the Sandwich Islands.

Time.	Latitude South.	Longitude West.	Variation East.	Winds, Weather, and Remarks.
1786. Jan. 23, Noon.	51 36	60 54		South. Light winds, and fine pleasant weather. New Island S. E. ¼ E. distant eight miles.
24	52 07	62 49	22 01	N. W. Fresh breezes and cloudy. No land in sight.
25	52 33	63 12	23 07	Ditto. Light breezes, and foggy.
26	53 43	63 54		W. S. W. Fresh breezes, and clear.
27	54 59	63 43		Variable. Strong gales and squally, with lightning to the S. W. Point St. Julian N. W. b. W. ¼ W. Passed a very strong rippling setting to the Northward.
28	55 29	64 00		W. b. N. to S. b. E. Strong gales, and squally. A heavy sea.

[A]

APPENDIX.

TABLE I. Continued.

Route of the King George and Queen Charlotte from Falkland's Islands to the Sandwich Islands.

Time.	Latitude South.		Longitude West.		Variation East.		Winds, Weather, and Remarks.
	°	′	°	′	°	′	
1786. Jan. 29, Noon.	55	30	64	07			S. S. E. to W. N. W. Fresh gales, with rain.
30	56	55	63	35			West. Fresh gales, and squally.
31	57	55	63	39	22	45	S. W. to N. W. Moderate and hazy.
Feb. 1	58	08	64	35	24	00	W. N. W. to S. b. E. Light winds, and foggy. Saw several penguins.
2	58	14	66	15			Variable. Fresh breezes, with rain.
3	59	07	66	59			Ditto. Fresh gales, and squally, with rain.
4	60	19	68	01			N. N. W. to W. S. W. Strong gales, and a heavy sea from the N. W.
5	59	27	68	02			Variable. Fresh breezes, with rain.
6	60	09	70	13	26	19	West. Fresh gales, and squally.
7	60	08	71	11	26	21	Variable. Fresh gales, with hail and rain, and a swell from the S. W.
8	59	55	72	03			S. S. W. to East. Moderate and cloudy.
9	59	14	74	05	26	34	Variable. Moderate and cloudy, with a swell from the S. W. Saw a penguin, a diver, and a quaker bird.
10	58	09	75	05	26	48	S. b. W. to S. W. b. W. Strong breezes, with sleet and snow.
11	56	37	75	45			S. W. Fresh gales, and squally.
12	56	42	75	55			S. W. to W. N. W. Moderate, and cloudy.
13	56	49	78	03			W. N. W. to S. W. Light winds, and cloudy.
14	55	49	79	40			S. W. Moderate, and cloudy.
15	56	23	81	13			N. W. Moderate and hazy, and a heavy sea from the N. W.
16	56	16	81	11			West. Light winds, and cloudy.
17	56	01	82	09			Ditto. Fresh gales and squally, with rain.
18	55	31	82	22			West to W. b. N. Fresh gales and squally, and a heavy swell from the westward. Passed some sea weed.

APPENDIX. iii

TABLE I. Continued.
Route of the King George and Queen Charlotte from Falkland's Islands to the Sandwich Islands.

Time.	Latitude South.		Longitude West.		Variation East.		Winds, Weather, and Remarks.
	°	′	°	′	°	′	
1786. Feb. 19, Noon.	55	37	83	22			W. N. W. to N. N. W. Strong gales and squally.
20	55	36	83	36			N. W. Strong gales, and squally, and a heavy sea.
21	54	27	81	54			Ditto. Ditto, ditto, with rain.
22	54	04	81	19	22	50	N. W. Fresh breezes, and clear. Cleaned ship.
23	53	19	81	32	22	53	Variable. Squally, with rain.
24	52	50	82	15			West to N. b. W. Strong gales, with rain, and a heavy sea from the northward.
25	53	23	83	44			N. W. Fresh gales, with rain.
26	53	00	84	09			Variable. Strong gales, with rain.
27	52	21	83	06			N. W. Strong gales, and squally, and a heavy sea from the N. W.
28	52	20	83	59			Ditto. Strong gales, and squally, with rain. Passed a piece of drift wood.
March 1	52	00	84	15	19	47	W. N. W. Fresh breezes, and clear.
2	50	22	83	24	17	32	West. Fresh gales, and cloudy.
3	48	36	82	32	15	02	Ditto. Ditto, ditto, and squally.
4	47	41	81	05			W. N. W. Fresh gales, and squally, with drizzling rain, and a heavy sea from the westward.
5	45	58	80	43			West. Fresh breezes, and pleasant weather. Cleaned ship.
6	45	30	79	53			W. N. W. Fresh gales, with rain, and a heavy cross sea.
7	44	20	79	49			West. Light winds, and hazy.
8	44	51	80	40			N. W. Moderate, and hazy.
9	44	25	82	12			West. Moderate, and cloudy.
10	43	33	82	10	12	41	Variable. Moderate, and hazy, and a swell from the S. W.
11	43	15	82	51			Variable. Moderate, and cloudy.

[A] 2

TABLE I. Continued.

Route of the King George and Queen Charlotte from Falkland's Islands to the Sandwich Islands.

Time.	Latitude South.		Longitude West.		Variation East.		Winds, Weather, and Remarks.
	°	′	°	′	°	′	
1786. Mar. 12, Noon.	42	53	83	02	15	07	Variable. Moderate, and pleasant.
13	43	05	84	18			N. W. Moderate, with foggy weather.
14	42	47	84	23			Variable. Light winds, and ditto, ditto.
15	42	14	85	04			Ditto. Fresh breezes, and squally unsettled weather.
16	40	53	85	36	12	06	S. W. to N. W. Fresh gales, with drizzling rain.
17	39	42	85	58			W. S. W. Moderate, and hazy.
18	38	06	86	56	10	52	Variable. Fresh gales, and dark cloudy weather, with a long swell from the S. W.
19	36	58	87	55	11	57	Ditto. Light winds, and hazy, and a heavy swell from the S. S. W.
20	36	38	88	05			Variable. Light airs, and pleasant weather. Saw a whale.
21	36	17	88	07	10	23	Ditto. Light winds, and pleasant weather.
22	35	14	88	46			West to South. Moderate, and pleasant.
23	34	11	90	00	9	19	Variable. Light winds, and fair.
24	33	29	90	37	8	14	Ditto. Moderate, and cloudy.
25	32	30	91	51			East. Moderate, and clear.
26	31	46	93	23	7	29	Ditto. Light winds, and clear. Saw a sail to the N. W. standing to the southward, but did not speak her.
27	30	46	94	26	7	10	Ditto. Moderate and pleasant weather.
28	29	20	95	42	6	29	Variable. Fresh gale, and pleasant weather. Saw a tropic bird.
29	28	00	96	44	6	36	East. Fresh breezes, and clear.
30	26	38	97	33			Ditto. Fresh gales, and clear pleasant weather. Several tropic birds about the ship.
31	25	07	98	33	4	32	E. S. E. Fresh gales, and clear.

TABLE I. Continued.

Route of the King George and Queen Charlotte from Falkland's Islands to the Sandwich Islands.

Time.	Latitude South.		Longitude West.		Variation East.		Winds, Weather, and Remarks.
	°	ʹ	°	ʹ	°	ʹ	
1786. April 1, Noon.	23	25	100	52			East. A fresh trade, and pleasant weather.
2	21	44	102	09			E. N. E. Moderate and clear.
3	20	21	103	39			East. Ditto, ditto. Saw several tropic birds.
4	19	17	104	28	4	19	Variable. Light winds, and hazy.
5	18	07	105	51			Variable. Fresh breezes, and hazy. Saw several tropic birds.
6	17	32	106	14			N. E. Light winds, and clear.
7	17	21	106	40	3	58	E. N. E. Ditto, ditto, ditto.
8	16	48	107	15	3	50	N. N. E. Light winds and hazy, with a long swell from the southward. Saw a land bird flying about the ship.
9	15	57	108	15			N. E. A fine breeze, and pleasant weather.
10	15	02	108	54	4	01	Ditto. A light breeze, and clear. Many tropic birds flying round the ship.
11	13	51	109	23			East. A fine breeze, and clear. Passed a turtle. Lowered the boat down; and upon taking of it up, found it to be a dead one. Many tropic and men of war birds about.
12	12	13	110	05	3	41	E. S. E. A fresh trade, and clear pleasant weather.
13	10	21	110	47			East. Ditto, ditto, ditto.
14	8	38	111	25	3	42	S. E. A fresh trade and cloudy, with showers of rain.
15	7	04	111	59			Variable. Moderate and clear. Many Porpoises about the ship. Caught a turtle, weighing 65 lbs.
16	5	45	112	38	3	25	East. A fresh trade, and pleasant weather. Passed many turtle. Numbers of birds about.

APPENDIX

TABLE I. Continued.

Route of the King George and Queen Charlotte from Falkland's Islands to the Sandwich Islands.

Time.	Latitude South.		Longitude West.		Variation East.		Winds, Weather, and Remarks.
1786.	°	′	°	′	°	′	
April 17, Noon.	3	07	113	22			S. E. A fresh breeze, and hazy. Saw a turtle. Many birds of the tern kind about.
18	1	29	113	57			Variable. Moderate, with rain. Passed a piece of sea weed. Saw a large flock of birds.
19	0	02	115	10	3	28	S. E. Moderate, and cloudy.
	North.						
20	1	20	115	40			Ditto. Ditto, and clear.
21	2	40	116	09	3	32	Variable. Moderate, and cloudy.
22	3	33	116	35			Ditto. Light baffling winds, with rain. Saw a whale.
23	4	28	117	10			Ditto. Very unsettled weather.
24	5	32	117	48			Ditto. Moderate and cloudy. Caught five bonitos, and three sharks.
25	6	11	117	59			Ditto. Moderate, with rain.
26	6	34	118	10			S. W. Light winds, and cloudy.
27	6	57	118	17			Variable. Light winds, with rain, and lightning in the N. E. board.
28	7	30	118	49			Variable. Light winds, with thunder and lightning. Passed a turtle. Many dolphins and bonitos about.
29	7	45	119	43			N. E. Moderate breezes, and cloudy. Many dolphins and bonitos about the ship.
30	8	22	120	42			Variable. Fresh breezes, and hazy. Caught several bonitos.
May 1	8	53	120	29			N. N. E. Moderate and cloudy. Caught a turtle.
2	9	45	121	46	2	55	N. E. A fresh trade, and pleasant weather. Caught six turtle; sent two of them on board the Queen Charlotte. Saw a whale.

APPENDIX.

TABLE I. Continued.

Route of the King George and Queen Charlotte from Falkland's Islands to the Sandwich Islands.

Time.	Latitude North.		Longitude West.		Variation East.		Winds, Weather, and Remarks.
	°	′	°	′	°	′	
1786. May 3, Noon.	10	49	123	12			N. E. Fresh gales, and cloudy. Caught ten turtle; sent four of them on board the Queen Charlotte.
4	12	09	125	12			N. E. Fresh gales, and hazy.
5	13	14	126	28			N. E. b. N. Ditto, and cloudy.
6	14	29	127	27			N. E. A fresh trade, and hazy.
7	15	53	128	38			Ditto. Ditto, ditto. Passed several turtle. Caught two of them.
8	17	13	129	41			N. E. A fresh gale, and hazy.
9	18	24	130	34			Variable. Fresh gales, and hazy.
10	19	33	131	27			Ditto. Ditto, ditto, and cloudy. Cleaned ship.
11	19	46	132	35			N. E. Fresh gale, and hazy. P. M. Being in the latitude of the Los Majos Isles, and about four degrees to the eastward of them, hove-to for the night. Passed some sea weed.
12	20	01	134	11			E. N. E. A fresh trade, and cloudy. Hove-to for the night.
13	19	56	135	48			East. A fresh trade, and squally. We still continue to heave-to for the night.
14	20	05	138	18			Ditto. Fresh gales, and cloudy. Hove-to as usual. Passed a large patch of sea weed.
15	20	01	140	07	7	21	E. b. N. A fresh gale, and hazy. Having passed directly over the spot, which the Spaniards laid them down; and not seeing any thing of them, stood on for the Sandwich Isles.
16	19	59	142	12	7	34	Ditto. Squally, with rain.
17	20	03	143	57			N. E. A fine breeze, and clear.
18	19	57	145	50	8	15	East. Ditto, ditto, ditto.

TABLE I. Continued.

Route of the King George and Queen Charlotte from Falkland's Islands to the Sandwich Islands.

Time.	Latitude North.		Longitude West.		Variation East.		Winds, Weather, and Remarks.
	°	′	°	′	°	′	
1786. May 19, Noon.	19	58	147	03	8	17	East. A fine breeze, and clear.
20	20	02	148	48			N. E. to East. Moderate and cloudy.
21	19	39	150	01			Ditto, ditto. Ditto and clear.
22	19	19	151	25	8	14	E. b. N. A fresh breeze, and hazy. Saw a man of war bird.
23	19	10	153	21			E. N. E. A fresh gale, and hazy. Many dolphins about the ship.
24	19	26	154	16			E. b. N. Ditto, and hazy. At noon the N. E. point of Owhyhee bore N. ¼ W. Distance about three leagues.
25	18	56					E. N. E. Moderate and hazy. The south point of Owhyhee E. b. S. about nine miles.
26							Variable, and light. Close in shore.
27							Ditto. Light breezes, and cloudy. At one P. M. came-to in Karakakooa Bay, Owhyhee.

TABLE II.

Route of the King George and Queen Charlotte whilst among the Sandwich Islands.

Time.	Latitude North.		Longitude West.		Variation East.		Winds, Weather, and Remarks.
	°	′	°	′	°	′	
1786. May 29, Noon.			156	06			Variable. Light breezes and cloudy. The northernmost land of Owhyhee in sight, N. b. E. six or seven leagues.
30	20	46	156	43	8	00	From South to E. N. E. A fresh breeze, and clear. The south point of the island of Tahorowa, S. S. E. six or seven leagues.
31							E. N. E. Fresh gales, and squally. The west point of Morotoi E. S. E. nine or ten leagues.
June 1	21	16	157	45			N. E. Fresh breezes, and hazy. At anchor in Woahoo.
5	21	18					Ditto. Ditto, ditto. The westernmost point of Woahoo in sight N. W. ¼ W. five leagues.
6	21	36					Variable. Very light winds. The north point of Atoui N. W. eight or nine leagues.
7	21	45					E. b. N. Moderate and hazy. The east point of Atoui E. b. N. five or six leagues.
8	21	57	160	15			E. S. E. Fresh breezes, and clear. At anchor in Yam Bay, at the island of Oneehow.

[B]

APPENDIX.

TABLE III.

Route of the King George and Queen Charlotte from the Sandwich Islands to Cook's River.

Time.	Latitude North.		Longitude West.		Variation East.		Winds, Weather, and Remarks.
1786.	°	′	°	′	°	′	
June 14, Noon.	23	10	160	45			N. E. Moderate and cloudy. The high land on the S. W. part of Oneehow bore S. E. b. S. ½ E. ten leagues.
15	24	14	160	24			E. N. E. Moderate and clear. Many birds of the tern kind about.
16	25	30	160	01			Ditto. Moderate and hazy. Saw many tropic birds.
17	26	36	161	22	12	00	E. b. N. Fresh breezes, and clear.
18	27	48	161	07	13	05	Ditto. Moderate and cloudy, with rain.
19	28	53	161	09	13	25	East. Ditto, ditto.
20	30	05	160	53			Ditto. Moderate and pleasant. Saw three whales.
21	31	05	160	37			E. S. E. to S. S. E. Moderate and clear.
22	32	04	160	08			South. Fresh gales, and hazy.
23	33	30	159	25			Variable. Fresh breezes, and squally.
24	34	18	158	51			Ditto. Fresh gales, and hazy.
25	35	57	157	49			Ditto. Strong gales, and squally, with rain.
26	36	59	156	48			N. W. b. W. Fresh gales, and cloudy.
27	38	14	155	56	15	48	Variable. Fresh breezes, and hazy.
28	38	51	154	54			N. W. Fresh breezes, and cloudy, with a head swell.
29	39	35	152	08			N. W. Fresh breezes, and hazy. Saw several seals.
30	40	39	151	36			W. N. W. Fresh gales, and thick foggy weather. Several seals about the ship.
July 1	41	20	151	18	16	30	W. S. W. Moderate and hazy. Passed a piece of drift wood, and saw several whales.
2	42	50	151	18			Ditto. Moderate, with thick foggy weather, and rain at times.
3	44	04	151	12			South to W. S. W. A fresh gale, and very foggy. Saw three whales.

TABLE III. Continued.

Route of the King George and Queen Charlotte from the Sandwich Islands to Cook's River.

Time.	Latitude North.		Longitude West.		Variation East.		Winds, Weather, and Remarks.
	°	′	°	′	°	′	
1786. July 4, Noon.	45	03	150	00	17	00	N. W. Fresh gales, and hazy.
5	45	31	148	45			Ditto. Ditto, ditto, ditto. Saw several whales.
6	45	59	147	40			Ditto. A moderate breeze, and hazy, and a swell from the northward.
7	46	11	147	08			N. W. to South. Light winds, and hazy.
8	47	30	147	32	17	40	Variable. Fresh gales, and hazy. Saw several wild ducks.
9	49	37	148	11			S. W. Fresh gales, and hazy. Passed a piece of sea weed, and saw a flock of ducks.
10	51	20	148	43			S. W. to S. E. Fresh gales, with foggy and rainy weather. Passed several pieces of the sea weed, and saw a flock of divers.
11	53	10	148	43			Variable. A fresh gale, and foggy. Passed several logs of wood, and pieces of sea weed.
12	54	21	147	37			W. N. W. Moderate and hazy. Passed several pieces of log wood, sea weed, and have seen several flocks of birds.
13	55	00	146	53			Variable. Light winds, with a thick fog. Passed vast quantities of birds feathers.
14	55	53	147	33			West to S. b. E. Moderate and foggy. Passed several pieces of drift wood, and saw vast flocks of birds.
15	57	02	148	32	22	21	S. W. Moderate and hazy. Saw several whales, seals, birds, and pieces of wood, and sea weed.

TABLE III. Continued.

Route of the King George and Queen Charlotte from the Sandwich Islands to Cook's River.

Time.	Latitude North.		Longitude West.		Variation East.		Winds, Weather, and Remarks.
	°	′	°	′	°	′	
1786. July 16, Noon.	58	13	150	31			Ditto. Fresh gales, and hazy. At 7¼ A.M. struck soundings 70 fathoms, light grey sand, with black specks.
17	58	23	149	43			Variable. Fresh breezes, and hazy. At 7 P. M. saw the land bearing N. W. ¼ W.
18	58	29	151	04			Ditto. A fresh breeze, and hazy, with rain. The southernmost land in sight S. W. twelve or thirteen leagues.
19					23	39	Ditto. Fresh gales, with constant rain. The west point of the Barren Isles N. N. E. two leagues.
20							East. Fresh gales, with frequent squalls, and constant rain. At 8½ P. M. came to an anchor in Cook's River.

TABLE IV.

Route of the King George and Queen Charlotte from Cook's River along the Coast, and from thence to the Sandwich Islands.

Time.	Latitude North.		Longitude West.		Variation East.		Winds, Weather, and Remarks.
	°	′	°	′	°	′	
1786.							
Aug. 13, Noon.	59	01					Variable. Light airs. The extremes of the Barren Isles S. W. and S. 38° W. Cape Elizabeth N. 80 W. five or six leagues.
14	59	09	150	11			Ditto. Light winds, and hazy.
15	59	23	149	59	24	30	Ditto. Thick hazy weather.
16	59	27	149	19			N. W. b. N. to W. S. W. Light winds, and hazy. Soundings in 56 fathoms, mud and sand.
17	59	48	148	30			Variable. Light winds. Saw the land bearing N. E. ¼ E. distant about two leagues.
18	59	42	148	24			Ditto. Light airs, and foggy. At anchor off the S. W. end of Montague Island in 43 fathoms, gravelly bottom.
19	59	12					Variable. Light winds. At 6¼ P. M. weighed, and made sail. The land N. E. b. N. seven or eight miles.
20	59	00					East to N. E. Squally, with rain.
21	59	10	148	24			N. E. Fresh gales, with thick rainy weather.
22	59	15	148	00			Ditto. Ditto. Squally, and a heavy sea from the N. E.
23	58	57	148	00			Ditto. Strong gales, and cloudy, with rain.
24	59	47	148	20			East. Moderate, with drizzling rain.
25	59	12	147	31			Ditto. Light breezes, and foggy. At 4 P. M. saw Montague Island, bearing N. 46° W.
26	58	26	146	39			E. N. E. Light winds, and foggy.
27	59	00	146	03	28	10	Variable. Moderate and pleasant.
28	59	15	146	05			N. E. Fresh breeze, and cloudy. Saw the land bearing W. ¼ N. 11 or 12 miles distant.

APPENDIX.

TABLE IV. Continued.

Route of the King George and Queen Charlotte from Cook's River along the Coaſt, and from thence to the Sandwich Iſlands.

Time.	Latitude North.		Longitude Weſt.		Variation Eaſt.		Winds, Weather, and Remarks.
	°	′	°	′	°	′	
1786.							
Aug. 29, Noon.	58	18	146	14			E. N. E. Freſh gales, with rain.
30	58	30	145	38			Variable. Freſh gales, and ſqually, with drizzling rain at times.
31	58	30	144	57			Ditto. Light winds, and cloudy.
Sept. 1	58	54	143	39			Ditto. Freſh breezes, and hazy.
2	58	49	142	41			Variable. Moderate, with drizzling rain.
3	58	18	141	08			North to S. S. E. Moderate and cloudy. Saw a ſhark.
4	58	30	140	33			Variable. Light winds, and cloudy.
5	58	16	140	28			Ditto. Ditto, ditto, ditto, with rain.
6	58	17	140	03			Ditto. Squally, with rain.
7	57	43	139	40			S. E. to N. E. Freſh gales, and ſqually, and a heavy ſea from the eaſtward.
8	57	33	138	39	24	00	Variable. Freſh gales, and hazy.
9	57	54	157	58			S. W. b. S. to S. E. b. E. Moderate and cloudy. The land in ſight extending from E. N. E. to N. N. E. ¼ E. A low point N. E. ¼ E. four or five leagues.
10	57	18	137	47			Variable. Freſh gales, with thick drizzling rain.
11	57	00	137	34			Ditto. Strong gales, and thick rainy weather, and a heavy ſea from the S. E.
12	56	49	133	08			Eaſt. Strong gales, and very hazy weather.
13	56	37	138	31			S. E. Freſh gales, and hazy, with rain, and a heavy ſwell from the S. E.
14	57	06	136	40			S. W. Moderate and hazy. The land in ſight. The eaſternmoſt part in ſight S. E. b. E. ¼ E. and the weſternmoſt ditto N. W. diſtance from the neareſt part two leagues.

TABLE IV. Continued.

Route of the King George and Queen Charlotte from Cook's River along the Coast, and from thence to the Sandwich Islands.

Time.	Latitude North.		Longitude West.		Variation East.		Winds, Weather, and Remarks.
1786.	°	′	°	′	°	′	
Sept. 15, Noon.	56	56	138	02			Variable. Strong gales, and hazy, with rain.
16	56	51	137	54			Ditto. Fresh gales, and cloudy.
17	55	14	136	45			West. A fresh gale, and cloudy.
18	53	46	134	06			N. W. A fresh gale, with clear pleasant weather. Saw the land.
19	51	58	132	39	24	18	Ditto. Fresh gales, and pleasant weather. The nearest land in sight N. b. E. eleven leagues.
20	51	09	130	36			Ditto. Fresh breezes, and pleasant, with a long swell from the N. E.
21	50	47	129	28			W. N. W. Light winds, and close weather. Saw an island bearing from N. E. ¼ E. to N. E. b. E. ¼ E. distance about six leagues.
22	50	02	127	48			N. W. Fresh breezes, and cloudy. Woody Point N. b. W. three leagues, and the rock lying off the Point N. b. W. ½ W. two leagues.
23	49	48	127	08	23	00	N. W. b. W. Moderate and pleasant. The land in sight extending from E. b. S. to W. N. W. ½ W. distance from the nearest part about four leagues.
24	49	27	127	13			Variable. Unsettled weather. P. M. a canoe with two men in her came off to the ship. The north point of King George's Sound N. E. six leagues, and Breakers Point N. 86° E. 10 leagues.
25	49	53	127	16			Ditto. Light breezes, and cloudy. The north point of the sound N. 63° E. about six leagues distant.

TABLE IV. Continued.

Route of the King George and Queen Charlotte from Cook's River along the Coast, and from thence to the Sandwich Islands.

Time.	Latitude North. ° '	Longitude West. ° '	Variation East. ° '	Winds, Weather, and Remarks.
1786.				
Sept. 26, Noon.	49 32	127 15		Variable. Heavy gales, with thunder, lightning, and rain. Carried away both clews of our foresail. The land in sight bearing N. b. W. ¼ W. five or six leagues.
27	49 33	127 19		Ditto. Squally unsettled weather, with frequent showers of hail and rain, and a heavy swell from the S. W. The north point of the entrance into the sound E. N. E. six or seven leagues.
28	49 32	127 11		Ditto. Moderate, with rain. The north point of the entrance N. 65° E. five leagues.
29	49 12	128 07	22 30	W. N. W. A fresh gale, and cloudy. The entrance of the sound N. 30° E. 15 leagues distance.
30	47 55	129 15		S b. E. Light airs and hazy, with a heavy swell from the N. W. Cleaned ship.
Oct. 1	47 53	130 24		W. N W. Fresh gales, and cloudy. A head sea.
2	46 48	131 06	19 00	Variable. Moderate and clear.
3	45 40	131 06		West. Moderate and foggy.
4	44 07	131 57		W. b. N. to N. N. E. Ditto, ditto.
5	44 06	132 42	19 27	Variable. Light winds, and cloudy.
6	43 08	132 42		Ditto. Fresh breezes, and cloudy.
7	43 06	133 17		Ditto. Strong gales, and squally.
8	42 33	133 17		S. W. Squally, with lightning and rain, and a heavy swell from the S. W.
9	41 49	132 58		Ditto. Squally, with rain.
10	40 32	133 31		West. Fresh gales, and cloudy.
11	39 27	133 12		Variable. Fresh gales, and squally, with a long swell from the S. W.
12	38 44	133 16		Ditto. Fresh gales, with rain.

APPENDIX. xvii

TABLE IV. Continued.

Route of the King George and Queen Charlotte from Cook's River along the Coast, and from thence to the Sandwich Islands.

Time.	Latitude North.		Longitude West.		Variation East.		Winds, Weather, and Remarks.
1786.	°	´	°	´	°	´	
Oct. 13, Noon.	37	01	133	45			N. W. b. W. Fresh gales, and pleasant.
14	36	24	134	16			Variable. Light winds, and cloudy. Caught a shark.
15	35	59	134	50			S. E. b. S. Light winds, and cloudy.
16	36	04	134	20			South. Moderate, and cloudy. Many tropic birds about.
17	35	55	135	04			Variable. Moderate, and cloudy.
18	34	08	135	41			North. Ditto, ditto.
19	34	26	136	22	11	17	Variable. Fresh breezes, and clear. Tropic birds and flying fish about.
20	34	22	137	44			S. b. E. Fresh breezes, and cloudy, with a swell from the Southward.
21	34	15	139	01			Variable. A fresh gale, and hazy. Saw some tropic birds.
22	34	00	140	54			Ditto. Fresh breezes, and hazy. Caught a dolphin.
23	33	40	140	54			S. S. E. Moderate and cloudy, with fogs at times.
24	33	22	141	32			S. E. Moderate and hazy, with rain at times.
25	32	57	142	16			S. S. E. A fresh breeze, with open cloudy weather. Caught a dolphin. Many tropic birds about.
26	32	36	143	35			S. E. b. S. A fresh breeze, and hazy.
27	32	24	144	12	11	46	S. S. E. Moderate, and hazy.
28	32	08	145	01			Variable. Light winds, and hazy. Cleaned ship.
29	31	05	145	27			E. S. E. A fresh gale, and cloudy.
30	29	49	146	24			S. E. A fresh gale, and squally. Saw a whale.
31	29	04	147	56			Ditto. A fresh breeze, and hazy.

[C]

TABLE IV. Continued.

Route of the King George and Queen Charlotte from Cook's River, along the Coast, and from thence to the Sandwich Islands.

Time.	Latitude North.		Longitude West.		Variation East.		Winds, Weather, and Remarks.
	°	′	°	′	°	′	
1786. Nov. 1, Noon.	28	14	148	35	12	09	East. Moderate and cloudy. A swell from the S. E.
2	27	15	148	56			E. b. S. Fresh breezes, and cloudy.
3	26	02	149	36			Variable. Squally unsettled weather.
4	24	54	150	02			Ditto. Ditto, ditto.
5	24	30	150	15			Variable. Light winds, and pleasant weather.
6	24	02	150	20			Ditto. Fresh breezes, and cloudy.
7	23	15	150	56			E. S. E. Moderate and cloudy. Saw some land birds. Many tropic birds about.
8	23	01	150	55			Variable. Unsettled weather.
9	22	47	151	00			Ditto. Strong gales and hazy, with rain.
10	22	52	150	38			Ditto. Strong gales, and squally, with lightning and heavy rain.
11	22	30	151	01			Ditto. Fresh breezes, with rain.
12	21	26	152	51			N. b. E. Moderate and pleasant. Caught a shark.
13	20	33	153	22			N. N. E. Ditto, ditto.
14	20	04	153	47			E. S. E. Light winds, and hazy.
15	20	08	154	35			East. Ditto, ditto, ditto. Saw the land bearing S. W. ¼ W. 12 or 13 leagues.
16	20	12	155	42			E. S. E. Moderate. Close in shore.
17	20	16					Variable. Light winds, and hazy. Standing along shore.
18							Ditto. Moderate and pleasant. Distance off shore about three miles.
19	20	26					Ditto. Strong gales, and cloudy. The S. W. end of Owhyhee south. Lightning and rain.
20	20	58					S. W. Fresh gales, with heavy rains. P. M. hove-to for a canoe with three men in. Hoisted her up, and took the men on board, they being very much fatigued.

TABLE IV. Continued.

Route of the King George and Queen Charlotte from Cook's River, along the Coast, and from thence to the Sandwich Islands.

Time.	Latitude North.	Longitude West.	Variation East.	Winds, Weather, and Remarks.
1786.	° ′	° ′	° ′	
Nov. 21, Noon.	21 10			W. S. W. Fresh breezes, and squally Mowee extending from S. S. E ¼ E. to S. W. ¼ S. distance five leagues.
22	21 07			E. S. E. Light winds, and pleasant. The west end of Mowee W. S. W.
23	21 32			Variable. Light winds, and pleasant. The extremes of Morotoi S. ½ E. and S. W. distant from the nearest part six leagues.
24	21 32			S. b. W. A fresh gale, and cloudy. The east end of Mowee S. b. E. ¼ E.
25	21 19			Variable. Light winds, and hazy. The east point of Mowee S. ¼ E. five leagues.
26	21 25			S. b. W. A fresh breeze, and clear. The east point of Mowee S. S. E. ½ E.
27	21 33			S. S. W. Moderate and clear. The extremes of Morotoi S. b. W. ½ W. and S. W. ¼ W. six or seven leagues distance.
28	21 17			Variable. Light breezes, and fine. The east point of Morotoi S. W. ¼ S.
29	21 26			E. b. N. Light airs, and hazy. The island of Woahoo in sight bearing from W. S. W. ¼ W. to West.
30	21 20			N. E. A fresh breeze, and hazy. The south point of Morotoi S. E.
Dec. 1	21 15			N. E. A fresh breeze, and cloudy. At five P. M. anchored in the bay in the south end of Woahoo in nine fathoms.
				N. B. From this to the 15th of March 1787, the vessels were at anchor, and off the islands of Woahoo, Atoui, and Oneehow.

TABLE V.

Route of the King George and Queen Charlotte from the Sandwich Islands to Prince William's Sound.

Time.	Latitude North.	Longitude West.	Variation East.	Winds, Weather, and Remarks.
1787.	° ′	° ′	° ′	
Mar. 15, Noon.	21. 31	159 02		S. E. b. E. Moderate breeze, and pleasant weather. The N. E. point of Atoui bore N. W. ¼ W. and the westernmost point in sight W. b. N.
16	22 40	158 35		S. S. E. Fresh breezes, and cloudy.
17	24 24	158 13		South to W. b. N. Fresh breezes, and cloudy, with rain.
18	26 02	157 52		Variable. Strong gales, with heavy rain and thunder and lightning, and a heavy sea from the southward.
19	27 23	157 47		S. S. W. Fresh breezes, and squally with rain.
20	28 47	157 47		S. W. Moderate, and hazy, with rain.
21	28 56	157 50		N. E. b. N. Light winds and hazy, and a swell from the N. W.
22	29 12	158 30		North. Moderate, and clear.
23	29 26	159 00		N. E. Light winds and cloudy, and a swell from the westward.
24	31 21	159 13		East. Fresh gales, with drizzling rain.
25	32 58	159 01		S. E. Fresh gales, with cloudy weather.
26	35 04	158 11		S. S. E. Fresh gales, with thick hazy weather.
27	36 02	153 08		S. S. W. Fresh breezes, and hazy.
28	37 20	157 02		Ditto, ditto, and clear.
29	38 38	155 55		S. S. W. A fresh breeze, and clear.
30	39 35	154 18		N. W. b. N. Strong gales and squally, with showers of hail.
31	39 25	153 45		N. N. W. Strong gales, and hazy.
April 1	40 16	152 56		S. S. E. A strong gale and cloudy, and a heavy swell from the N. N. W.
2	42 17	152 01		South. Fresh gales and squally, with rain.

TABLE V. Continued.

Route of the King George and Queen Charlotte from the Sandwich Islands to Prince William's Sound.

Time.	Latitude North.	Longitude West.	Variation East.	Winds, Weather, and Remarks.
1787. April 3, Noon.	44 51	150 00		S. S. W. Strong gales with rain, and a heavy following sea. Saw a whale, and several divers.
4	46 03	149 09		S. W. Fresh gales and squally, with rain.
5	46 52	149 27	18 10	Variable. A fresh breeze, and hazy. Caught a porpoise.
6	47 54	149 23		Ditto. A strong gale, with rainy weather. Caught a diver.
7	47 22	148 25		North. A fresh breeze and cloudy, with showers of hail and snow.
8	47 40	147 23		N. N. W. Fresh breezes and cloudy, with snow. Passed several pieces of sea weed.
9	48 25	147 16		From N. to S. b. W. Fresh breezes and hazy, with rain. Passed sea weed, a seal, and a flock of gulls.
10	50 04	147 17		S. W. b. S. A fresh breeze, with a thick fog. Passed sea weed, drift wood, and a diver.
11	51 21	147 23		Variable. Thick foggy weather. Saw a whale.
12	52 46	146 55		W. S. W. A fresh gale, with fair weather. Passed several patches of sea weed, and logs of wood.
13	54 06	146 54		Variable. Fresh gales, with sleet and snow. Saw several flocks of gulls.
14	55 41	146 56		Ditto. Moderate and cloudy. Saw two whales, and a flock of gulls.
15	57 14	147 09		W. S. W. A fresh gale, and cloudy, with showers of snow. Passed drift wood, sea weed, whales, gulls, and divers.

TABLE V. Continued.
Route of the King George and Queen Charlotte from the Sandwich Islands, to Prince William's Sound.

Time.	Latitude North.		Longitude West.		Variation East.		Winds, Weather, and Remarks.
	°	′	°	′	°	′	
1787. April 16, Noon.	58	10	147	18	19	00	Variable. Moderate and cloudy, with showers of snow.
17	58	25	147	23			Ditto. Moderate and hazy, with showers of snow at times. Saw a seal.
18	59	13	148	04			S. S. W. Fresh gales, with drizzling rain and sleet. Passed several patches of sea weed.
19	7	40	147	24			W. b. S. Strong gales, and cloudy, with sleet, and a heavy sea from the S. W.
20	58	48	148	29			Variable. Fresh breezes, with snow. Saw a large flock of wild geese.
21	59	11	148	40			East. Strong gales, with snow and sleet. Saw a flock of shags.
22	59	00	149	02			E. b. N. A fresh gale, with sleet and rain. Saw many whales, gulls, divers, shags, and many other kinds of birds.
23	59	11	148	15			Variable. A fresh breeze, with snow. Many whales and birds about.
24	59	50	148	24			Ditto. Fresh breezes, and hazy. The extremes of Montague Island E. b. S. five miles, and N. b. E. ½ E. four leagues.
25							Variable. At anchor in Prince William's Sound from this to July 31, 1787.

TABLE VI.

Route of the King George (after parting Company) from Prince William's Sound to Portlock's Harbour.

Time.	Latitude North.		Longitude West.		Variation East.		Winds, Weather, and Remarks.
	°	′	°	′	°	′	
1787. July 31, Noon.	59	27					W.S.W. Light airs, and hazy.
Aug. 1	59	03	147	15	27	00	S. b. W. Moderate and cloudy.
2	58	49	144	09			S.E. Strong gales, with thick rainy weather.
3	57	59	141	02			Variable. A fresh breeze, and cloudy, and a heavy sea from the S.W.
4	57	12	138	20			S. b. W. A fresh breeze, and pleasant weather.
5	57	23	138	07			Variable. Very light airs, and clear. The land in sight. A high mountain bearing N.N.W. ¾ W. distance 25 or 30 leagues.
6	57	48	136	35			N.W. Fresh breezes, and clear pleasant weather. At anchor in Portlock's Harbour from this to the 23d of August 1787.

APPENDIX.

TABLE VII.
Route of the King George from Portlock's Harbour to the Sandwich Islands.

Time.	Latitude North.		Longitude West.		Variation East.		Winds, Weather, and Remarks.
	°	′	°	′	°	′	
1787. Aug. 23, Noon. }	57	35					Variable. Light winds, and pleasant. Mount Fair Weather bearing N.W.b.N. 25 leagues.
24	57	05	138	42			S.E. Moderate, with thick rain, and a head swell.
25	56	18	138	49			S.W.b.W. A fresh breeze, with a thick fog and rain.
26	54	31	138	48	24	00	W.b.S. Strong gales, with drizzling rain
27	52	22	138	48			N.W. Strong gales, and fog, with drizzling rain. Saw several whales.
28	50	06	138	37			West. Fresh gales, with drizzling rain. Passed a seal, several logs of wood, and patches of sea weed.
29	48	02	138	28			N.b.W. A fresh gale, and hazy.
30	46	08	138	07			North. A fresh breeze, and cloudy.
31	44	30	137	50	18	00	N.N.W. Moderate and hazy.
Sept. 1	43	32	137	39			Variable. Moderate and cloudy. A great many birds about.
2	42	52	137	24			Ditto. Light winds, and cloudy. Caught a shark and two bonitos.
3	42	05	135	58			S.W. Moderate and fair. Saw two Arctic gulls.
4	40	39	135	45			Variable. Squally, with rain.
5	38	49	136	49	15	15	West. A fresh breeze, and clear.
6	37	32	135	14			Variable. Moderate and pleasant.
7	36	05	135	26			N.W. Moderate and fair.
8	34	50	135	43			N.b.W. Moderate and hazy.
9	33	33	136	02	12	45	N.E.b.E. Ditto, and clear.
10	32	11	136	22			E.N.E. Moderate breezes, and close weather.
11	31	00	136	41			N.b.E. A fresh breeze, and hazy.

TABLE VII. Continued.
Route of the King George from Portlock's Harbour to the Sandwich Islands.

Time.	Latitude North.		Longitude West.		Variation East.		Winds, Weather, and Remarks.
	°	′	°	′	°	′	
1787. Sept. 12, Noon.	29	51	136	59	11	22	Variable. Light winds, and pleasant. Saw several tropic birds.
13	28	56	137	11			N. N. E. Light winds, and clear.
14	28	17	137	26			Variable. Light winds, and cloudy.
15	27	51	137	35			Ditto. Fresh breezes, and cloudy.
16	26	42	136	25			S. W. b. W. A fresh breeze, and open cloudy weather, and a swell from the westward.
17	25	48	136	12	9	45	W. b. S. Moderate, and cloudy.
18	24	49	136	33			N. W. Ditto, ditto, and a swell from the N. W.
19	23	22	137	27			N. E. b. N. A fresh breeze, and clear.
20	21	54	139	18			N. E. A fresh gale and squally, with rain.
21	20	37	140	55			E. N. E. A fresh gale, and cloudy.
22	20	17	143	07	8	00	Ditto. A fresh breeze, and hazy.
23	20	10	145	15			E. N. E. A fresh gale, and cloudy.
24	20	02	147	3			Ditto, ditto, ditto, and hazy.
25	19	49	149	03			E. N. E. A fresh gale, and cloudy.
26	20	05	151	32			Ditto. A fresh gale, and hazy. Many tropic birds and land birds about.
27	20	03					E. b. N. Moderate and clear, with a long following sea. The island of Owhyhee in sight, the east point bearing S. b. W. ¼ W. distance about twelve or fourteen leagues.
28							Variable. Squally unsettled weather. Five miles off shore.
29	20	12					East. Moderate and cloudy. Caught two sharks. Distance off shore four or five miles.

TABLE VII. Continued.
Route of the King George from Portlock's Harbour to the Sandwich Islands.

Time.	Latitude North.	Longitude West.	Variation East.	Winds, Weather, and Remarks.
1787. Sept. 30, Noon.	° ′	° ′	° ′	E. b. N. Moderate and cloudy, the south point of the island of Mowee W. S. W. ¼ W.
Oct. 1				Variable. Squally, with showers of rain. The extremes of Morotoi S. ¼ W. and S. E. b. E. ¼ E. Distance from the nearest part about seven leagues.
2	21 58			E. b. N. Moderate and fair. The extremes of Woahoo S. 38° E. and S. 73° E. From the nearest part eight leagues.
3	21 51			Variable. Moderate, and fair. Atooi from E. b. N. to N. N. E. Town of Wymoa N. E. b. E. four leagues.
4				Variable. Light airs. At anchor in Yam Bay in the island of Oneehow, from this to the 8th of October 1787.

APPENDIX. xxvii

TABLE VIII.

Route of the King George from the Sandwich Islands to China.

Time.	Latitude North.		Longitude West.		Variation East.		Winds, Weather, and Remarks.
	°	′	°	′	°	′	
1787. Oct. 8, Noon.	21	26	161	36	9	00	East. A fresh gale, and pleasant weather.
9	20	10	162	43			E. N. E. Moderate, and clear.
10	18	40	163	50			East. A fresh breeze, and hazy. Saw a tern.
11	16	48	165	07			Ditto. A fresh gale, with rain.
12	15	12	166	39			E. N. E. A fresh gale, and cloudy.
13	14	07	168	37			N. E. b. E. A fresh gale and hazy, with a following sea. Saw several tern.
14	13	17	172	22	9	30	E. N. E. A fresh gale and cloudy, with a heavy following swell.
15	13	47	174	24			Ditto. A fresh breeze, and cloudy.
16	13	45	176	15			E. b. N. Moderate and cloudy, and a following swell.
17	13	51	178	13	13	59	Ditto. A moderate gale and squally, with rain.
18	13	55	179	53			Variable. Fresh gales and squally, with rain.
19	13	40	181	29			E. b. N. Moderate, and cloudy. Caught a land bird of the plover kind.
20	13	46	184	45	13	40	Variable. Squally unsettled weather, with rain, and sharp lightning in the southern and western boards.
21	13	42	186	43			Ditto. Moderate, and clear. Saw two tropic birds.
22	13	54	187	51			E. S. E. Light winds, and cloudy, with a swell from the N. E.
23	13	28	190	34			E. N. E. Light winds, and fair weather.
24	13	28	190	34	13	15	Ditto. A fine breeze, and cloudy. Many tropic birds about, and saw two land birds.

TABLE VIII. Continued.

Route of the King George from the Sandwich Islands to China.

Time.	Latitude North.	Longitude West.	Variation East.	Winds, Weather, and Remarks.
1787. Oct. 25, Noon.	13 54	194 00		E. b. N. Squally, with frequent showers of rain. Saw a booby.
26	13 44	195 38		Variable. Squally, with rain at times. Caught a noddy.
27	13 26	197 05		East. Moderate, and cloudy.
28	13 24	199 03	11 7½	E. N. E. Ditto, ditto.
29	13 56	200 51		East. Moderate and cloudy, but squalls at times, with rain, and lightning in the southern board.
30	13 20	202 30		E. N. E. Moderate, and hazy.
31	13 29	203 56	10 8½	N. E. b. E. Ditto, and cloudy.
Nov. 1	13 29	207 51	8 12	N. E. Moderate, and fair.
2	13 42	209 08		Variable. Fresh breezes and squally, with rain. Saw a duck.
3	14 29	211 36		N. E. Fresh gales, and fair pleasant weather.
4	15 12	214 07	7 18	N. E. b. N. Fresh gales, and hazy. The island of Tinian, one of the Ladrones, in sight, extending from S. 30° E. to S. 60° E. Our distance from the west point about 10 leagues.
5	16 00	216 35		N. E. A fresh gale, and cloudy, with rain at times.
6	16 58	219 10		N. E. b. N. A fresh gale, and clear.
7	17 30	221 37		N. E. A fresh gale and cloudy, with light squalls, and rain at times.
8	17 52	223 46		N. E. A fresh gale, and fair pleasant weather.
9	18 33	226 13		N. E. b. E. A fresh breeze, and fair. Saw many tropic birds.
10	19 06	228 29		N. E. A fresh gale, and cloudy, with squalls at times.

APPENDIX. xxix

TABLE VIII. Continued.

Route of the King George from the Sandwich Islands to China.

Time.	Latitude North.		Longitude West.		Variation East.		Winds, Weather, and Remarks.
	°	′	°	′	°	′	
1787. Nov. 11, Noon.	19	42	231	08			N. E. A fresh gale, and fair, with a very heavy swell from the northward.
12	20	30	233	04			N. N. E. Strong gales, and fair, with a heavy sea from the northward.
13	21	10	237	06			N. E. b. N. Strong gales, and cloudy.
14	22	10	238	05			N. E. b. E. Fresh gales, and cloudy. P. M. passed the Bashee Islands. At noon the island of Botel Tobago Xima bore from W. N. W. to W. about four leagues distant. A heavy sea from the N. E.
15	22	03	240	26			N. E. b. N. A fresh breeze, and hazy, with frequent puffs off the land. The south point of the island of Formosa E. b. S. five leagues, and the north part in sight N. b. W. ¼ W. four leagues.
16	22	07					N. b. E. Strong gales, and hazy, with a heavy sea from the northward.
17	22	28					N. N. E. Strong gales, and hazy. Sounded 20 fathoms. Light grey sand.
18							North. Moderate, and hazy. The island of Pedro Blanco N. E. b. N. four miles. Soundings in 24 fathoms, muddy sand. A. M. took a pilot on board out of a fishing-boat.
19							N. N. E. A fresh breeze, and hazy, with rain at times. The Grand Lama in sight, bearing S. E. b. S. 13 or 14 miles.

TABLE VIII. Continued.

Route of the King George from the Sandwich Islands to China.

Time.	Latitude North.	Longitude West.	Variation East.	Winds, Weather, and Remarks.
1787. Nov.20, Noon.	° ′ 22 10	° ′	° ′	North. Light winds, and cloudy. At 5 P. M. came-to, the island of Macao bearing West, in $8\frac{1}{2}$ fathoms, muddy bottom. At 6 A. M. weighed; and at $\frac{1}{2}$ past 10 A. M. came-to again, with the best bower, in nine fathoms muddy bottom, Macao bearing N. W. $\frac{1}{4}$ N. five or six leagues.
21				North. Light breezes, and fair. At 1 P. M. weighed, and made sail towards Macao. And at $\frac{1}{2}$ past 4 came-to in Macao Roads, with the best bower, in $4\frac{1}{2}$ fathoms, muddy bottom. The peak of Lantoon E. b. N.

TABLE IX.

Route of the King George and Queen Charlotte from China, to parting Company off Java Head.

Time.	Latitude North.	Longitude West.	Variation East.	Winds, Weather, and Remarks.
1788.	° ′	° ′	° ′	
Feb. 10, Noon.	21 37	246 21		Variable. Fresh breezes, and fine weather. At $\frac{1}{2}$ past 9 A. M. the S. E. end of the Grand Ladrone bore N. E. $\frac{1}{2}$ N. eight leagues.
11	20 02	246 09$\frac{1}{4}$		N. E. to E. Fresh breezes, and fine weather.
12	18 55	246 08$\frac{3}{4}$		E. b. S. Fresh breezes, and open cloudy weather.
13	18 01	246 35$\frac{1}{4}$		S. E. to E. Moderate breezes, and fair. At $\frac{1}{2}$ past 7 A. M. saw a strange sail to the N. E. standing to the south.
14	17 44	246 17$\frac{1}{4}$		Variable. Moderate, and cloudy. P. M. spoke the sail we saw this morning; she is called the Lowden, Captain Berkely, from Macao, bound to the Mauritius.
15	16 32	245 56	2 17	E. N. E. Moderate, and cloudy.
16	15 31	246 01		N. E. to E. Moderate breezes, and clear.
17	14 23	246 43		Variable. Fresh breezes, and hazy.
18	13 01	247 28		N. E. b. N. to E. N. E. Moderate breezes, and fair.
19	11 40	248 36	1 46	N. E. b. N. A fresh breeze, and cloudy, with a following sea.
20	10 01$\frac{1}{2}$	250 35		Ditto. A fresh gale, with fine weather. The island of Pulo Sapata in sight S. W. b. W. $\frac{1}{4}$ W. two or three miles distance, and a small rock in one with Sapata N. W. b. W. $\frac{1}{2}$ W.
21	8 42	252 17	2 52	N. E. Fresh breezes, and clear.
22	7 03	253 20		Ditto. Fresh gales, and hazy.
23	5 28	254 17		N. E. b. E. to E. Moderate breezes, and fair.
24	4 09	254 21	1 59	E. N. E. Moderate, and clear. Passed a large piece of drift wood.

APPENDIX.

TABLE IX. Continued.

Route of the King George and Queen Charlotte from China, to parting Company off Java Head.

Time.	Latitude North.	Longitude West.	Variation East.	Winds, Weather, and Remarks.
1788.	° ′	° ′	° ′	
Feb. 25, Noon.	2 35	254 26		E. N. E. to N. N. E. Moderate breezes, and hazy. The south point of the island of Anamba in sight E. N. E. distant ten or eleven leagues; and the island of Pulo d'Omai N. E. b. N. four leagues.
26	1 11	254 45½		N. N. E. Light winds, and close weather. The island of Pulo Panjang in sight, the south point bearing S. W. ¼ S. distance about six leagues.
27	0 11	254 25		N. E. to N. N. E. Light winds, and clear. The easternmost point of the Damonis Islands in sight, W. ¼ S. nine leagues.
28	1 11	250 40		N. N. E. Moderate, with lightning. At 11 A. M. spoke the Queen Charlotte, when Captain Dixon informed us his surgeon was dead. The extremes of the three islands in sight, N. E. b. E. ¼ E. and S. E. b. E. ¼ E. Distant from the nearest part four leagues. Islands off the north point of Banca S. S. W. 11 leagues N. N. E. Moderate, and cloudy.
29	2 12	254 42		N. to N. N. E. Fresh breeze, and clear. The north point of Banco in sight N. W. b. N. Sumatra extending from S. W. ¼ S. to S. E. b. E. ¼ E. four leagues.
March 1		254 5		Variable. Fresh gales, with rain. At ¼ past 1 P. M. passed a shoal bearing from Mount Monopin S. E. b. S. four or five leagues. At 7 P. M. came-to in eleven fathoms water, muddy bottom. At 5 A. M. weighed, and made sail. The 2d point on the Sumatra shore W. ¼ N. five miles.

APPENDIX. xxxiii

TABLE IX. Continued.
Route of the King George and Queen Charlotte from China, to parting Company off Java Head.

Time.	Latitude South.	Longitude West.	Variation East.	Winds, Weather, and Remarks.
1788.	° ′	° ′	° ′	
Mar. 2, Noon.	3 9	253 56		Variable. Light winds, with heavy rain. At 3 P.M. passed a Dutch man of war lying at anchor. The 1st point on the Sumatra shore S.E. ¼ S. Spoke the Lansdown Indiaman, Captain Storey. At 7 P.M. came-to in eleven fathoms mud. At 5 A.M. weighed, and made sail. Lusepara S.E. four leagues.
3	3 c6			Ditto. Light winds, and sultry. At 6 P.M. the Lansdown struck on a shoal, and stuck fast. Anchored in 5¼ fathoms, and sent boats to assist the Lansdown. South point of Sumatra S. b. W. ¼ W. three leagues. At 3 A.M. got the Lansdown into deep water without any damage.
4	3 5c			Ditto. Light airs, and hazy. Half past P.M. weighed, and came to sail; Sumatra extending from N.W. ¼ N. to S.W. ¼ S.
5	3 51			Ditto. Light airs, with calms. During these 24 hours, several times under weigh.
6	4 17			Ditto. Light airs, with rain. P.M. weighed, and came to sail. At 11 P.M. anchored in nine fathoms muddy bottom.
7	4 39			Ditto. Light winds, and cloudy, with sharp lightning. At 3 P.M. weighed, and made sail, Sumatra bearing from S.W. b. W. ¼ W. to W. ¼ S. six leagues. At 1 A.M. anchored in ten fathoms water. Weighed, and made sail at 8 o'clock, and anchored at 11 A.M. Sumatra N.W. ¼ N. to N.W. six leagues.

[E]

APPENDIX.

TABLE IX. Continued.
Route of the King George and Queen Charlotte from China, to parting Company off Java Head.

Time.	Latitude South.	Longitude West.	Variation East.	Winds, Weather, and Remarks.
1788.	° ′	° ′	° ′	
Mar. 8, Noon.	4 54			Variable. Light airs, and cloudy. At 2 P. M. weighed and stood to the southward. At 7 came-to in 11 fathoms, the Sisters bearing South. At 8 A. M. weighed and made sail, the Sisters from S. W. b. S. to S. W. ¼ S. 7 miles.
9	4 55			Ditto. Fresh gales and squally, with rain. At 1 P.M. anchored in 13 fathoms water. At 3 weighed, and made sail. At 6 fresh gales and squally, came-to in 13 fathoms. The Sisters S. b. W. 5 miles, and a high island to the Westward of the Sisters S. S. W. six leagues.
10	5 04			Ditto. Light winds, and sultry. At 1 P.M. weighed and made sail. At ½ past 6 came-to in 10 fathoms. The Sisters S. b. E. ¼ E. and S. S. E. ½ E. two miles.
11	5 07			From S. b. E. to S. W. Moderate and cloudy. Half past 3 P. M. weighed and made sail. At ½ past 5 came-to in 11 fathoms. The Sisters S. E. b. E. two miles. At ½ past 6 A. M. weighed and made sail. At 10, anchored in 11 fathoms water, the Sisters bearing E. b. S. two miles.
12	5 26			Variable. Moderate, and hazy. At 7 A. M. weighed and made sail. At noon, North Island S. S. W. seven miles. Cape St. Nicholas S. b. E. eight leagues, four miles from the Sumatra shore.

TABLE IX. Continued.
Route of the King George and Queen Charlotte from China, to parting Company off Java Head.

Time.	Latitude South.	Longitude West.	Variation East.	Winds, Weather, and Remarks.
1788.	° ′	° ′	° ′	From N. to N. W. Squally, with rain. At 2 P. M. came-to in 11 fathoms, North Island S. b. W. ½ W. five miles.
Mar. 13, Noon.				At 5 A. M. weighed and made sail. At 8 moderate and cloudy. North Island S. b. W. 1¼ mile. At 10 anchored on the Sumatra shore in 3½ fathoms. Warped off into 17 fathoms, and made sail.
14, 15				N. N. W. Light winds, with frequent squalls and rain. At 3 P. M. anchored in eight fathoms. North Island N. N. E. three miles. Found several Dutch vessels riding at anchor. Employed wooding and watering.
16				Variable. Cloudy, with squalls and rain. At 8 A. M. weighed and got under sail. From this to the 23d, working up to Cracatoa, where we filled our water.
24		6 23	—	Ditto. Squally, with rain. At half past 4 A. M. moderate and fair, weighed and made sail. At noon Prince's Island from S. W. to S. W. b. W. four leagues, and the Peak of Cracatoa N. b. W. six leagues.
25		6 35		W. N. W. to N. W. Fresh breezes, and cloudy. At 4 P. M. Prince's Island from S. W. b. W. to W. N. W. three leagues. At 8 anchored in 35 fathoms, muddy bottom. North point of Prince's Island W. b. S. five leagues. South point of Java S. W. At 5 A. M. weighed and made sail. At noon the north point of Prince's Island N. W. b. W. ¼ W. four leagues.

TABLE IX. Continued.
Route of the King George and Queen Charlotte from China, to parting Company off Java Head.

Time.	Latitude South.	Longitude West.	Variation East.	Winds, Weather, and Remarks.
1788.	° ′	° ′	° ′	
Mar. 26, Noon.	6 42			Variable. Moderate breezes, and fair weather. Half paſt 6 P. M. came-to in 40 fathoms muddy bottom. The ſouth point of Prince's Iſland S. W. ¼ W. four leagues, and the ſouth point of Java S. W. b. S. ſix leagues. At 8 A. M. weighed and came to ſail. At noon a freſh gale and hazy. Java Head S. b. W. four miles.
27	7 47	254 23		N. W. to W. N. W. Freſh gales and cloudy.
28	8 59	254 56		N. W. Freſh gales, and hazy.
29	10 15	255 23		From N. to N. W. Squally, with rain. Saw a ſail in the N. E. quarter.
30	11 09	255 59		N. E. Light breezes and hazy. Spoke the Queen, Douglas, from China, all well. This day agreed to part company with the Queen Charlotte.

APPENDIX.

TABLE X.
Route of the King George (after parting Company with the Queen Charlotte) to St. Helena.

Time.	Latitude South.		Longitude West.		Variation West.		Winds, Weather, and Remarks.
	°	′	°	′	°	′	
1788. Mar. 31, Noon.	11	37	256	28			Easterly. Light winds, and fair weather.
April 1	12	17	257	28			E. N. E. Moderate, and cloudy.
2	13	24	259	00			E. S. E. Fresh gales, and cloudy.
3	15	13	261	10			Ditto. Ditto, ditto.
4	16	02	263	18			Ditto. Fresh breezes, and fine weather.
5	16	33	265	04			East. Ditto, ditto.
6	17	16	266	55			Easterly. Fresh gales, and cloudy.
7	17	54	268	38			Ditto. Ditto, and fair weather.
8	18	2	269	54			Ditto. Moderate breezes, and cloudy.
9	18	57	272	54			East to N. E. Fresh breezes, and hazy.
10	19	21	274	14			Easterly. Squally, with rain.
11	19	38	276	32			E. S. E. Fresh breezes, and cloudy weather.
12	19	55	278	52			Ditto. Ditto, and fine weather.
13	20	04	280	41			E. b. S. Moderate, and ditto.
14	20	16	282	51			E. S. E. Fresh gales, and clear.
15	20	38	285	15	4	38	Ditto. Moderate, and clear.
16	20	57	286	34			S. E. Light winds, and fine weather.
17	21	46	288	44			S. S. E. Fresh breezes, and clear. A swell from the S. W.
18	22	28	290	52			S. b. E. Fresh gales, and hazy.
19	22	58	292	31			S. E. Moderate wind, and cloudy. A swell from the S. W.
20	23	29	294	17			E. N. E. Moderate, and clear.
21	23	47	296	30	9	6	Northerly. Fresh gales, and cloudy weather.
22	24	28	297	47			Variable. Moderate, and hazy.
23	24	35	299	07			S. S. W. Fresh gales, and cloudy. A heavy sea from the southward.
24	24	55	300	25			Variable. Fresh gales, and open cloudy weather.
25	5	2	302	19	15	17	S. S. E. Moderate breezes, and fine weather.

TABLE X. Continued.

Route of the King George (after parting Company with the Queen Charlotte) to St. Helena.

Time.	Latitude South.	Longitude West.	Variation West.	Winds, Weather, and Remarks.
1788. April 26, Noon.	26 26	304 08		S. S. E. Fresh gales and clear.
27	27 15	306 26		Variable. Ditto, ditto.
28	28 07	308 34		East. Ditto, ditto.
29	28 38	311 13		Ditto. Ditto, ditto. Strong lightning to the S. W.
30	29 16	312 56		E. b. N. Fresh breezes, and cloudy.
May 1	29 36	314 55		Variable. Ditto, and clear weather.
2	29 46	315 41		Ditto. Moderate, and hazy.
3	28 53	317 03		S. W. Squally, with rain.
4	29 45	318 46		S. b. W. Fresh gales, and cloudy weather, with a heavy sea.
5	30 40	321 15		South. Fresh gales, and clear.
6	31 03	322 43		Variable. Moderate, and cloudy.
7	32 01	325 09		N. b. E. Moderate breezes, and clear weather.
8	32 33	326 36		Variable. Fresh gales and squally, with lightning.
9	33 20	328 39		Ditto. Fresh gales, and cloudy weather.
10	33 24	329 52		Ditto. Ditto, and squally. Tried soundings with 100 fathoms line. No ground.
11	34 23	330 34		Variable. Light airs, with calms and cloudy weather. A heavy swell from the W. S. W.
12	35 04	333 39		Ditto. Fresh breezes, and clear. Saw high land bearing N. W. 27 leagues.
13	35 06	33 03		E. N. E. Moderate breezes, and clear. Land in sight from N. b. E. ¼ E. to N. b. W. 20 leagues.
14	35 47	336 48		N. E. Light breezes, and clear. The land in sight North 18 leagues. Passed several strong riplings of a current.

TABLE X. Continued.

Route of the King George (after parting Company with the Queen Charlotte) to St. Helena.

Time.	Latitude South.		Longitude West.		Variation West.		Winds, Weather, and Remarks.
1768.	°	′	°	′	°	′	
May 15. Noon.	35	46	339	13			N.N E. Fresh breezes, and cloudy. Saw a large seal, and numbers of gulls and ganets.
16	36	20	339	24			Variable. Strong gales, and squally. Saw a sail in the N. W. quarter.
17	35	47	339	02			Ditto. Very strong gales, and squally. Lay-to.
18	35	25	338	38			W. b. N. Fresh gales, and cloudy. Saw large flocks of gulls and ganets.
19	35	53	338	38			Variable. Fresh breezes, and hazy weather.
20	35	43	339	55			N. W. Moderate and cloudy.
21	35	47	340	27			Variable. Ditto, ditto. Passed a large piece of wood covered with barnacles. Passed through a strong ripling of a current.
22	35	22	340	51			Variable. Fresh gales, and cloudy weather.
23	35	28	341	15			N. W. b. W. Fresh breezes, and squally.
24	34	46	342	25			Westerly. Ditto, and open cloudy weather. Saw a sail to the southward standing to the northward.
25	34	03	343	37			Variable. Moderate and cloudy. A ship in sight. Hoists a French jack at the mizen-topmast-head.
26	33	20	344	15			Ditto. Light winds, and clear. Many porpoises.
27	32	36	344	48			Ditto. Moderate, and hazy.
28	32	29	344	54			Northerly. Fresh gales, with rain. Great numbers of Albetrosses.
29	31	43	346	8			Variable. Fresh breezes, and squally, with lightning and rain.
30	29	45	348	3			S. W. Fresh gales, and fine weather.
31	28	01	350	13			S. S. E. Ditto, and squally.

APPENDIX.

TABLE X. Continued.

Route of the King George (after parting Company with the Queen Charlotte) to St. Helena.

Time.	Latitude South.		Longitude West.		Variation West.		Winds, Weather, and Remarks.
1788. June 1, Noon.	26	36	351	36			S. E. Fresh breezes, and cloudy weather. A vast quantity of porpoises about.
2	25	34	352	41			S. b. E. Moderate, and cloudy.
3	24	44	353	26			Variable. Light winds, and cloudy.
4	23	50	352	49			Ditto. Ditto, and clear weather.
5	22	30	352	18			Northerly. Fresh breezes, and clear.
6	21	21	353	51			Southerly. Ditto, and hazy weather.
7	20	09	355	24			S. E. Fresh breezes, and cloudy.
8	19	00	357	58			S. S. E. Ditto, ditto. A heavy swell from the southward.
9	17	52	359	10			S. E. Fresh breezes, and cloudy weather.
10	16	30	360	38			Ditto. Ditto, ditto.
11	15	55	363	16			Ditto. Ditto, ditto.
12	15	55	365	30			S. E. b. E. Ditto, ditto. At noon saw St. Helena bearing W. S. W. three leagues. At 5 P. M. anchored in the road in 13 fathoms water.

THE END.

www.ingramcontent.com/pod-product-compliance
Lightning Source LLC
Chambersburg PA
CBHW051843300426
44117CB00006B/246